Other Stephen King books by Stephen Spignesi

The Complete Stephen King Encyclopedia
The Stephen King Quiz Book, Vols. 1 & 2
The Lost Work of Stephen King, Vols. 1 & 2
The Essential Stephen King

STEPHEN KING

AMERICAN MASTER

A CREEPY CORPUS OF FACTS
ABOUT STEPHEN KING & HIS WORK

STEPHEN SPIGNESI

PERMUTED
PRESS

A PERMUTED PRESS BOOK

ISBN: 978-1-68261-606-2
ISBN (eBook): 978-1-68261-607-9

Stephen King, American Master
A Creepy Corpus of Facts About Stephen King & His Work
© 2018 by Stephen Spignesi
All Rights Reserved

Cover art by Dean Samed

PERMUTED
PRESS
Permuted Press, LLC
New York • Nashville
permutedpress.com

Published in the United States of America

Life is like a wheel. Sooner or later, it always comes around to where you started again.

Stephen King

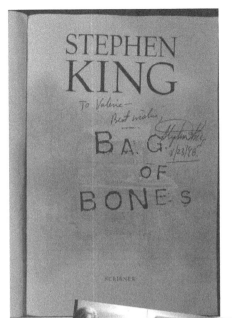

Dedication

For Valerie

Photo by George Beahm. © 1998. Used by permission.

I'd say that what I do is like a crack in the mirror.
If you go back over the books from Carrie *on up,*
what you see is an observation of ordinary middle-class
American life as it's lived at the time that
particular book was written.

Stephen King
The Paris Review

CONTENTS

PART II
The Creepy Corpus

Top 10 Lines from Stephen King Novels

10. "Oh, there's nothing in the attic."
9. "I know it sounds crazy but that Water Pik is after me!"
8. "Stop making fun of my ability to levitate butcher knives—or you'll be sorry!"
7. "I've got a feeling that that small green dot on your skin will be larger by Chapter 8."
6. "This is a losing battle. Let's just paint the walls blood red."
5. "This seems awfully large for just a turkey leg."
4. "I've bought a lot of suits in thrift shops before—but this was the first one that ever tried to strangle me."
3. "Since my wife died, our love life has been great."
2. "The company's been sold. You're working for General Electric now."

And the #1 line from Stephen King novels...

1. "I've been a veterinarian for 30 years and I'm telling you—that's no ordinary poodle!"

From *Late Night with David Letterman*, Thursday, April 27, 1989

INTRODUCTION:
PULLING BACK THE SHEET...

You've been here before. Sure you have.
Needful Things

Greetings...and Happy Horrors!
I have been writing about Stephen King's work for quite some time now. In fact, I remember the day I officially began researching and writing about King: It was Tuesday, March 13, 1984. This was the day my first book, *Mayberry, My Hometown*, was published, and it was also the day my niece Jennifer was born.

It was on that day that I decided what my next book would be: *The Complete Stephen King Encyclopedia*. It would take me five years to complete it, while publishing two volumes of *The Stephen King Quiz Book* in the interim, based on the research I was doing for the *Encyclopedia*.

The limited-edition title of the *Encyclopedia* was *The Shape Under the Sheet: The Complete Stephen King Encyclopedia*. That title came from a metaphor King used in his Introduction to *Night Shift*, in which he explained that the horror writer takes you in a room and shows you the shape under the sheet, and that that shape is your own dead body. *Bingo!* I thought, and commandeered it for my own book, since what I was doing was metaphorically showing King readers all the shapes under all the sheets in all of King's work.

I've been a Stephen King fan since spring 1977. That was when I came across a yellow paperback called *The Shining*. I consumed it in one large gulp. That was the beginning.

This book is a continuance of my interest in, reading of, and study of the work of Stephen King. Unlike my other books about King (*The Lost Work of Stephen King* and *The Essential Stephen King*) this book is more of a browsing book in that it can be flipped through, read cover to cover, or used to look up something specific.

I guess you could say that this book is a good-humored acknowledgment of the influence of that insane asylum called the internet. This is not a "lists" book, but its use of bullet points of fact does nod to similarly-designed features on too-many-to-count websites. There are in-depth entries when warranted, but mostly this is King info in an easily digestible form which I hope will ensorcell you. It makes an enchanting companion to my own denser works, as well as the works of many other King scholars, including the late, great Rocky Wood, Tony Magistrale, Bev Vincent, George Beahm, Robin Furth, Tyson Blue, Kevin Quigley, Andrew Rausch, Justin Brooks, Michael Collings, and many others. Long days and pleasant nights to them all.

A Note About Spoilers: You won't find any here, if I could avoid them in any way at all. And if I do reveal a conclusion or a plot twist, it will be prefaced by [**Spoiler Alert**] in bold. I add details as needed without intentionally giving away endings or key plot points.

Also: Some of the material in *Stephen King, American Master* appeared in different forms in my 1990 book *The Complete Stephen King Encyclopedia*, my 1998 book *The Lost Work of Stephen King*, and my 2001 book *The Essential Stephen King*, all of which are now long out of print. I did a great deal of in-depth Stephen King research for those books and wanted to share some of it with *Stephen King, American Master* readers who may have never seen or even heard of my previous King books.

Stephen Spignesi
New Haven, Connecticut

SCARE STORIES: REASSESSING AMERICA'S MOST POPULAR WRITER

by Stephen Spignesi

Because of his immense popularity, King has earned the ire of literary elitists the world over. While popularity doesn't necessarily equal greatness... one of the many wonders of democracy is that every once in a while, the masses get it right. King's genius can be found in many places, particularly in his ability to take the metaphorical and make it literal. It's a literary device that, in our time, only Franz Kafka and Dr. Seuss managed to pull off so well....Just this once, the Academy [awarding the Nobel prize] should bestow the award upon someone people actually read.

Andrew Ervin
"Nobel Oblige"

He was a major writer for me as a kid, and as an adolescent. I was thrilled every time a Stephen King book came out. I'd spend pocket money on hardbacks. Man, they were the first hardbacks that I demanded my parents get for me. I remember buying IT *and thinking it was the most epic horror novel—that it was the* Ulysses *of horror.*

Bret Easton Ellis
Author, American Psycho

Time continues to prove that his books are far more than pop-cultural phenomenons—he is increasingly and deservedly respected as one of the greatest authors this country will ever produce.
J. J. Abrams

Most of the old critics who panned anything I wrote are either dead or retired.
Stephen King

Consider this:

>...and surrounding everything like an auditory edging of lace, the soothing, silky hiss of lawn sprinklers.

Is that not beautiful phrasing? It's from *The Regulators.*

I'm certain it didn't come easy. Just the "auditory edging of lace" construction had to have taken some time to craft into that perfect expression. And the alliteration— *surrounding, soothing, silky, hiss, sprinklers*—is just perfect, isn't it? This took time and skill to write.

Or how about this?

>Romantics compare the cycle of the seasons to the cycle of human life, a comparison I never really trusted. And yet now...I find something in it, after all. Sooner or later, life takes in its breath, pauses, and then tilts towards winter. I sense that tilt approaching. When the idea threatens to become oppressive, I think of the woods in New England tilting into winter— how you can see the whole expanse of the lake, not just the occasional wink through the trees, and hear every movement on the land that slopes down to the

water. You can hear every living thing, no matter how cunning, before snow comes to muffle the world.

Or this?

> I have stridden the fuming way
> of sun-hammered tracks and
> smashed cinders;
> I have ridden rails
> and bummed Sterno in the
> gantry silence of hobo jungles:
> I am a dark man.

This is fine writing. Evocative, well crafted, powerful...but what would you have thought if I had told you before you read them that the author of these passages was Stephen King?

In all likelihood, you would have been surprised, and you would have likely admitted that your positive reaction to the passages was unexpected.

Why?

Because Stephen King's a horror writer, after all.

He writes that *stuff.*

Y'know, stories about possessed dogs, and murderous vampires, and haunted cars, and dead cats coming back to life, and clown monsters that live in sewers, and "fans" who chop off the feet of the writer they love. (And if my references are not recognizable, I just alluded to *Cujo, 'Salem's Lot, Christine, Pet Sematary, IT*, and *Misery*.)

How could a guy who writes stuff like that craft the engaging, lyrical passages that you just read?

The truth is this: the perception that Stephen King is only a horror writer is a myth—or, more accurately, a misperception. And as is often the case over the past few decades, we can blame popular culture for that, specifically the plethora of movie adaptations of King's stories.

King himself has told a story more than once in which a fan recognizes him, comes up to him and says, "You're Stephen King! I love your movies!" For a while, I believe he made a point of telling these folks that he was a writer first and foremost and that those movies came from his books. Oftentimes, though, the profound meaning of that would fly right over their heads.

King has also been telling an ironic story recently about an incident in a grocery store in Florida. A woman recognized him and said, "You're Stephen King. I can't stand your books," or something along those lines. King says he then asked the woman if she had seen the movie *The Shawshank Redemption*. Her face lit up and she replied, "Oh yes! I loved that movie." He then flipped over his hole card and said, "I wrote that story." She glared at him, said, "No, you didn't," and walked away.

This is the problem in a nutshell. King is too often perceived as a horror-movie-maker, period. Sure, his real fans know he writes novels and short story collections as his main artistic focus, but people really don't read all that much these days. In fact, books are at the bottom of the entertainment pyramid, with movies, TV, music, and sports viewing above them.

I've been writing about Stephen King for going on thirty years now. My first book about him was *The Complete Stephen King Encyclopedia*. I followed that with *The Lost Work of Stephen King*, and *The Essential Stephen King*. As a Practitioner in Residence at the University of New Haven, I taught King's work in a course called "The New Gothic Horror of Stephen King." We read King's nonfiction book *On Writing*, several of his short stories, and his novel *The Shining*, but I also introduced my students to his nonfiction essays, poetry, book reviews, and even a one-act play he wrote—*An Evening at God's*—which we actually performed in class.

I've written about many other topics, but my King work sometimes garners particular responses from people: "I don't like that horror stuff" or "How can he write that gory stuff?" or "His movies are too much for me."

When I bring up his non-horror writings, these self-appointed (and mistaken) critics are almost always open to the idea that he writes more than just horror, but in every case, they are completely surprised and commonly react with "I had no idea!"

For almost three decades now, I have introduced students and ordinary readers to my thesis that King is so much more than a pulp fiction writer by stating, with confidence, that Stephen King is the Charles Dickens and Edgar Allan Poe of our time, and by proclaiming, with certainty, that his best work will survive the next hundred years.

Dr. Michael Collings, a dear friend, superb writer, fellow academic, and Stephen King authority (and contributor to this book), once told me something that has stayed with me, and that I've returned to many times over the years: "William Shakespeare was the Stephen King of his time."

That assessment can elicit a sea-change shift in someone's perception of King and his role in modern letters as an American writer. Sometimes, an artist's popularity is toxic to his reputation. The thinking goes, "Anyone who's that popular can't be good."

And in many cases, this is true. There's no denying that lowest common denominator marketing can often result in a less than high caliber product.

But then, if we extend that reasoning to anything enormously popular, the Beatles should be dismissed as junk; Andy Warhol should be ignored as a one-trick pony; and Michael Jackson should be tossed aside as a flavor of the month with no acknowledgement of the groundbreaking influence he had on popular music, music videos, fashion, and more. And certainly no one should ever go see *Cats*. (Or *Hamilton*, for that matter.) The cultured class seems to accept that popularity can equal greatness when it comes to other forms of art, yet some will glance askew at books that sell millions of copies and think, *junk*.

Oftentimes, this way of thinking is just plain wrong, especially in the case of the work of Stephen King. Emily Dickinson's genius was largely unrecognized until after her death. She sold only eight poems during her life. Vincent Van Gogh was unable to support himself with his art, and died broke, a suicide. Sometimes artistic quality and longevity is unrecognized during an artist's lifetime.

Yet consider this: Stephen King is unique. He is probably the only living writer who has achieved the trinity of success: popular, academic, and collector. Most highly successful writers are very popular, but their work is not taught or collected. King's work hits the bestseller lists; some of it is taught at high school and college levels; and much of it is passionately collected by fans in signed, limited editions (often of books they already own. I know one King fan who has five different editions of 'Salem's Lot.)

King is, of course, a master storyteller.

But in addition to being able to weave a narrative spell over the reader, he also has keen insight into the human psyche, the "monsters within," as he's described it. He knows Modern Man and Modern Woman, with all their glories, and failings, and as Woody Allen puts it, their "quirks and mannerisms."

Is King a literary writer? First of all, what, precisely, is a literary writer? And who decides what's literature and what is...something else?

When Stephen King won an O. Henry Award for his Hawthorne-inspired short story, "The Man in the Black Suit," we nodded our heads and said, "Of course. King's short stories are outstanding."

When Stephen King was awarded the National Book Award for his "Distinguished Contribution to American Letters," many of us who had been touting the merits of King's writing for decades felt vindicated.

When President Barack Obama awarded Stephen King the National Medal of Arts in 2015, many of us knew it was warranted and we posted the picture of King with the President on our Facebook pages. When King was awarded the 2018 PEN Award, fans nodded in approval.

And when a new Stephen King short story appeared in the esteemed magazine, *The New Yorker*, King aficionados weren't surprised.

The difficulty many people have juxtaposing King's work with the concept of literature can be summed up in one word: genre.

Much of King's mainstream work—novels, short story collections—can be considered genre fiction, or actually multiple genre fiction. He writes horror, but he also writes science fiction, westerns, thrillers, suspense, and fantasy. That's a given.

But he also tackles—even in his familiar titles (*IT*, *The Shining*, *The Stand*, *The Dead Zone*)—heavy sociocultural topics and themes, including domestic abuse, depression, addiction, childhood trauma, marital discord, mental illness, toxic guilt, and much more.

When Jonathan Franzen published *The Corrections* in 2001 with its complex time and place narrative shifts, it was widely praised for its genius. When King did a similar thing fifteen years earlier in 1986 in *IT* (which I ranked as his magnum opus in *The Essential Stephen King*) the comments focused on the fact that all the major monsters appeared, some for the last time in King's fiction. The excellence of the writing, including the sheer brilliance of the metaphor—childhood trauma that manifested as a cyclical, supernatural monster—was oftentimes dismissed or ignored because *IT* was, after all, a horror novel and King was, after all, a horror writer.

And consider this: undeniably "literary" writer David Foster Wallace, author of the book everyone owns but many have not read (yet), *Infinite Jest*, taught King's novel *Carrie* in his "English 102: Literary Analysis I: Prose Fiction" class at Pomona College. His margin notes in the King paperback are available online.

Isn't *that* interesting? And it begs the question, if Stephen King is not literature, then why did America's leading literary writer, the late David Foster Wallace, teach King to his writing students? If anyone might have an understanding of literature, one would assume it would be Wallace, yes?

So, is what Stephen King writes literature?

Yes.

Granted, some of his novels are just down-and-dirty thrillers or horror stories, writing that isn't often considered within the classic context of "serious literature." (Let's just play along and pretend that that distinction makes sense.) And that's absolutely fine. But keep in mind that if anything classified as "horror" were eliminated from, let's say, school curricula, authors on the chopping block would include Edgar Allan Poe, William Faulkner, Henry James, Joyce Carol Oates, Bram Stoker, and, of course, William Shakespeare.

But not all of King's stories and novels are roller coaster rides.

Some are naturalistic, nuanced, insightful stories that highlight the glories and nightmares of the human condition.

Take, for example, his story "Premium Harmony," which first appeared in the November 9, 2009 issue of *The New Yorker*. It begins:

> They've been married for ten years and for a long time everything was O.K.—swell—but now they argue. Now they argue quite a lot. It's really all the same argument. It has circularity. It is, Ray thinks, like a dog track. When they argue, they're like greyhounds chasing the mechanical rabbit. You go past the same scenery time after time, but you don't see it. You see the rabbit.

"Premium Harmony" is about the deterioration of a marriage, and it asks the question, "What if you hated your wife...and she just up and died?"

Ray's wife dies in the ignominious location of a gas station convenience store. She has a heart attack and, as the EMT tells Ray, "She didn't die unattended." This was in response to a discussion by onlookers about whether or not they were going to have to do an autopsy on her.

Real people, in a real place, faced with a real tragedy, who have lives to get on with, and a clerk who is probably hoping they get the body out of there quickly so it doesn't block access to the cash register.

And all of it witnessed by the "grieving" spouse—who only cries when he opens the car door and realizes his dog Jack has died from the heat in the closed car.

There's a reason King is published in *The New Yorker*, *Tin House*, *The Atlantic*, *Granta*, *Esquire*, *Harper's Magazine*, *The Virginia Quarterly Review*, *Playboy*, *McSweeney's*, *The Paris Review*, and *Antaeus*.

Stephen King is talented and prolific. He also has, perhaps, a once-in-a-generation imagination. He creates extraordinarily memorable characters and inserts them into horrifying, heart wrenching, often tragic situations and circumstances—and then tells us what they're feeling, flawlessly illustrating what they're going through.

Stephen King writes—for all his haunted cars and gruesome deaths—about the human condition.

In other words, he writes literature.

Excerpts from: *The Regulators*, "Leaf-Peepers," "The Dark Man," "Premium Harmony" by Stephen King

PART I

Say Hello To My Esteemed Guests...

AN INTERVIEW WITH RICHARD MATHESON: ABOUT STEPHEN KING

I interviewed the late, great Richard Matheson for my *Complete Stephen King Encyclopedia*, and I reprint the interview here with the kind and gracious permission of his son Richard Christian Matheson, the superb writer of the "Battleground" episode of King's *Nightmares & Dreamscapes* TV series, and *Big Driver*, the TV film of King's novella.

Stephen Spignesi: Thank you for visiting *The Shape Under the Sheet*, Mr. Matheson. Since you are one of the three primary influences on Stephen King's writing (along with John D. MacDonald and Don Robertson), your thoughts and opinions are of great interest to us all. Let's start with this: How, specifically, do you feel that your work has influenced Stephen King?

Richard Matheson: I gather, from what Stephen King has said himself, that reading my work—in particular *I Am Legend*—indicated to him that horror need not be (indeed, in my point of view, should not be) confined to crypts and ancient cellars. When Lovecraft was writing, that sort of thing was in vogue. These are modern times. The approach to horror must accommodate these times. Since I was unable to write "old fashioned" horror stories (I tried it on a number of occasions and, in spite of it being very difficult, the results are not that great—i.e., *Slaughter House*), I wrote as contemporaneously as I wanted to and found it more successful. This approach to horror, so I gather, had its effect on Stephen, and he went on to become its most successful exponent. I have not read about him that extensively, so I may be repeating what has already been said but he, also, became a distinctly *regional* writer. This is important and I think a valuable approach to this genre. I suppose this could have been done in the "old fashioned" mode, but it certainly works well done in a contemporary style.

SS: Of the King works that you've read, do you have a personal favorite?

RM: No particular favorite. I have enjoyed them all from *Carrie* on. I was impressed right from the start. *Carrie* was remarkable in that he kept mentioning some horrendous event which took place and kept the entire book leading to it—which can be very perilous if you don't pay it off properly—and then *did* pay it off in spades. I think *'Salem's Lot* is great, and was sorry I didn't get to do the [film] script on it—or on any of the books, for that matter. I would have enjoyed it.

SS: How often are you in contact with Stephen King?

RM: I am not in contact with Stephen very often. My wife, my son Richard, and I had dinner with him out here some years ago and enjoyed his company; he is a very friendly person. Richard has seen him at conventions.

SS: Do you have any opinions on what Stephen King is *really* like?

RM: I can't say I really have any idea at all what he is "really" like. I suggest a reading of his work. What a writer writes is a dead giveaway of what is going on inside. In my case it is—or, I hope, was—a sense of paranoia. In Stephen's case—who knows? Not me.

SS: What are your thoughts on the film adaptations of King's work?

RM: I thought *Carrie* was well done. I thought the TV version of *'Salem's Lot* was well done. Of course, I always miss the parts that are left out; trying to make a film out of a long novel is usually a waste of time—witness *Dune* and *Ghost Story*. Both marvelous books, both inferior films because of what had to be left out.

I thought *The Shining* was a poor film. It was a marvelous—is a marvelous—novel. I thought Kubrick lost most of it in his usual attempt to be abstruse. For instance, I keep telling people to read Clarke's novelization of *2001*, which is perfectly understandable while the film is rather incomprehensible until viewed about ten times and discussed for a year or two.

I thought *The Dead Zone* was the best King film so far. Cronenberg did an excellent job, the performers were perfect. I haven't seen any of the later films, except part of *Cujo* which I didn't care for.

SS: Your son Richard seems to be the leading practitioner of the "short-short," and his fiction is often closer to mainstream than horror. What are your thoughts on your son's work?

RM: I admire Richard's horror short-shorts. When they succeed—this form, I mean—the impact can be tremendous. He has been impactful in many of his stories. For instance, who would dare do a story in which each sentence is *one word*! Incredible. [Note: The story referred to is Richard Christian Matheson's "Vampire," from his collection *Scars and Other Distinguishing Marks* (Tor paperback, 1988).]

SS: It seems Stephen King has transcended his own name and become a popular culture archetype—a brand name for horror. What do you think of the ongoing Stephen King phenomenon—this unprecedented popularity for a living American writer?

RM: The Stephen King phenomenon is, I think, simply this. The groundwork for it was laid by a number of writers—myself included, I presume. The market and tastes of the public—synonymous, I suppose—reached a peak of "expectation" and "desire," even, perhaps, "need" for this type of product, and Stephen was there to become its spokesperson. His writing style, his attitudes, his ideas made him *the* writer to end up on the top of the mountain.

Stephen King is a brilliant writer but, if the need were not there, if he had begun writing in the 1930s, or, perhaps, the 1980s, it would be in such perfect sync with the market for this genre.

He would always have become a successful writer because of his talent. But a phenomenon is something else. More is required. In particular, the Time. Suppose the Beatles had come forth in the 1940s? Nothing. This, perhaps, saying nothing in that the Time and the Artist are so inextricably bound together. Stephen King, the Phenomenon, without the time he emerged from, would not have become a Phenomenon. The Time, without Stephen King, would have still demanded *someone*, and someone might well have emerged. Happily, when the craving was there, so, too, was Stephen with his talent, and the phenomenal period of his success began. Bottom line: the man is an enormous talent and the time was right for his spectacular literary ascent.

RICHARD CHRISTIAN MATHESON REMEMBERS THE FACE OF HIS FATHER

Stephen King should have a shoulder strap holding that word processor. It's like he's picking off these strange sort of Fahrenheit solos and just zapping, and it's very rock—it's very rock-oriented. I got a lot of my playfulness with language from King. He convinced me that you could do it…can we call it "heavy-metal language"?
R. C. Matheson

RC Matheson (l.) and his father Richard Matheson. Photo © RC Matheson, All rights reserved. Used by permission. [FPO]

This is an excerpt from a very lengthy interview I did with R. C. for my *Complete Stephen King Encyclopedia* in which he talks about his father's influence on the work of Stephen King. Many thanks to R. C. for allowing me to reprint this in this volume.

I think Stephen King took the best of my father, which was a very strong narrative and character kind of "drive," and then he added something which I think my father did less of, which was a much more in-depth search of his characters. And King also did a *lot more* characters. My father tended to orient his stuff toward one guy. When Stephen King is involved in idea formation—that process when he begins to develop story ideas and characters—he calls the character he sees "The I-Guy." And then this I-Guy becomes a bunch of other people as time goes on and he begins to name the characters in the story. I think my father stuck much more with that I-Guy. With King, it was almost like having a teacher who loves F. Scott Fitzgerald showing you things about Fitzgerald that you never saw. And in his case, the way he showed you was through his writing.

Because I knew that my father was an influence, I could see that seminal patch cord to my dad. I'd see my dad in King's writing, and I was very well aware of the dynamic between the two of them. King would send letters to my dad occasionally and say, "I'd like you to read my new book." Not that my dad was a present-day mentor, but he had really been a voice that King had paid attention to. And I looked at what King did, and could see the directions my father had kind of laid down. And I liked it. It appealed to me.

I guess what I learned from King was characters, and I think had my father approached his fiction with more of a "people" fabric rather than the "individual man" fabric, an "idea" fabric, you probably would have gotten work a lot like King's.

WILL PEOPLE STILL BE READING STEPHEN KING IN 2068?

By Bev Vincent

Bev Vincent is the author of several books about Stephen King's work, including *The Dark Tower Companion* and *The Stephen King Illustrated Companion*. He has been writing *Stephen King: News from the Dead Zone* for *Cemetery Dance* magazine since 2001 and is currently providing "historical context" essays for Richard Chizmar's *Stephen King Revisited* project. Follow him on Twitter at @BevVincent or visit bevvincent.com.

I n late 1997, I had the opportunity to talk to Stephen King at length for the first time. We were driving around Bangor and, during the course of our conversation about authors we enjoyed, I mentioned an interview I'd encountered recently in which Jonathan Kellerman said he thought King would be read in schools in fifty years, the way Poe is read now.[1]

After a few seconds, King, who was driving, responded, "That's great. But you know what? In fifty years, I probably won't give a shit!" A typical Kingian self-effacing response, in the same vein as his comment in the afterword of *Different Seasons* that most of his novels "have been plain fiction for plain folks, the literary equivalent of a Big Mac and a large fries from McDonald's." But as I approached this essay, that moment came back to me. Fifty years is an interesting, albeit arbitrary, chunk of time. Long, but not too long. When our conversation took place, it was conceivable that I'd live to see whether Kellerman's prognostication came true.

However, as it turns out, I don't need to survive to the ripe old age of eighty-six to find out if Kellerman was right. King is already being read in school, despite some concern at the middle and high school level about the suitability of his stories because of strong language and scenes of horrific violence. (If you search for King's name in the context of high school, you'll mostly find articles about his books being challenged for removal from school libraries.[2])

Still, a number of high schools have King short stories listed as part of the curriculum, generally for honors English classes, and guides exist for teachers who want to integrate his stories into their syllabi. One of these guides, written *before* Kellerman's interview,[3] *A Teacher's Guide to Selected Horror Short Stories of Stephen King: From the Anthologies Night Shift, Nightmares and Dreamscapes, and Skeleton Crew*, while acknowledging the issues pertaining to content, argues that even reluctant read-

---

1   Kellerman's exact quote is: "I do think Stephen King will be read in high school textbooks in coming generations and venerated in much the same way we venerate Poe." *The Book Report*, November 24, 1997.

2   King addresses this issue in "Adventure in Censorship Is Stranger than Fiction," originally published as a guest column in the *Bangor Daily News* in 1992 and available on his official website.

3   In fact, the first ever book written about King's work was *Teacher's Manual: Novels of Stephen King* by Edward J Zagorski, published in 1981.

ers will enjoy his work, which can be used as a springboard to the classic novelists of horror and suspense. That might seem like a backhanded compliment, but the fact is that King isn't *yet* a classic novelist. He's a producing author who is still finding new and interesting things to say. Classic status requires some distance, in much the same way that "magnum opus" does.[4]

"In terms of popularity, he is a major contemporary author who has mastered the craft of creating horror and suspense stories, both genres with long historic and literary roots. Such writers as Charlotte Brontë, Emily Brontë, Mary Shelley, Bram Stoker, William Shakespeare, Edgar Allan Poe, Nathaniel Hawthorne, Herman Melville, Robert Louis Stevenson, Wilkie Collins, and Charles Dickens are just a few examples of classic writers who won similar popular acclaim in their day," the introduction to this guide states.[5] Not bad company to keep.

If you move beyond high school, to the more permissive and less cloistered world of university, not only will you find King stories in the syllabi, you'll find entire classes devoted to King and his works. Tony Magistrale, whose name you may recognize, and who also appears in this volume, held a class called *The Films and Novels of Stephen King* at the University of Vermont nearly twenty years ago. The University of North Carolina Wilmington has offered a graduate level course on King's work, and Purdue University currently offers an upper-level class on King's short stories. Academic papers and PhD theses have been written about his work.[6] [Note from Stephen Spignesi: Bev is

---

4   And, yes, my first book does discuss the Dark Tower series as possibly King's magnum opus, but that's part of a discussion and not a definitive assessment.

5   A Teacher's Guide to Selected Horror Short Stories of Stephen King: From the Anthologies *Night Shift, Nightmares and Dreamscapes,* and *Skeleton Crew* by M. Jerry Weiss. Penguin USA 1995.

6   For example: "The haunted house of memory in the fiction of Stephen King," Will Napier, University of Glasgow, 2008, and "Standing up with the King: A critical look at Stephen King's epic," Jenifer Michelle D'Elia, University of South Florida 2007, to name just two.

right about this. I myself taught a popular course at the University of New Haven called "The New Gothic Horror of Stephen King."]

As early as the 1980s, literary critics believed King's work merited closer scrutiny than any other "popular" fiction. Several were published as part of the Starmont Studies in Literary Criticism series, with contributions from Magistrale, Michael R. Collings, and other critics. Biographies aside, over a hundred books have been published about aspects of King's work.

●

This discussion about King's longevity as a writer is not limited to the academic environment, despite the proclamations of self-appointed gatekeepers of the Western literary canon. Harold Bloom, in an introduction to a collection of essays devoted to King in the Modern Critical Views series,[7] complained that he had suffered through his reading of various King works, and later derided the decision by the National Book Foundation in 2003 to present King with the award for distinguished contribution to American letters.[8]

Writers don't remain popular simply because they're part of a high school or university curriculum. King continues to be immensely popular: hundreds of millions of copies of his fifty-plus novels and collections are in print in English alone, and he has been translated into over forty languages, from Albanian to Vietnamese.

Hundreds of millions of copies. It's hard to conceptualize that many books. Let's try this experiment: If we assume the average volume

---

7   The inquiring mind wonders why Mr. Bloom would want to be associated with a book containing critical evaluation of a man's work that he so clearly disdains.

8   Bloom didn't criticize only King...he also lambasted J.K. Rowling and then went on to decry university classes where Aphra Behn, the first Englishwoman known to earn her living by writing, was taught instead of Shakespeare, and declaring that a number of poets (all female, by the way) simply couldn't write.

is two inches thick, you could make a stack of his English-language books that, if tipped over, would extend more than halfway around the planet. Those books aren't going to go away, even in the unlikely event that any go out of print, a concept that is becoming increasingly difficult to define in this era of modern publishing. And millions more of them are printed every year.

According to Kevin Quigley in *Chart of Darkness*, King's books have reached the number one position on the *New York Times* bestseller list more than any other author in history—with well over thirty appearances in that slot. That represents a track record of loyal readership spanning multiple decades. His popularity is so unprecedented that the *Times* had to change its rules in 1996 when multiple installments of *The Green Mile* serialized novel took over the list simultaneously.

Though it's difficult to look fifty years into the future in this fast-changing world, King has been publishing for that long *already* (his first professional sale was in 1967), and the novels and stories he wrote in the 1970s are still being read as avidly today as his most recent works. Elements from his books (and the films based upon them) have become cultural touchstones. "Here's Johnny" would have been an internet meme, had there been memes and an internet to spread them when Kubrick's adaptation of *The Shining* came out. Celebrity stalkers are instantly compared to Annie Wilkes. Stories about scary dogs inevitably reference *Cujo*. Self-driving cars run amok will no doubt be compared to Christine. Coulrophobia has hit new levels in recent years thanks to Pennywise V 2.0.

Let's take a stroll through King's earliest novels to explore whether they're still relevant today. Are contemporary teenagers cruel to each other? Our awareness of bullying and shaming is higher now than it was in 1974. In this day and age, would a man torment his family when subjected to the pressures of alcoholism and isolation? Certainly. Do people shoot up schools in 2018? Sadly, yes. Are we prone to eradication by a super-virus? Oh, yeah. Could an insane person take control of the U.S. government and launch a first nuclear strike? Don't get me started. The only difference is that if Greg Stillson used a baby to shield himself from an assassin today, his political prospects would probably survive the controversy.

Supernatural novels like *'Salem's Lot* are affected a bit by changes in technology. Small towns are no longer as isolated as they were in the 1970s. It would be difficult to imagine that story in the modern era, with live streaming and Twitter. However, that doesn't negate the book's fundamental truths about life in rural America and the way people interact. And there's nothing wrong with considering King's second novel a "period piece," in much the same way that we know that *Dracula* wouldn't play out the same way if it were set in the twenty-first century. In fact, one of the inspirations for *'Salem's Lot* was a discussion about what would happen if Stoker's vampire showed up in New York City in the 1970s.[9]

Here's more evidence of the universality of King's novels—because that's what we're talking about, after all. Stories and novels survive because something about them continues to be relevant. The smash hit movie of 2017 was Chapter 1 of *It*, which broke box office records one after the other. Here's an adaptation of a thirty-year-old novel that still strikes a chord with viewers today. More to the point, the screenwriters moved the timeframe of the story forward over thirty years, from 1958 to 1989, without having to change much about the story. Everything that was important in the original timeframe was still meaningful in the later setting.

Even a novel like *Cell*, which is heavily reliant upon technology that was current when it was written but will probably seem as foreign to future readers as the oversized cell phones in the earliest episodes of *The X-Files* are to us now, contains an underlying truth. The notion that a foreign entity could hack our technology and turn it against us is

---

9   During that discussion, Tabitha King said he'd get run over by a cab at the New York Port Authority and that would be the end of him. King joked that he would survive a few weeks before Efram Zimbalist, Jr. and the FBI dragged him off, a victim of modern surveillance.

perhaps even more frightening today than it was a dozen years ago. In addition to this high-concept description of the novel, it is propelled by a fundamental and universal idea: a father's drive to rescue his son.

In 2017, we saw a resurgence in cinematic adaptations of King's novels. In part, this was inspired by the multitude of new venues for these adaptations. The rise of original content on pay services like Netflix and Hulu, and on premium cable channels like Spike TV and the Audience Network, means that the old schism between feature film and made-for-TV adaptation no longer exists. Netflix was willing to take a chance on a feature length adaptation of *Gerald's Game* without having to deal with the messy details of distribution, for example, and Audience Network was able to create a brutally graphic adaptation of *Mr. Mercedes* without bowing to the demands of network Standards and Practices. However, none of these projects would have proceeded if the source material wasn't popular and relevant. *Gerald's Game* was a more than twenty-year-old novel when Mike Flanagan adapted it, but the underlying story is as pertinent today as in the early 1990s.

The fact that so many of King's books and stories have been adapted to film—and *re*-adapted and sequelled—will also increase his legacy. Movies—even bad ones—have a way of persisting. *The Shawshank Redemption* is already in heavy rotation on Turner Classic Movies, and regardless of your thoughts about the Kubrick adaptation of *The Shining*, it's a movie that is going to be watched for generations to come. This vast library of films and TV series is going to keep King's name in the common consciousness, in much the same way that even now there is a cadre of King fans who know his work primarily through its adaptations. Some of these fans go on to read the books, and will continue to do so.

King is different from most other authors in the way he has become a recognizable figure. Thanks to his movie and TV cameos, television commercials and countless televised interviews, King is a personality, as instantly recognizable as Agatha Christie, Edgar Allan Poe, Mark Twain or Ernest Hemingway.

The list of King's awards for individual works is long. In 2015, President Obama awarded King the National Medal of Arts, the highest award for artists given by the US government, for "his remarkable storytelling with his sharp analysis of human nature."

Another indicator of popularity is parody. You don't lampoon something unless you expect people to recognize the reference. There have been numerous parodies of King's work (including on *The Simpsons*) over the years. Songs have been inspired by his novels and stories. Amateur filmmakers option his stories so they can showcase their skills. He has created such a vast, interlinked universe of characters and places that it is sometimes discussed with the same reverent tones used for Marvel and DC characters. The success of *Stranger Things* is, in large part, due to its unabashed homage to King's books from the 1980s. It's hard to imagine his reputation running out of steam any time soon.

King is not only a producer of popular works, he is also an avid consumer. He reads voraciously and across genres, and also enjoys films and TV series. For a number of years, he wrote about his passion for popular culture in a regular column in *Entertainment Weekly*, culminating in a series of "year's best" articles about books, movies and television. His book reviews continue to appear in venues like the *New York Times*. His connection to contemporary culture means that he continues to keenly observe it, and it is that observation that provides fodder for his work. On occasion, there has been an eerie prescience to his fiction: the domestic terrorism scene at the end of *Mr. Mercedes*, for example, presaged similar events in recent years. Even when he's writing about things happening now, he's looking to the future. Just look at *The Dead Zone*. Just look.

●

Since we can't peer into the future to see what 2068 will look like, let's perform the reverse experiment and turn our sights on the past. Five authors held the top position on the *New York Times* bestseller list during 1968: William Styron, Fletcher Knebel, John Updike, Arthur Hailey, and Helen MacInnes. How many do you recognize? How many are still being read today?

Styron, author of *The Confessions of Nat Turner*, would go on to write *Sophie's Choice* and a number of other books, but he's hardly a household name. MacInnes, author of *The Salzburg Connection*, wrote a number of subsequent novels, but her name is probably not well known outside the mystery genre. In 1968, Arthur Hailey was in his heyday for *Airport*, and he wrote a number of bestsellers thereafter. People are probably more familiar with the spoof *Airplane!* than with the Hailey novel itself these days, but he's still fairly well known. I've never heard of Knebel (*Vanished*), but Updike's name will be known to just about everyone, and his 1968 novel *Couples* put him on the cover of *TIME* magazine.

Here are some other authors who released new books in 1968 whose names will be familiar to most readers: Isaac Asimov, Agatha Christie, Arthur C. Clarke, August Derleth, Philip K. Dick, John Irving, John D. MacDonald, John le Carré, Norman Mailer, Alice Munro, Mordecai Richler, Robert Silverberg, Jack Vance, Gore Vidal, and John Wyndham. A couple of them are still publishing today.

What does this tell us? Nothing specific about King, but the fact that so many authors from fifty years ago are remembered and read today bodes well for King's legacy. Regardless of where you come down on the question of King's literary merit—is he more akin to Agatha Christie or Alice Munro?—longevity is still very much a possibility half a century hence.

●

What factors contribute to an author's work's endurance? Does it matter if an author is prolific? No—there are a number of classic novels that were either the only work by an author or part of a small output, whereas Dickens produced an impressive body of work. How much does it matter if an author is popular in his or her time? John Dickson Carr published a ton of books and gained a measure of acclaim, but few people recognize his name—or the titles of any of his books—today. Is popularity and accessibility contrary to literary merit? Some critics would have you think so, but Mark Twain was hugely popular in his time and is still being read today. Is King's use of "common language" and pervasive use of contemporary cultural references detrimental? That remains to be seen—copies of his books, if published in 2068, might need to be annotated. But King would deny any charges that he uses common language and is, by his own admission, greatly interested in language. In the first foreword to *On Writing*, King recounts a conversation with Amy Tan in which the two authors lament the fact that no one ever asks them about language. "They ask the DeLillos and the Updikes and the Styrons, but they don't ask popular novelists," he writes.

That book, *On Writing*, may play a large part in King's literary legacy. Even people who do not regularly read King's fiction have lauded it as an exceptional writing guide. His thoughts on the craft of writing are timeless.

●

People who have adapted King's work feel confident of his legacy. J. J. Abrams, executive producer of the Hulu series *11/22/63* and creator of the series *Castle Rock* based on King's famous fictional town, says, "Time continues to prove that his books are far more than pop-cultural phenomenons—he is increasingly and deservedly respected as one of the greatest authors this country will ever produce."[10]

What does King say about his legacy (other than "I probably won't give a shit.")? In 2006, he said that neither critics nor authors them-

---

10   "How Stephen King scared a generation of storytellers into existence," Anthony Brenzican, *Entertainment Weekly*, September 12, 2017.

selves have much to say about how their work will be regarded in the future. "In the end, after you're gone, the work finds its own level," he said. So long as he doesn't end up being treated like a "sociological artefact" like a Halloween mask, he's content. "Some of the books which everyone sneered at for being disposable, such as Agatha Christie, have actually survived the longest on the bookshelves."[11]

In response to a question about how he saw his place in the literary tradition of Poe, Stoker and Lovecraft, King said: "I'm not one to think about legacy, but I would like it if people said of me, 'His writing faithfully reflected the America he lived in.'"[12]

He was more expansive when asked what people would say about him after he was gone. "It would be nice if people said, 'He worked hard. He left a rich legacy of novels and did the right things in the community.'"[13] When asked if he thought people would be reading *The Stand* in fifty years, King replied, "That would be really nice. They might read *The Shining*. They might read *'Salem's Lot*. I think horror novels and fantasy novels have a longer shelf life than other kinds of books. I think of big bestsellers from when I was a kid, like *Seven Days in May* and the novels of Irving Wallace. You get a blank look if you mention those names. That's what happens to most writers. People move on."

I don't think there's any question that readers will still be scaring themselves silly and enjoying King's novels in 2068. The only question is: in what form will they be read? How prevalent will hardcopy novels be in that mystical future era? What new technologies will have evolved that we can't imagine today? Whatever they are, I am confident that Stephen King's books will be available on them.

---

11   I Want to Share My Nightmares, Nigel Farndale, *The Telegraph*, November 12, 2006.
12   Can a Novelist Be Too Productive?: Q. & A. With Stephen King, *The New York Times*, September 1, 2015.
13   The Last Word: Stephen King on Trump, Writing, Why Selfies Are Evil, Andy Greene, *Rolling Stone*, June 9, 2016.

REGRET AND REDEMPTION IN
THE GUNSLINGER

By Robin Furth

Robin Furth is the author of the acclaimed *Dark Tower Concordance* and works as Stephen King's research assistant.

Spoilers Warning: This essay refers to events that take place in all of the Dark Tower novels, including Book VII.

Please Note: All *Gunslinger* excerpts used below are drawn from the 2003 edition unless otherwise stated.

INTRODUCTION

In his introduction to the fifth Dark Tower novel, *Wolves of the Calla*, Stephen King tells us the subtitles for the first seven books of his magnum opus.[14] They are *Resumption, Renewal, Redemption, Regard,*

---

14   *The Wind Through the Keyhole*, which Stephen King published in 2012, is
       subtitled *A Dark Tower Novel*. Although it was written after the seventh

Resistance, and *Reproduction*. For *The Dark Tower*, the seventh and final installment of Roland's quest, the subtitle is *Revelation, Redemption, Resumption*. What these subtitles indicate (and what Constant Readers have always known), is that the Dark Tower novels are not just a series of adventure stories. In the tradition of John Bunyan's seventeenth century Christian allegory, *Pilgrim's Progress*, The Dark Tower novels are an account of one man's search for redemption. Each subtitle summarizes the spiritual and moral development that Roland undergoes as he transforms from a dangerous, Tower-obsessed loner into a chivalric knight. (Note: A Constant Reader is a devoted King fan. He or she probably owns all (or almost all) of King's works and has read them multiple times. King often addresses his fanbase this way. It is a playful and affectionate term.)

To those reading the Dark Tower books for the first time, the subtitle of *The Gunslinger* may prove initially puzzling. What is Roland resuming, and why? *The Gunslinger's* subtitle, "Resumption," refers to an aspect of Roland's character arc only hinted at in the 1982 and 2003 versions of *The Gunslinger*, but which is made plain in the final book of the series. Although he does not know it, Roland is trapped in a time-loop. The Dark Tower he quests for is not a structure but a god, and that god is determined to hold the gunslinger accountable for all of his sins. Roland has not lived through the events of *The Gunslinger* once but many times, and he is damned to relive his quest—resuming it over and over—until he finds a way to atone and change.

Nowhere in the Dark Tower series is Roland's need for transformation more obvious than in the first book, *The Gunslinger*. It is in this novel that Roland's actions are especially repugnant, but it is also in this book that the foundations of his transformation are laid. Through a series of carefully placed flashbacks, and through his burgeoning re-

---

and final installment of the Dark Tower saga, in terms of the chronology of Roland's journey, it sits between *Wizard and Glass* and *Wolves of the Calla*. However, since it was not included in King's 2003 introduction to *Wolves of the Calla*, I have not included it in this essay.

lationship with a vulnerable young boy named Jake Chambers, Roland begins to understand how he has transformed from an idealistic and naïve apprentice gunslinger into a cynical and hardened killer.

In *The Gunslinger* we first meet Roland Deschain, the last of Mid-World's elite clan of warriors, descended from the land's semi-mythical hero, Arthur Eld.[15] Described as a man of "blacks and whites,"[16] as well as a "plodder and a bludgeoner,"[17] Roland is portrayed as an embittered loner who has suppressed the memory of his past in order to focus on his quest for an elusive, fey structure called the Dark Tower. The Tower is the linchpin of the time/space continuum, and Roland wants to climb to its top and question whatever god or demon resides there. When we initially join Roland on his quest, he is trekking across Mid-World's endless Mohaine Desert, single-mindedly pursuing a sorcerer called the man in black. Roland believes that the man in black can lead him to the Tower, and our gunslinger will stop at nothing—not even murder—to catch his quarry.

In this initial Dark Tower novel, Roland is courageous and his skill with the gun is legendary, but he lacks the idealism and morality of the traditional hero. He is, in essence, an anti-hero. But as in all good tales, Roland is not a static character, and his personality is complex. Although he often seems heartless, there is a romantic side to his nature which allows him to learn from his mistakes and—ultimately—to change. And over the course of the Dark Tower novels, Roland Deschain changes profoundly. As the series progresses, we begin to discover that Roland's journey is not just *outward*, toward a mythical place

---

15   Please note: In the 1982 edition of *The Gunslinger*, Roland is not given his last name, "Deschain." In the first chapter of this early edition, he is referred to as "the gunslinger" only. Later on in the text we learn his first name.

16   "He had laid his fuel in a pattern that was not artful but only workable. It spoke of blacks and whites. It spoke of a man who might straighten bad pictures in strange hotel rooms." (7)

17   "They both knew he was not flashingly intelligent like Cuthbert, or even quick like Jamie. He was a plodder and a bludgeoner. Even Alain was better at studies."

called the Dark Tower, but also *inward*. The landscape he traverses is both literal and symbolic, and his quest is not just to find the linchpin of time/space, but also to redeem his corrupted soul.

In *The Gunslinger*, Roland's sins are many. He has forced sexual relations with a woman, he murders the entire population of a town (including his lover, Allie), and he lets a trusting child drop to his death. Suspicion and killing are never far from his mind. Within the first few pages of Chapter I ("The Gunslinger"), Roland meets a red-haired border dweller named Brown, who shares water and food with the gunslinger and gives him shelter for the night. But despite these kindnesses, murder is not far from Roland's mind:

> "I started to tell you about Tull."
> "Is it growing?"
> "It's dead," the gunslinger said. "I killed it." He thought of adding: *And now I'm going to kill you, if for no other reason than I don't want to have to sleep with one eye open* (17).

In the lengthy confession that follows, Roland tells Brown about his adventures in the town of Tull. He begins by describing his love affair with a scarred barkeep named Allie, and his confrontation with a strung-out weed-eater who'd been brought back from the dead by the man in black. But when Roland begins to recount his interactions with a mad female preacher named Sylvia Pittston, the tale becomes dark.

Before Roland's arrival in Tull, Pittston had already engaged in sexual relations with the man in black, and now Pittston believes that she is pregnant. But Roland maintains that the "demon" inside her is no more than her own sexual desire. He proceeds to remove this demon by penetrating her with the barrel of his gun:

> "The price of my flesh would be your life, gunsling-
> er. He has got me with child. Not his, but the child of

a great king. If you invade me ..." She let the lazy smile complete her thought. At the same time she gestured with her huge, mountainous thighs. They stretched beneath her garment like pure marble slabs. The effect was dizzying.

The gunslinger dropped his hands to the butts of his pistols. "You have a demon, woman, not a king. Yet fear not. I can remove it" (61).

Despite Pittston's resistance (she recoils from him in terror, stabs the sign of the Eye at him, and locks her legs together "like a vise"), Roland pries her legs apart and slides the barrel of his gun into her body.

The scene makes for uncomfortable reading, since both Roland's violence, and Pittston's arousal, are obvious. Pittston makes "strange, lustful keening noises" and her breath comes in "savage grunts" (58). But while her body may respond to Roland's aggression (her "huge body tried to suck the invader in" and she eventually orgasms), she remains "terrified" and quite consciously fights him. Even as her breath becomes rough, she continues to scream "No! No! No!" and beats his head with her fists. At the end of the interaction, she seems to "wilt and grow smaller" (59). Although Pittston is initially a powerful and frightening figure, by the time Roland is finished, she is reduced to a pitiful victim who weeps with her hands in her lap. When Pittston demands that Roland leave, saying that he has killed the child she carried, Roland maintains that her pregnancy was an illusion. "'No child,'" he says. "'No angel, prince, no demon'" (59).

Even if Pittston's pregnancy was an illusion, her desire for revenge is very real. Calling Roland "Satan" and "The Interloper," she sets her congregation on him like a pack of rabid dogs. Although the people of Tull are only armed with stones, chunks of wood, forks, and knives, Roland instantaneously begins shooting: His reaction was automatic, instantaneous, inbred. He whirled on his heels while his hands pulled the guns from their holsters, the butts heavy and sure in his hands" (61).

What makes this scene so disturbing is not only Roland's almost unearthly skill at killing, but also the way he can, without remorse, even kill his lover, Allie. In the 2003 edition of *The Gunslinger*, this murder is made a little less cold-blooded, since Allie begs to be shot. (Uttering the sinister magic word *nineteen*—one of the many psychological traps left by the man in black—she prompted Nort to divulge the secrets of the afterlife and she can't live with the knowledge).

> It was Allie, and of course it had to be Allie, coming at him with her face distorted, the scar a hellish purple in the lowering light. He saw that she was held hostage; the distorted, grimacing face of Sheb peered over her shoulder like a witch's familiar. She was his shield and sacrifice. He saw it all, clear and shadowless in the frozen, deathless light of the sterile calm, and heard her:
>
> "Kill me, Roland, kill me! I said the word, *nineteen*, I said, and he told me...*I can't bear it-*"
>
> The hands were trained to give her what she wanted. He was the last of his breed and it was not only his mouth that knew the High Speech. The guns beat their heavy, atonal music into the air. Her mouth flapped and she sagged and the guns fired again. The last expression on her face might have been gratitude. Sheb's head snapped back. They both fell into the dust. (61-62)

In the 1982 edition, Allie's death is much more horrific, since she doesn't beg Roland to kill her, but begs Roland *not* to shoot:

> ...It was Allie, and of course it had to be Allie, coming at him with her face distorted, the scar a hellish purple in the lowering light. He saw that she was held hostage; the distorted, grimacing face of Sheb peered over her shoulder like a witch's familiar. She was his

shield and his sacrifice. He saw it all, clear and shadow-
less in the frozen deathless light of the sterile calm, and
he heard her:

"He's got me O Jesus don't shoot don't don't
don't—"

But the hands were trained. He was the last of his
breed and it was not only his mouth that knew the
High Speech. The guns beat their heavy, atonal music
into the air. Her mouth flapped and she sagged and the
guns fired again. Sheb's head snapped back. They both
fell into the dust. (1982 edition, 59)

Over and over, Roland's killing spree is described as both graceful
and heartless. He moves "like a dancer to avoid the flying missiles"
even as his innocent lover's body lies "crucified" in the dust. Trained
well in the art of war, Roland never misses when he shoots. Each blast
of his pistols finds "a vital spot" as his hands pick targets "with ease and
dreadful accuracy" (62). Despite the constancy of the attack, his fingers
reload "with a rapidity that had…been trained into [them]" (63). All
around him, men, women, and children "fell like ninepins in a game of
Points" (63). "Transmogrified into an Eye and a Hand," in other words
a scope and a trigger, Roland lets "his hands do their reloading trick"
though his mind is "far away and absent" (64).

For Roland, killing is a religious experience, and he is a prophet of
death, come to teach Pittston's congregation about his personal creed:

Could he hold up a hand, tell them he had spent a
thousand years learning this trick and others, tell them
of the guns and the blood that had blessed them? Not
with his mouth. But his hands could speak their own
tale. (64)

When it comes to words, Roland may be a reticent man, but when it comes to death, he is fluent. Toward the end of the attack, Pittston runs at Roland, waving two crosses and screaming "DEVIL! CHILDKILL-ER!" Roland shows his disdain for her religion by "blowing the roods to splinters." He then puts four more bullets into Pittston's head (65).

Even with Pittston dead, the congregation continues to run at him like a "vicious clot" (65). Someone throws a knife and the hilt strikes Roland between the eyes, knocking him over. Roland's aim is thrown off and he misses one target, but then downs eleven. Lying among his spent shells, being stabbed and kicked and hit, Roland throws his at-tackers off and shoots some more. When a small boy cut him across the calf, Roland "blew his head off" (66).

Although Roland's shooting spree began in self-defense, it ends in blatant murder. Even when the final townsfolk turn and try to flee, he continues to aim and fire:

> They were scattering and he let them have it again, back-shooting now. The ones left began to retreat to-ward the sand-colored, pitted buildings, and still the hands did their business, like overeager dogs that want to do their rolling-over trick for you not once or twice but all night, and the hands were cutting them down as they ran. The last one made it as far as the steps of the barber shop's back porch, and then the gunslinger's bullet took him in the back of the head (66).

Like "overeager dogs that want to do their rolling-over trick for you not once or twice but all night," Roland's hands continue to aim and fire until every man, woman, and child is dead. The fact that Roland's hands are like "overeager dogs" implies that they are not completely under his control. Who do they show their trick to, if not Roland him-self? Although he could have mounted his mule and left town (who could have followed him, and who could have shot at him when no one else had a gun?), Roland begins "back-shooting," which, almost by definition, is butchery.

After the killing is over, Roland follows the zigzagging trail of death, counting his victims. Without regret, he realizes that he "had shot and killed thirty-nine men, fourteen women, and five children. He had shot and killed everyone in Tull" (66). He then returns to Allie's honkey-tonk, where he "ate hamburgers, and drank three beers while the light failed. That night he slept in the bed where he and Allie had lain." (67) Roland has "no dreams" and no nightmares, either. When he awakes the next morning, "The wind was gone and the sun was its usual bright and forgetful self." The bodies of his victims have disappeared, "gone south like tumbleweeds with the wind." (67)

After recounting his Tull experiences to the border dweller named Brown, Brown asks Roland if the confession has made him feel better. But Roland doesn't understand why he should feel remorse. Brown responds that being human means feeling regret after committing murder:

> Just as he was about to get up and spread a pallet in the corner, Brown said, "There. You've told it. Do you feel better?"
>
> The gunslinger started. "Why would I feel bad?"
>
> "You're human, you said. No demon. Or did you lie?"
>
> "I didn't lie" (67).

At the close of "The Gunslinger," Roland is still the same man he was in the opening lines: a loner obsessed with his quest who is an accomplished gunman able to kill without regret. However, in Chapter II, that picture begins to change.

The Way Station: *Khef* and the Waters of Life

At the beginning of "The Way Station," Roland is the same unyielding character we left at the end of "The Gunslinger." Only now

Roland is trapped in the heart of the Mohaine Desert and has run out of water. Though he is desperate and stumbling, he tries to remember the pride that was beaten into him as a child:

> …He didn't want to fall, even though there was no one to see him. It was a matter of pride. A gunslinger knows pride, that invisible bone that keeps the neck stiff. What hadn't come to him from his father had been kicked into him by Cort, a boy's gentleman if there ever was one. Cort, yar, with his red bulb of a nose and his scarred face (74).

As so often happens in the Dark Tower novels, the desiccated landscape Roland travels through also symbolizes his emotional state. In High Speech, the term *khef* means "the sharing of water." It also implies birth, life force, and the emotional bonds that join people to one another. *Khef* is, in essence, the water of life (*Concordance*, 528).

When Roland traveled toward Tull, he was completely alone. His youthful ka-tet[18] of gunslingers was dead and he had little desire to bond with others. *Khef* was in short supply. In the landscape, too, water was scarce. As we were told in the previous chapter, "It was ugly country. It had showered twice since he had left Pricetown, grudgingly both times. Even the timothy looked yellow and dispirited" (18).

Yet after Roland's rampage in Tull, where he killed his lover Allie, as well as every other man, woman, and child in the town, what little life-water remained in the landscape has dried up completely. Now, that dryness is killing him. Sixteen days after leaving Brown's hut, his water skins are empty and he is "very likely a dead man" (74). Even the seemingly indestructible devil-grass is "stunted and yellow" (74). Exhausted and disorientated, Roland falls and skins his hands. He then

---

18   Ka-tet: Ka-tet means a group of people bound by fate. Usually the bonds of ka-tet are formed by allegiance and love.

becomes obsessed with the drops of blood rising to the surface of his abraded skin:

> …He looked at the tiny beads of blood on his flaked skin with disbelief. The blood looked no thinner; it looked like any blood, now dying in the air. It seemed almost as smug as the desert. He dashed the drops away, hating them blindly. Smug? Why not? The blood was not thirsty. The blood was being served. The blood was being made sacrifice unto. Blood sacrifice (75).

If Roland has a God at this point in his development, it is the Old Testament's vengeful Jehovah. His killing of the final fleeing citizens of Tull was retaliation, or in the words of Exodus, "Eye for eye, tooth for tooth, hand for hand, foot for foot" (*King James Bible*, 21:24). As such, those slaughters were justified. But in this passage, Roland speaks of a blood debt. In other words, the price for spilling blood in Tull is payment in blood: "And almost all things are by the law purged with blood; and without shedding of blood is no remission." (Hebrews, 9:22).

But why would Roland—who by his own admission felt no regret over the Tull massacre—feel that his own spilled blood is a necessary atonement? Perhaps because Roland is a more complicated character than he at first seems. He was not always alone, as he was not always a heartless killer. As Roland plods across the hardpan, disorientated and hallucinating, he has a vision of himself as a very small boy. In this vision, he is in his castle bedroom. His mother has tucked him into his bed beneath the window of many colors.

In this memory, which replays "maddeningly, like a dog chasing its own tail," it is raining outside, and his mother is singing a nursery rhyme to him, a nursery rhyme which is also about rain:

The rain in Spain falls on the plain.
There is joy and also pain
but the rain in Spain falls on the plain....

We walk in love but fly in chains
And the planes in Spain fall in the rain.

In this hallucination, water and love—the two aspects of *khef* which now are missing in his life—are in abundance. (73-74) Already, the harsh gunslinger culture of Gilead had begun to take its toll on Roland—his mother was not allowed to sing to him at bedtime "because all small boys born to the High Speech must face the dark alone" —but the waters of *khef* had not yet dried up in him, or in the world around him (74). Beyond the beautiful, multicolored window it is raining, giving the landscape, and the people in it, much needed sustenance. By the time Roland is fourteen, he will hate his mother and reject the nurturing she represents in favor of his father and the gun, but now, at the moment where Roland faces the prospect of his own demise, he remembers his mother's love and a different, gentler way of being.

Jake, the Way Station, and *Khef*

The hallucinatory recollection of maternal love that assails Roland in the desert prefigures an important encounter. Stumbling forward, Roland comes across a way station, which was originally a stopping place on the old coach line. Standing outside the station is a person whom Roland at first takes to be the man in black, but soon realizes is an altogether different creature. The ultimate repercussions of this meeting will prove to be enormous.

He got up, holding his hands to his chest, and the thing he'd seen earlier was almost in front of him, so close it made him cry out—a dust-choked crow-croak.

It was a building…surrounded by a fallen rail fence… someone sat in in the shadow…. And the building seemed to lean with the burden of his weight….

Him, then. At last. The man in black.

…He came the last quarter mile at a jolting, flat-footed run…

"You're covered! You're covered! Hands up, you whoreson, you're—"

The figure moved restlessly and stood up. The gunslinger thought: *My God, he is worn away to nothing, what happened to him?* Because the man in black had shrunk two full feet and his hair had gone white . . .

He sucked the white-hot air into his lungs and hung his head for a moment. When he raised it again, he saw it wasn't the man in black but a boy with sunbleached hair (77).

The boy Roland meets is Jake Chambers. When Roland collapses moments later, Jake saves Roland's life by giving him water. Unlike Roland or the people in Roland's world, Jake has not yet been desiccated by the waterlessness of the desert. His "arms were thin, but the skin, although tanned, had not dried and cracked" (80). Roland realizes that if circumstances were reversed and he had been Jake, *"[I] would have taken one of my guns and shot me right where I lay,"* but Jake is a very different kind of being (80). After giving Roland water, Jake offers the gunslinger some food.

It soon becomes apparent that Jake comes from our world, and the last thing he remembers is being hit by a car and dying. Expressing his fear of this strange new lonely place where he has unexpectedly found himself, Jake is on "the verge of tears" (81). But rather than respond with sympathy, Roland's cold retort is "'Don't feel so sorry for yourself. Make do'" (81). Jake, in turn, responds with bewildered defiance, "I didn't ask to be here" (81).

But Jake's more sensitive nature does not leave Roland unmoved or unchanged. In Jake's company, Roland—who until now has chosen to neither ruminate upon nor evaluate his own actions—has an unusual moment of self-reflection. In this reverie, Roland grudgingly expresses some guilt for the murders he has committed, and betrays a budding concern about what kind of future this boy will have with only himself as a companion. He also begins to question the rightness of his quest:

> The gunslinger ate another piece of the meat, chewing the salt out of it before swallowing. The boy had become part of it, and the gunslinger was convinced he told the truth—he had not asked [to be part of the man in black's game]...He himself...*he* had asked for it. But he had not asked for the game to become this dirty. He had not asked to turn his guns on the townsfolk of Tull; had not asked to shoot Allie, with her sadly pretty face...had not asked to be faced with a choice between duty and flat-out murder. It was not fair to ring in innocent bystanders and make them speak lines they didn't understand on a strange stage. *Allie,* he thought, *Allie was at least part of this world, in her own self-illusory way. But this boy...this Goddamned boy...* (82).

Already we sense that Roland and Jake's interaction will end in tragedy, but we also suspect that something new is happening to our gunslinger. He is gaining self-awareness.

Despite Roland's coldness, the gunslinger and the boy begin to build a relationship. In order to learn more about Jake's past, Roland hypnotizes him with a bullet. As Jake's eyes close, he looks so vulnerable that Roland once again has a vision of his almost-forgotten mother, as well as her protectiveness and her love: "He once more seemed to hear his mother singing, not the nonsense about the rain in Spain this time, but sweeter nonsense…as he rocked on the rim of sleep: *Baby-bunting, baby dear, baby bring your basket here…*(84).

Suddenly Roland, the man without remorse, has a premonition of terrible crimes to come. His mouth fills with "the smooth, loden taste of soul-sickness" and he is assailed with a sense of self-disgust. The shell he has been using to hypnotize Jake suddenly feels "horrific," like "the spoor of a monster" (84). Dropping the shell in his hands, Roland squeezes it "with painful force" (84). For the first time since our initial encounter with him, Roland does not mindlessly accept his ability to kill, but damns himself for it. He realizes that had the bullet exploded at that moment, "he would have rejoiced at the destruction of his talented hand, for its only true talent was murder" (84).

Trying to come to grips with these new-found emotions, Roland reminds himself that "[t]here had always been murder in the world" but such thoughts prove to be of little comfort. Throughout history, men like him have committed murder, rape, and other "unspeakable practices" in the name of "the good, the bloody good, the bloody myth, for the grail, for the Tower." (84) These sacrificial horrors will not end now, and they will not end with him. Amid these thoughts, Roland once more hears the "sweet sound of his mother's voice." However, rather than listen to that gentle love song again, Roland "brushed the song, and the sweetness of the song, aside" (84).

But despite his best efforts, Roland cannot halt the growth of this new self-awareness or the new emotions that this young and vulnerable boy are beginning to arouse in him. Roland begins to remember that he, too, was once a boy. He, too, was once able to love and be loved. Watching Jake sleep, Roland contemplates his own boyhood, "which usually seemed to have happened to another person…but which now seemed poignantly close" (89).

Quite appropriately, the first person that Roland thinks about during this unexpected reminiscence is his brutal teacher, Cort, the man who shaped Roland's adult personality. Described as "a violent midnight carouser," Cort had loved and trained three generations of apprentice gunslingers, but his teaching methods were both cruel and merciless (173):

> ...he thought of Cort—Cort, an ageless engine of a man, his face stitched with the scars of bricks and bullets and blunt instruments. The scars of war and instruction in the arts of war. He wondered if Cort had ever had a love to match those monumental scars. He doubted it (90).

Cort's job was to prepare young warriors for the treacherous times they lived in. He taught them to fight ruthlessly, because if they did not learn this lesson well, they would either fail their test of manhood and be sent west in disgrace, or they would die under another's guns.

Although Cort's reality is the one Roland has adopted as his own—it is his armor and his protection—the deep places of Roland's mind contain other, less comfortable memories of companionship and love. Watching Jake sleep, Roland, "who was not a man to dwell on the past" and who had only "a shadowy conception...of his own emotional make-up" (90), is suddenly overwhelmed by memories of a carefree time, and the green, fragrant land of his youth:

> It seemed to the gunslinger that if he closed his eyes he would be able to hear the croaking of the first spring peepers, smell the green, almost summer smell of the court lawns after their first cutting (and hear, perhaps, the indolent click of wooden balls as the ladies of the East Wing, attired only in their shifts as dusk glimmered toward dark, played at Points), could almost see Cuthbert and Jamie as they came through the break in the hedges, calling for him to ride out with them...(93).

Bemused, Roland—the man who has survived the Mohaine Desert—laughs. That water-rich world is long dead. "*I am the last of that green and warm-hued world,*" he thinks without self-pity. The world he knew had moved on mercilessly, and he—to survive—has moved on mercilessly with it (91).

Jake As a Trap Left by the Man in Black

While in the cellar of the way station, Roland encounters a speaking demon in the building's sandstone foundations. Speaking in the sacred language of High Speech, Roland demands that the demon speak. What the demon offers is a warning, "While you travel with the boy, the man in black travels with your soul in his pocket" (96).

Roland leaves the cellar. When he is halfway across the stable yard, Jake screams and runs to him, crying. He hugs Roland, and Roland feels the boy's "face, hot against his chest." The "rapid beating of the boy's heart" so near his own awakens unexpected emotions. Roland begins to realize that he loves Jake, but he also realizes that this love "was, of course, what the man in black must have planned all along" (96).

Jake's love and Jake's need will inevitably vie for Roland's attention and Roland's commitment to his quest. If he succumbs to Jake and the requirements of surrogate parenthood, he will fail and the man in black will elude him. Roland, the warrior, has spent his life avoiding the traps set for him by his enemies. And, "Was there ever a trap to match the trap of love?" (96).

But despite what he fears, Roland cannot help but care about this boy who—in some unacknowledged way—reminds him so much of his own younger, more innocent self. Roland and Jake leave the way station together. As their relationship grows and the waters of *khef* are drawn from the deep human well of commitment, the landscape around them grows greener:

> They were three days out of the way station; the
> mountains were deceptively clear now. They could see
> the smooth, stepped rise of the desert into foothills…
> Further up, the land gentled off briefly again, and for
> the first time in months or years the gunslinger could see
> real, living green. Grass, dwarf spruces, perhaps even wil-
> lows, all fed by snow runoff from further up. (98)

The waters of *khef* have returned. However, Roland realizes that if he is to pursue his quest, this greenness will not last: "Beyond [the green] the rock took over again, rising in cyclopean, tumbled splendor" (98). The fact that Jake is not slowing him down does not bode well for the future. A plethora of "more sinister possibilities" flood the gunslinger's mind. Roland knows that the man in black drew Jake into this world, and that "the boy had been placed in his path. "If Jake's purpose is not to slow Roland down, what sin of betrayal or murder might await up ahead to damn him?" (98, 99).

But for the moment, Roland and Jake's relationship is superficial-ly unchanged. Like a careful guardian, Roland takes care of the boy. When Jake reels and falls due to heat exhaustion, Roland—who up until now has refused to pause in his quest—insists they rest each af-ternoon (100). He is surprised that "his previous maddening sense of hurry" is gone, but he is also more sure than ever that the man in black now "wanted to be caught" (101).

Once more watching Jake sleep, Roland thinks of his old friend Cuthbert, and of his hawk, David, who was the first of many beings he befriended and then sacrificed. Remembering these things, "[t]he gunslinger's stomach seemed to rise painfully against his heart, but his face didn't change" (102). He knows that another trap, like the one in Tull, awaits him.

Directly after this section, the story moves into flashback mode. We return to Roland's eleventh year, and we see his first encounter with love and treachery. In Roland's experience, one inevitably leads to the other.

Hax: A Lesson in Betrayal

In section VIII of Chapter II, "The Way Station," we return to Roland's eleventh year. This flashback is extremely timely, since it shows Roland's first experience of treachery, and his first lesson in the brutal reality of what it means to be an adult gunslinger. In essence, it is the first step in Roland's development from childhood trust to adult mercilessness.

At the beginning of this section, Cort is teaching falconry to his apprentices. When Roland's friend Cuthbert is slow to unleash his falcon (he is too busy talking), Cort "walked over to where the boys stood...and swung his huge and twisted fist at Cuthbert's ear. The boy fell over without a sound" (102). When Cuthbert cries Cort's pardon, Cort swings at the boy again. This time Cuthbert bleeds as he falls. Cort demands that Cuthbert speak the High Speech, the language of gunslingers. "Speak your Act of Contrition in the speech of civilization for which better men than you will ever be have died, maggot" (103).

Cuthbert stands. There are tears in his eyes, but his lips are pressed together "in a tight line of hate which did not quiver" (103). In "a voice of breathless control," Bert admits that he has "forgotten the face of [his] father, whose guns [he] hope[s] someday to bear" (103). As Bert speaks his contrition, Roland sees that the hawk, David, has taken down his prey. He tosses the bird some rabbit flesh, but when Roland tries to re-leash it, "The hawk whirled, almost absentmindedly, and ripped skin from Roland's arm in a long, dangling gash" (104). Pointing to the dripping slash on Roland's arm, Cort tells him that he pissed the bird off. "The hawk does not fear you, boy, and the hawk never will. The hawk is God's gunslinger" (104).

After thumping Bert again (this time for sticking out his tongue behind his teacher's back) Cort dismisses the boys, saying that their "stupid maggot faces" are going to make him puke (105). Bert, he says, must go without supper and breakfast as punishment for his failures. However, Bert and Roland have no intention of obeying Cort in this, even if they obey him in everything else. They sneak into the kitchens where the head cook, Hax, who is "no friend of Cort's," gives them each a thick slice of pie (106).

Physically and temperamentally, Hax is Cort's opposite. He loves all children impartially, "even…the boys who had begun the way of the gun, although they were different from other children—undemonstrative and always slightly dangerous, not in an adult way, but rather as if they were ordinary children with a touch of madness" (106). But kindly as he seems, Hax has a darker side. While eating their pie in a secret corner under the stairs, Roland and Cuthbert overhear Hax in a treasonous conversation with a guard. Hax secretly serves John Farson (also called *the good man*), who is the enemy of the gunslingers. With the guard's help, Hax plans to poison the town of Taunton.[19]

Upon discovering the head cook's treachery, young Roland's first reaction is bewilderment. "*Hax?…Hax who put a poultice on my leg that time? Hax?*" (109). A "taste of warm despair" rises in Roland's throat, but instead of exploring this confusion and despair, Roland reacts in a way that, in later life, will become all too common. His "mind snapped closed, cutting the subject off" (109). Whatever is left of the dove inside Roland dies in the talons of the apprentice gunslinger, the hawk-in-training. When Roland glances over at his friend Cuthbert, he sees the very same emotionless gaze that will later characterize Roland when faced with dealing death. Though Hax was the boys' friend, feeding them when they were hungry, caring for them when they were injured, he is a traitor and must die.

When Roland exposes Hax's treachery and his father reminds him that Hax will now hang, Roland—who until now has been calm—explodes in anger. We cannot help but suspect that under Roland's adult emotional distance is childhood's simmering rage: "I wanted to kill him—both of them! Liars! Snakes!…They hurt me…They did something to me. Changed something. I wanted to kill them for it" (105).

---

19   In the 1982 version of *The Gunslinger*, Hax helps to poison the town of Farson.

Roland and Cuthbert ask to see Hax hang, and as part of their training, they are allowed to do so. Before they leave, Cort gives the boys bread to place under Hax's feet. "When it's over," Cort says, "each of you will put this beneath his shoes. Mind you do exactly as I say or I'll clout you into next week" (113).

Interestingly, it is only when Roland climbs the hangman's steps and faces the gibbet that he begins to understand the enormity of his responsibility, and that gunslingers are not the shining heroes he once thought them to be. What he is being trained to become is neither valiant nor beautiful, but dogged, emotionless, and exacting:

> They walked slowly toward the gibbet, and the birds took wing, cawing and circling like a mob of angry dispossessed peasants. Their bodies were flat black against the pure dawnlight of the In-World sky.
>
> For the first time Roland felt the enormity of his responsibility in the matter: this wood was not noble, not part of the awesome machine of Civilization, but merely warped pine from the Forest o'Barony, covered with splattered white bird droppings. It was splashed everywhere—stairs, railing, platform—and it stank . . .
>
> Roland shook his head slowly. There was a lesson here, he realized, not a shining thing but something that was old and rusty and misshapen. It was why their fathers had let them come. And with his usual stubborn and inarticulate doggedness, Roland laid mental hands on whatever it was.... (114).

Roland and Cuthbert descend from the scaffold, although they know full well that if Cort had been present, he "would have knocked them both sprawling," forced them back up the platform, and "put the noose around each of their necks in turn, [and]...made them stand on the trap to feel it" (115). If either of them had wept in fear or lost control of their bladder, Cort would have struck them again. Although the thought of such punishment is frightening, Roland believes that his teacher's harshness would be justified. Suddenly hating his own childhood and its accompanying weakness, young Roland wishes for "the long boots of age" (115).

In the end, Roland and Cuthbert— already inured to violence— decide that watching a man hang "wasn't such of a much" (116). Already becoming the "formidable" man his father predicts he will be (111), Roland decides he will pass his test and become a gunslinger, even if this means that someday he will have to play the part of hangman.

After this flashback is finished, and the story returns to Roland and Jake climbing the mountains in pursuit of the man in black, Roland thinks back to the gallows tree, and the fact that every adventure seems to end "upon the killing ground" (120). Despite all that he has experienced and all the evil he has done in the name of his mission, Roland has a brief hope that this time his quest will be different—surely when one searches for the Dark Tower, *ka* (destiny) must "show its true face" (119). But for Roland, at this point in his development, the face of *ka* is the face of death:

> The boy, the sacrifice, his face innocent and very young in the light of their tiny fire, had fallen asleep over his beans. The gunslinger covered him with the horse blanket and then curled up to sleep himself. (119-20)

If duty calls for it, Roland acknowledges that he will let Jake die as he has let so many others perish before him.

Roland's premonition of impending tragedy and betrayal is buttressed when, more than a week later, Roland and Jake close in on the man in black. In the shadow of a giant stone boulder, Jake begins to tremble violently and his face goes pale. He begs Roland to go back.

When Roland refuses, Jake has a terrible epiphany. "You're going to kill me," Jake says, "you're going to kill me...*And I think you know it...*" (150). Roland speaks "the lie on his lips." He says, "'You'll be all right,' and a greater lie yet: 'I'll take care'" (150). Yet when the gunslinger and the boy face the man in black moments later, the sorcerer laughs at Roland. "We'll speak on the other side, I think," he says. His eyes flicking to Jake, he adds, "Just the two of us" (152).

Chapter IV, "The Slow Mutants": Roland's Coming of Age Battle and the Rejection of the Mother in Favor of the Gun

After their brief encounter with the man in black, Roland and Jake's relationship enters a new phase. What trust they had is now broken. Not only does Roland realize that betrayal awaits, but so does Jake. What is happening in their relationship is symbolized by the transformation of the landscape through which they travel. Gunslinger and boy have now entered the black tunnels below the Cyclopean Mountains. Although in the distance they can hear the thunder of a subterranean river, nothing grows here and the way ahead is barren rock. Roland and Jake drink, but the waters of *khef* have become dangerous. "They... drank from its flat, mineral-salted depth, hoping there was nothing in it that would make them sick or kill them" (162).

During the long hours of pumping a handcar along underground tracks, Jake asks Roland about his coming of age, and Roland tells him the story of how he won his guns. Like the story of Hax's hanging, it is a tale of deceit and treachery. Not surprisingly, that year, in Roland's home city of Gilead, the waters of *khef* were in short supply. The season of Full Earth, which should have been abundant, came "to the land like a vampire lover" (169). It killed the tenant farmers' crops, "turning the fields of the castle-city of Gilead white and sterile" (169).

Just as the waters of *khef* had disappeared from the land, the bonds of *khef* no longer held among men: "In the west, some miles distant and near the borders that were the end of the civilized world, fighting had already begun." (169). The green, abundant land of Roland's childhood was gone:

> The center had frayed like a rag rug that had been washed and walked on and shaken and hung and dried. The thread that held the last jewel at the breast of the world was unraveling. Things were not holding together. The earth drew in its breath in the summer of the coming eclipse. (169)

This terrible and dangerous year also happened to be the time of Roland's sexual awakening. As fourteen-year-old Roland was on the way to the roof to masturbate (he had not yet slept with a woman), he passed his mother's chamber. Outside her door, he met with his father's trusted sorcerer and advisor, Marten Broadcloak. Marten was "dressed with a suspicious, upsetting casualness—black whipcord trousers almost as tight as leotards, and a white shirt open halfway down his hairless chest." (170). His hair was tousled, as if after love-play. Telling Roland that his mother wanted to see him, he ushered Roland into Gabrielle's chambers.

By this point in his life, Roland's mother was almost a stranger to him, but she was "a beloved stranger" (171). But Roland's recent sexual arousal made it obvious to him that Gabrielle and Marten were having an affair. For Roland, love and betrayal were once again riveted together. Only now it was also lust that appeared treacherous, since it had made both his mother and Marten disregard their duty to the hierarchies of Gilead.

Roland—who up until this point in his life had been a child—has a sudden adult realization. A "game" is being played, a "charade." But what Roland doesn't yet know is "who is playing with whom" (171). For Marten, Roland feels a sudden "amorphous fear" as well as "an inchoate hatred" (171). But Roland's emotions for his mother—and all that she represents—also become tainted. We already know that

Roland is destined to commit matricide (118), though how and when this will happen we do not discover until the fourth Dark Tower novel, *Wizard and Glass*.

After a verbal confrontation with Marten, in which Roland reminds the sorcerer that he is nothing more than his father's "bondsman" and that he owed fealty to the line of Deschain, Marten mockingly tells Roland to "go and find your hand" (172). Roland leaves, but he does not go to the roof. Instead, he storms to Cort's cabin. Kicking in the door, he cries out in High Speech, "Cort, I want you, bondsman," and demands to take his test of manhood. Cort—a squat man runneled with scars and thick with muscle—tries to dissuade him. "You are early, puler," Cort says casually, though he uses the formal interchange of High Speech. "Two years early at the very best, I should judge. I will ask only once. Will you cry off?" (174).

Cort knows only too well that failing the test means banishment, no matter what the cause, but Roland the boy is as intransigent as Roland the man will be. Although Cort suspects that Roland has been played for a fool, and that Marten—a servant of the Good Man— wants to terminate the line of Deschain and have Roland sent west in disgrace, Roland is blinded by his own rage. No matter what the risk, he is determined to win his guns so that he can kill the man who has dishonored the Line of Deschain and made his father into a cuckold. With regret, Cort finally agrees. "One hour," he says in a voice that is both dry and businesslike. "And the weapon of your choice" (175).

Despite his inexperience and youth, Roland wins his guns. He defeats Cort by a clever ploy. Instead of using a traditional weapon in the Square Yard confrontation, Roland uses the hawk, David, who over the last three years he has befriended. Roland knows that David will be killed in this confrontation, but he is willing to make this sacrifice, since his own future hangs in the balance:

> "I think you die today," he said, continuing to stroke [the hawk]. "I think you will be made a sacrifice,

like all those little birds we trained you on. Do you remember? No? It doesn't matter. After today I am the hawk (176-77).

Not long after winning his guns, Roland will be sent east with two of his *ka*-mates, since the Good Man's forces—deprived of Roland's humiliation and banishment—now seek to kill him. The story of Roland's Hambry adventures—and his love affair with a beautiful girl named Susan Delgado—unfolds in Book IV of the Dark Tower series, *Wizard and Glass*. In terms of Roland's fate, that tragic tale is but a continuation of the character arc begun in *The Gunslinger*. Roland proves to be an excellent soldier and strategist. At age fourteen, he outwits men much older and more experienced than himself, including the Big Coffin Hunters, led by the elderly failed gunslinger, Eldred Jonas. However, in terms of his heart, Roland is less successful.

Although Roland seems to both love and lust for Susan, he somehow cannot completely shed the disgust he felt upon realizing his mother had followed the way of desire rather than duty. While trapped in the treacherous seeing sphere called Maerlyn's Grapefruit, Roland comes to believe that he must choose between Susan's love and his quest for the Dark Tower. He chooses the Tower, and as a result Susan—who, because of her affair with Roland, has been branded a traitor to her town—is burned to death on a Charyou Tree fire. She dies proclaiming her love for him.

To be a hawk, or "God's gunslinger," as Cort so aptly calls it, is a lonely and dangerous fate:

> You cannot friend a hawk…unless you are half hawk yourself, alone and only a sojourner in the land, without friends or the need of them. The hawk pays no coinage to love or morals (176).

By the age of fourteen, Roland had chosen the way of the hawk, and it is one he follows relentlessly. He does not question the way of the gun until his fateful meeting with the boy Jake at the way station. However, as we suspected all along, Roland does not change easily, and his relationship with this lonely lost boy is destined to end in tragedy.

By the end of Chapter IV, "The Slow Mutants," Jake—who had once been trusting—has grown cynical. He knows that, to Roland, he is ultimately no more than "a poker chip" in the high stakes game being played with the man in black (187). When Roland responds to Jake's anxiety offhandedly, he is secretly horrified at himself. For the first time in his life, he fears the "self-loathing" that lies in wait for him (188). That self-loathing does not take long to blossom.

After a long journey in the dark, Roland and Jake reach the end of the tunnel beneath the Cyclopean Mountains. But in order to return to the light—the pinprick of which they see ahead of them—they must first cross a trestle track on foot. This track, which is rotten with age, crosses a vast abyss. At the bottom of the abyss flows a powerful river.

Ninety feet from the trestle's end, a shadow steps out of the darkness and its silhouette blocks the daylight. It is the man in black. The sorcerer laughs loudly and Jake begins to totter, his arms gyrating. As Jake falls, Roland faces a final test. It is one that will determine the trajectory of the rest of his life:

> Metal ripped and sloughed beneath them; the rails canted through a slow and dreamy twisting. The boy plunged, and one hand flew up like a gull in the darkness, up, up, and then he hung over the pit; he dangled there, his dark eyes staring up at the gunslinger in final blind lost knowledge.
>
> "Help me."
>
> Booming, racketing: "No more games. Come now, gunslinger. Or catch me never."

All the chips on the table. Every card up but one.
The boy dangled, a living Tarot card, the Hanged man,
the Phoenician sailor, innocent lost and barely above
the wave of a stygian sea (203-4).

For a moment, Roland hesitates. Once again Jake calls for help, and the man in black pronounces that if Roland pauses in his quest "Then I shall leave you." Enraged and blind to everything but his quest, Roland cries out, "*No! You shall NOT!* Leaping over Jake, he lands "in a skidding, plunging rush toward the light" (204). In the dreadful silence that follows, Jake speaks. "Go then. There are other worlds than these" (205). The trestle collapses and Jake falls to his death.

Standing "drunkenly, pallid as a ghost" (205), Roland realizes that he has crossed over into "damnation" (204). Ahead of him await "further degradations of the spirit...that might make this one seem infinitesimal," yet he will continue to "flee the boy's face," trying to "bury it in cunts and in killing" (205). Yet ultimately Roland knows that in the end, when he enters life's "final room," it will be Jake's face "looking at him over a candle flame" (205).

In memory of his "Isaac," his innocent sacrificial victim, Roland gathers wood. Then he and the man in black hold palaver in an ancient bone-strewn killing ground which Roland calls a *golgotha*, or "place-of-the-skull" (1982 edition, 197). Over the course of one endless night, the man in black reads Roland's future with a deck of tarot cards and then gives him a terrifying glimpse of the multiverse. When Roland awakes, he is ten years older. His black hair is finer, and it has thinned and gone gray at the temples. The lines in his face are deeper and his skin rougher. The man in black, who he sacrificed so much to follow, has been reduced to a skeleton.

Taking the man in black's jawbone, Roland sets his back toward the rising sun. He has passed his own internal Rubicon, and his journey forward appears bleak. However, he will not abandon his quest. Heading toward the ocean, Roland declares, "I loved you Jake." Sitting by the water's edge, Roland turns his face toward the light and dreams of reaching the Tower and "winding his horn, to do some final unimaginable battle" (231).

CONCLUSION

In the Dark Tower series, the force that controls men's lives is *ka*, or fate, and Roland's interaction with Jake Chambers has altered the gunslinger's *ka*. When we leave him at the end of *The Gunslinger*, Roland—the heartless killer—has changed. He realizes that he loved Jake, and he regrets letting the boy tumble to his death. Although Roland is still devoted to his quest, he believes that he has damned himself. But it is only in this darkest hour that Roland's redemption can begin.

In the opening scene of the second Dark Tower novel, *The Drawing of the Three*, Roland dreams he is drowning. But to Roland, this is a good dream, since he is the one drowning, not Jake: "he found this a relief because it would be far better to drown as Jake than to live as himself, a man who had, for a cold dream, betrayed a child who had trusted him" (5). As Roland tries to scramble out of the frothy waves to save his weapons, he is attacked by a monster he dubs a "lobstrosity." In *The Gunslinger*, Roland wished for "the destruction of his talented [right] hand," since "its only true talent was murder" (84). In *The Drawing of the Three*, Roland gets his wish. The monster clips off most of his right big toe and the first two fingers of the gunslinger's dominant right hand, depriving him of his trigger finger.

Roland's wounds soon become septic. Dying of blood poisoning, Roland crawls up the beach, where he finds two magical, free-standing doorways. Through these doorways he enters the minds of two people from Jake's home city of New York. The first is a junkie named Eddie Dean from 1987, who is addicted to heroin just as Roland is addicted to his quest for the Tower. The second is Odetta Holmes/Detta Walker, a young African-American woman from 1964, who has lost her legs from just above the knee. Just as Roland has two selves—the heartless killer and the romantic who wishes to atone and change—Odetta/Detta has two selves, one of whom is a socially conscious civil rights activist and another who is a dangerously enraged sadist.

Finally, through a third doorway, Roland enters the mind of a psychotic serial killer named Jack Mort. Roland forces Mort to take his own life, symbolically destroying the part of himself that is also a kind of serial killer. But before he does this, Roland prevents Mort from murdering Jake. (Ultimately, by saving Jake in this world, he prevents Jake from dying in Mid-World.)

At the end of *The Drawing of the Three*, Roland—who has been sick in body as well as mind and spirit—has been renewed. He has expiated the sin of killing Jake, and he now has two new traveling companions. But it is in the third Dark Tower novel, *The Waste Lands*, that Roland's debt to Jake is repaid and his redemption truly begins.

In a Speaking Ring much like the circle of stones where Roland saved Jake's life back in *The Gunslinger*, Roland, Susannah, (formerly Detta/Odetta) and Eddie create a doorway-between-worlds. Through it, they draw Jake into Mid-World. During Jake's symbolic rebirth, Roland risks his life to snatch the boy from the monstrous demon that guards such portals. Once Roland and Jake have been reunited, Roland promises Jake that he will never let him fall again. Throughout the rest of the series, Roland keeps this promise. As we learn when Roland reaches the Tower at the end of the seventh book of the series, he has not yet expiated all of his sins. But in this particular iteration of his journey, he has come a step closer to redemption.

WORKS CITED

The Gunslinger. 1982. New York: Plume-Penguin, 1988.

The Gunslinger. 2003 (revised edition). New York: Plume-Penguin, 2003.

The Drawing of the Three. 1987. New York: Plume-Penguin, 1989.

The Waste Lands. 1991. New York: Plume-Penguin, 1989.

IT: KING'S MASTERPIECE HITS THE BIG SCREEN (WELL, HALF OF IT, ANYWAY...)

by Tyson Blue

Blue Bio (with apologies to Linda Ronstadt)

Tyson Blue, a true *eminence grise in the world of horror criticism,* has been writing and publishing reviews in the genre since the 1970s. He is considered an expert on the work of Stephen King and the various media projects related thereto, and has lectured extensively on the subject around the country. His *The Unseen King* was for years considered the definitive work on King's early and unpublished material. His work appeared in *Cemetery Dance, Twilight Zone, 2 AM,* and he was Contributing Editor for *Castle Rock: The Stephen King Newsletter* for most of its run in the late '80s. He has also written a number of short stories for various anthologies. He lives with his wife, Janice, near Rochester, New York and practices law in his spare time.

IT, Stephen King's epic novel about a group of kids in a small city in Maine and their decades-spanning battle with a monstrous, child-devouring creature that lives in the sewers below, has always been one of my favorite of King's novels. Not so much for the monster stuff, although that's terrific—I loved it more for the segments dealing with the children's lives, the things they do when they're not chasing IT.

If you wanted to know what my childhood in the small New England mill-town of Franklin, New Hampshire, was like, read *IT*. We ran around town, playing "guns"—not army, not cowboys, but "guns" and said things like "Jeezum Crow!", and drank Moxie (which figures more in 11/22/63 than it does in *IT*, but hey! It's my review!).

More to the pertinent point, we played in a wooded area with streams running through it, dotted with large, cone-shaped wells that led down to the sewers that carried waste from the houses atop the hill to the east of where we played, before it was ultimately dumped into the waters of the Merrimack River, which formed from the intersection of the Winnipesaukee and Pemigewasset Rivers right behind the high school, whence it headed on down into Massachusetts and, ultimately, the Atlantic. Those wells reminded me of nothing so much as the wells leading to the lair of the Morlocks in the 1959 version of *The Time Machine*, directed by the great George Pal. And decades later, when King described the wells which dotted the Barrens in Derry, I knew exactly what they looked like.

In other words, it was the "kid stuff" that made *IT* one of my favorite King novels. And that's why I like Andy Muschietti's 2017 film, *IT: Chapter One*, so much—it got the "kid stuff" right.

The film used locations in Port Hope, Ontario, about an hour east of Toronto, to stand in for the fictional town of Derry, Maine, which is in itself a combination of Bangor and Stamford, Connecticut (mostly Bangor). Port Hope is completely convincing as a mid-sized New England city, aided in no small part by the inclusion of such Bangor references as the Paul Bunyan statue and the Thomas Hill standpipe, a Bangor landmark which figures prominently in the novel's climax (it remains to be seen whether or not it will play as important a role in the second film, shooting in Canada as this is being written). Having grown up in a small New England city, I can tell you that the atmosphere is perfectly recreated.

Although the earliest portions of King's novel took place in 1957 and the "contemporary" part in 1984, the *Chapter One* film is set in 1988, with the second part presumably set in 2019, the year the film is tentatively set for release. This is does not significantly affect the basic story—there are, unfortunately still bullies and their victims, high schools are still home to winners and losers, popular kids and everyone else, and so all that is really needed to make the transition is to change hairstyles, clothing, films on the theater marquee, and so forth.

Cell phones were in their infancy at that time, having first been practically developed in 1983, and would not have been in wide use. In addition, although the Internet as we know it was created in 1981, its use was very limited and the modern Internet would not come into being until 1995, so the novel's plot could transfer to the screen relatively intact, without the vast changes these modern advances would have imposed on the film.

The story focuses on the Losers Club, a group of seven youngsters drawn together by their ostracism from Derry society, or rather Derry school society. And this ostracism takes place for many of the same reasons it does today—being poor, overweight, black, Jewish, gawky, nerdy, sickly, being a girl with a bad reputation or just plain not fitting in.

Muschietti has assembled a fantastic cast of young actors to portray the Losers, and all of them do a spectacular job. Sophia Lillis turns in a breakout performance as Beverly Marsh, one of the greatest characters King has ever created. (Lillis also appears in the HBO series *Sharp Objects*, playing the main character played by Amy Adams, as a young person.) Finn Wolfhard, fresh from his standout performance in the first two seasons of the Netflix series *Stranger Things*, which bears more than a passing resemblance to IT, is great as Richie Tozier, the would-be wiseguy comedian of the group.

The rest of the ensemble are stellar as well. Jason Lieberher is Bill Denbrough, whose brother Georgie is killed in spectacular fashion by IT at the film's iconic beginning, which closely resembles the novel. Jeremy Ray Taylor is Ben Hanscom, whose secret adoration for Beverly fuels much of the film's understory. Chosen Jacobs is Mike Hanlon, a young black man who is trying to fit into a town that hates him, particularly a gang led by the sociopathic Henry Bowers (Nicholas Hamilton). Jack Dylan Grazer is Eddie Kaspbrak, a boy whose asthma may be in large part psychosomatic, and engineered by his bizarre mother, Sonia (Molly Jane Atkinson). Wyatt Oleff is Stan Uris, a young Jewish boy seeking to please his rabbi father and dealing with his own refusal to believe in the supernatural things that are happening around him, including a particularly scary manifestation of IT.

In 1990, the novel was adapted as a two-part, four-hour TV movie, which featured Tim Curry as the title character in his guise as Pennywise the Clown, a performance which set a very high bar for anyone to try to replace Curry in anyone's mind in the role. Muschietti wisely chose to create his own unique take on the character.

Bill Skarsgård, a member of the Swedish Skarsgård acting dynasty, is Pennywise. His IT primarily manifests as a more Victorian-appearing clown, who never really has a purely funny aspect. With his perpetual snaggle-toothed grin and steady, unblinking yellow eyes, his Pennywise is always sinister. When he appears, it is almost always suddenly, his head thrust forward, moving quickly until he is right in the face of one of the Losers. This makes him a scary, dangerous presence, always threatening.

And although we never see him in his true form, it is obvious from the start that IT is a creature never before encountered, although he takes on the aspect of the things each of the Losers fears most—for Eddie, a leper, for Mike, the victims of the fire at The Black Spot, a segregated nightclub burned down by bigots in the town's past. For Stan, IT is the eerie, twisted flautist in a painting hanging in his father's office at the temple. Ben sees IT as a headless boy killed in an explosion at the Derry Ironworks, whose head ended up in the branches of a tree, as shown in an illustrated history of the town he finds in the library.

Only Beverly sees IT's true form, its deadlights, near the film's climax, but for much of the film she has to deal with her father, whose interest in her may be more than normal paternal concern.

IT's minions are a teen gang, led by the aforementioned Henry Bowers, a mullet-wearing psychopath whose sadistic crimes may be a way of acting out his hatred of his brutal police officer father. He even scares his three cohorts, as shown by their reaction when, early in the film, he pulls a knife and starts to carve his name in Ben Hanscom's belly, casing Ben to break free and flee into the Barrens, which actually leads to the formation of the Losers Club.

As the Losers coalesce, they piece together what they have seen and begin to get a picture of the cycle of child death that has plagued Derry since its creation. They also intuit the way the adults in the town turn a blind eye to the situation, and realize that anything that gets done about IT will have to be done by them.

Another classic scene from the novel is the Apocalyptic Rockfight, in which the Losers fend off an attack by Bowers and his gang on Mike Hanlon by pelting the four with rocks until they flee, with Bowers vowing revenge.

One major change the film makes is moving the entrance to IT's realm from the sewers to the House on Niebolt Street, home to the leper seen by Eddie. The Losers descend into the well on a rope in search of Beverly, who was taken by the creature after IT had temporarily caused the group to fracture. They are reunited in their desire to rescue Beverly.

While they are separated, IT is able to fight them off. Bill is led astray by an image of his dead brother, Georgie. Mike is attacked and injured by Bowers, who has tracked him down after murdering his father with a knife. Stan is attacked by IT, whose huge, tooth-bedizened mouth battens on him and threatens to eat him.

It is only when the Losers all reunite and awaken Beverly that they can successfully take on IT, wounding it and driving IT down the well, at least severely injured and hopefully dead.

The film has a long, gentler denouement, where they all gather a few weeks after the confrontation underground, at which time, their memories of the events already beginning to fade, they all swear a blood oath to return if the killings ever begin again and to finish IT once and for all, or die trying.

And, since most of us have read the novel, we know that, 27 years later, IT does in fact come back, and the adult Losers, minus one, will find themselves drawn back to Derry to face the monster one last time. (And if you're one of those whiners who don't like spoilers, I don't coddle you people, you should have known that, so go away!) But we'll all have to wait until at least September 6, 2019, to find out how it comes out in the cinematic world.

For now, though, we have *IT: Chapter One*, as it is revealed to be titled at the end, and a most enjoyable film it is—scary and exciting, and poignant and affecting all at the same time.

And, as in the novel, I liked the kid stuff the best. And in this one, the kid stuff is done amazingly well.

This one's for my pal, Harlan Ellison. I miss you, kiddo.

THE STEPHEN KING IMMERSION PHENOMENON

by Kevin Quigley

Kevin Quigley is a novelist and Stephen King monographer, whose books *Chart of Darkness*, *A Good Story and Good Words*, and *The Illustrated Stephen King Movie Trivia Guide* (co-written with Brian Freeman and Hans-Åke Lilja) explore the untapped or lesser-known avenues of Stephen King's vast universe. Kevin also runs Charnel House, one of the longest-running Stephen King websites on the internet, focusing on full-length book reviews and up-to-date news. Kevin is a graphic designer in Boston where he lives with his husband Shawn.

I n the far-flung past of the mid-1980s, Stephen King expert Dr. Michael Collings wrote an essay on King's then-newest novel, *IT*, titled, "A Concatenation of Monsters." The essay does a deep dive into what makes *IT* work, exploring the unusual crossroads of the mythic and historic, of narrative fiction merged with loose autobiography, and more. After pulling back the critical veil and admitting how much the novel moved him, Collings calls *IT* King's "comprehensive masterpiece," and concludes that the book "transcends itself to stand as the most powerful novel King has yet written."

So let's talk about transcendence and the work of Stephen King. Collings' point about *IT* is that the book stands as a masterpiece on its own—the novel is, for the most part, an objectively fantastic work. But it's the audience response, that untouchable, unquantifiable *feeling* the book gives the reader, that makes it transcend itself. It's more than simply being swept away by the story or being invested in the characters. It's the way so many of King's novels have of making you feel like you're *part* of the story, like these things are happening to you—not in some recounted past, but *right now*. We're in Ben Mears' raiding party in *'Salem's Lot,* we're in those sewers with the Losers Club in *IT,* we're working the midway in *Joyland,* and we're inmates in the Dooling Correctional Facility for Women in *Sleeping Beauties.*

IT manages to pull off the near-impossible, firmly inserting us into the Losers Club in 1958, and then bringing us back into the circle in 1985, ready to grow young again. The book's multiple concurrent finales across two timelines and several locales serve as the epitome of that transcendence—you're not *reading* the work so much as *absorbing* it, the words sometimes actually getting in the way of your experience. While *IT* might be one of the best examples of this phenomenon, it's by no means unique in King's canon: the man has a knack for this sort of thing.

Witness *Carrie*, right at the start. It's a short book and we just barely get into the lives of these fascinating characters...but the scenes in which Carrie uses her telekinesis seem to *drag* the reader into the book, heightening and expanding the very experience of reading. Much has been made of King's "cinematic" text; he uses those tools bluntly here, wielding the word *flex* like a stage direction, signaling to the reader that something awesome is about to happen. It's that full immersion in the text, that sense that the book is pulling you along for the ride. Reading itself is secondary to the experience of being *in* the book, as though the spaces between the words are themselves telekinetic.

Over the next few years, it's psi phenomena that King would go to most readily to achieve this magnetic momentum. See Danny's clairvoyant flashes in *The Shining*, Charlie McGee's pyrokinetic events in *Firestarter*, or Johnny Smith's psychic episodes in *The Dead Zone*: there's a particular heat, of friction, that comes through in these sequences. It's not just moments of excitement or horror, either. There are two moments in *The Dead Zone*—when Johnny is holding Denny, the baby, and when he touches old wood and gets sepia-toned memories of the long past—that emerge quietly out of the narrative, that also retain this unusual feel of transcendence. It's not telling. It's not showing. Despite the fact that these moments center on supernatural elements, these sequences feel like breathing, like autonomic responses inside the reader that King simply spelunked into consciousness.

Beyond psi abilities and King's unique touch describing them, witness his evolving take on romantic love. King mastered the art of characters falling in love early on: Sue and Tommy in *Carrie* are in love before the book begins, and despite Sue's reservations, theirs seems a mostly healthy, happy young relationship. King uses these relationships as a springboard for drama: Larry and Lucy in *The Stand*, Arnie and Leigh in *Christine*, even Johnny and Sarah in *The Dead Zone*. Not until the fourth book of the *Dark Tower* series does the romantic relationship become the *point* of the story. Amidst all the talk of thinnies and harriers and the Crimson King, Roland and Susan's young relationship takes center stage, emerging as Stephen King's only real stab at the romance genre (despite snippets in *Misery*). The moments this pair are together generate the same sort of *frisson* that the psi occurrences in King's earlier books did. Incongruously, Roland and Susan's relationship is both remarkably real against the epic, myth-making backdrop, and elevated into something like myth itself. If the Mohaine is the apotheosis of all deserts, then Roland and Susan's love affair is the apotheosis of clandestine relationships. Upon each meeting, there's that same pull, the sense that the words are getting in the way of experiencing the story as it unfolds. It's so immersive, it almost feels like voyeurism.

Despite Roland and Susan's tragic end, it's the sheer joy and thrill of their togetherness that makes us one with the story. Though Stephen King is primarily known as a horror writer, this utilization of joy as a story element is one of the most vital in his toolbox. Witness Rose Mc-Clendon's first look around her own apartment in *Rose Madder*: King stops the momentum of the book to focus on this seemingly simple moment. In doing so, he elevates the moment to something that functions on a different level than both the violent drama of the beginning of the novel and the magical realism that comprises the latter half. It's a tricky take, because to treat it like something outsize would overwhelm its fragility; to sweep by it would be to ignore its essential power. Through his understanding of the character and her circumstance, King is able to place the reader in that apartment with her, an unseen empathic guest exploring Rosie's first genuine moment of self since the beginning of the book.

On a subtler scale, we can turn to Dev Jones in *Joyland*. The book's ostensible "A" story is that of the ghost haunting Joyland's Horror House, and of the killer who might still prowl Joyland's grounds. The "B" story, however, is at times the more engaging of the two: the story of Dev Jones getting over his breakup and learning to be his own person again. It's a bit of a pale echo to Rosie McClendon's more intense tale of escaping systematic abuse at the hands of her psychopath husband, but because *Joyland* is a gentle book with occasional crescendos of action and emotion, Dev's story feels just as vital and just as electric. The short novel revolves on the hinge of Dev "wearing the fur": putting on the Howie the Happy Hound costume and entertaining children at the park. The parallels to *Rose Madder* again assert themselves: here again, it's simple joy driving those moments of transcendence; Dev's happiness in wearing the costume supersedes all other worry and thought, just as Rosie standing in her own apartment had done.

The plot and/or situation might be how we describe King's books to people, and the incredibly well-drawn characters are how we identify with the narrative, but these moments are why we keep coming back for more—not just to new stories, but to revisiting the old ones. We could examine each novel individually and single out these moments of elevation, of transcendence. Every time Edgar Freemantle paints a picture in *Duma Key*, we feel it. Every time Bobbi Anderson reveals a new power or new gadget in *The Tommyknockers*, we feel it. Every time Pete Riley gets dragged into another game of Hearts in *Hearts in Atlantis*, we feel it. Maybe their actions don't line up with our lives, but the feelings they evoke? Like Bob Dylan wrote in "Tangled Up in Blue," they flow off the page as if they're already written on our souls. These are good moments and bad, thrilling moments and quiet. These are the moments that are already in our psyches and hearts and lives, just waiting for some talented scrivener to bring them out in the open, and to share them with the world. All we can do is race to read faster, to keep up with what's already there.

13 STEPHEN KING BOOKS YOU MUST HAVE ON A DESERT ISLAND

By Stanley Wiater

Stanley Wiater has been interviewing and writing about Stephen King since 1979. He is the co-author, with Christopher Golden and Hank Wagner, of *The Complete Stephen King Universe*. He lives in western Massachusetts, less than a day's drive from Bangor, Maine.

1. *'Salem's Lot:* Simply stated, the best modern vampire novel ever. Period.

2. *The Shining:* Even more bluntly stated, the most terrifying haunted hotel novel ever written. Period.

3. *Misery:* King at the top of his game with this relentlessly suspenseful psycho—and still deeply, truly psychological—thriller.

4. *The Stand: Complete and Uncut:* If King never wrote another novel, his Constant Readers would somehow have no complaints.

5. ***Different Seasons:*** A brilliant collection of novellas, the literary form where King has no rivals.

6. ***Danse Macabre:*** An indispensable guide to every form of modern horror in the mass media, sprinkled throughout with some delicious, if still tender and raw, autobiography.

7. ***The Dead Zone:*** If you have half a heart, this novel will bring you to tears. If you have half a soul, it will shock you to your core.

8. ***Pet Sematary:*** During our very first interview, King confessed he had in fact written something that was so darkly hardcore he had no plans of ever publishing it. Later, to settle a contract dispute with the publisher, that manuscript became *Pet Sematary*.

9. ***On Writing:*** The best contemporary memoir of what it takes to be a writer, as well as an incredible guide to dealing with the craft of writing itself.

10. ***Stephen King Goes to the Movies:*** Not only does this collection contain five of his most acclaimed short stories—including *Rita Hayworth and Shawshank Redemption* and "1408"—we get a unique "behind the scenes" view of every film adaptation from King himself.

11. ***Skeleton Crew:*** Not only a great collection of short stories, herein you will also be treated to *The Mist*—which is so incredible, it has already been adapted into a feature film and a television series.

12. ***IT:*** Some Constant Readers will forever declare *The Stand* is King's masterpiece. We say this *IT* is truly *it*.

13. ***The Dark Tower:*** Okay, this last one is a bit of a cheat. For the Constant Reader, we recommend you bring along *all* of the titles in *The Dark Tower* series. Even at the risk of sinking your lifeboat or raft.

BEING A STEPHEN KING FAN: NOT EASY BUT OH SO REWARDING!

By Hans-Åke Lilja

Hans-Åke Lilja is the founder of *Lilja's Library—The World of Stephen King*, a leading Stephen King fan website for the past 22 years. Lilja has just released his third Stephen King-connected book, *Shining in the Dark*, both in the US and internationally. His first two King-themed books are *Lilja's Library—The World of Stephen King* (2010) and *The Illustrated Stephen King Movie Trivia Book* (2013). Lilja has also conducted two lengthy interviews with Stephen King. Lilja lives with his family in Sweden.

I've been a Stephen King fan for as long as I can remember. Well, almost. I got my first book when I was thirteen years old. It was a Christmas present and an attempt by my parents to get me to read something other than comics. I'm not sure why they picked *Carrie*. Maybe someone recommended it to them. I got it, read it, and liked it. Not as much as comics, though. Soon after, I was supposed to read a book in school for a book report. Not being an avid reader, I didn't have a clue what to read. But then I saw a copy of *Cujo*. The one with the dog fangs on the cover. I'm sure you know it. And I thought that if I'm going to spend time reading a book, it should at least have a cool cover. *Cujo* did. But it had so much more. And while I read the book, a love for King's work developed, and I have never looked back.

For a number of years, I read every book by Stephen King that had been translated into my native language: Swedish. And I had a lot to catch up on. But I did, and a collection of Swedish books started to form. But as the 90s rolled around, I had read all the books that had been translated and I realized two things. The first was that the Swedish publisher didn't rush the translations of the books. It could be years before a book was translated. And second, there were a lot of books that hadn't been translated. What eventually pushed me over the edge and got me reading the books in English for good was the fact that the third *Dark Tower* book was released and I didn't have the patience to wait to find out what happened to Roland and the others. After reading a few books in English, I also noticed that I enjoyed hearing King's voice (which is somewhat lost in a translated text, no matter how well translated it is) in the stories.

When 1996 rolled around, the internet became accessible to everyone. I was a student at the time and spent a lot of time in front of a computer. As I surfed the net, I started to find other King fans online. Sites and forums that talked about King and his work. Being from the small country of Sweden, where I usually learned about a book when it showed up on the shelves in the stores, a brand-new world opened itself to me. I could now find out about books released in the US. I could get the bookstores here in Sweden to order them for me (English books were not all that common in Swedish bookstores back then). Some of the first books I ordered were the six installments of *The Green Mile*. Each month, I got a new book. The bookstore where I ordered them wanted to wait and order them all at the same time, when the last one was out, but I didn't go for that. I wanted them as soon as I could, and they arranged that for me.

As time moved on and I got more and more used to finding info on the internet, I started to feel that I wanted more. I wanted sites that listed all of King's books, that listed all the stories. I wanted sites that reported news about King and his work. But that was hard to find. Remember, this was back in 1996 and the internet was new. Most sites had revolving skulls, red text, and black backgrounds. In short, the internet was new and we were all unsure how to use it. But I was twenty-six and thought I had the world under my arm and could do anything. So when I didn't find the King site that I was looking for, there was never any doubt about what to do. I created the site I wanted and "Lilja's Library—The World of Stephen King" was born.

The first version of the page didn't look very exciting. And it was far from what I wanted, but it was there and it was alive and I decided that I was going to do the best I could with it. Little did I know that I would write this twenty-one years later and still be running the site.

But here we are and the site is bigger than ever. I have met King three times, interviewed him on the phone twice, and released three books connected to King's work, the latest of which will be released in at least five different languages. Who would have believed that twenty-one years ago? Well, not me. But I love every second of it and feel like I could go on for another twenty years. But as with everything in life, there have been ups and downs. Times when other things have taken up my time and the site has been neglected. Not totally, but some, and sometimes more than I wanted. But luckily those times have been few and short. And Stephen King has always been a presence in my life since back in 1983 when I discovered him. I don't think there's been a day since then that I haven't done or thought about something connected to King or his work. Sometimes it might just have been as little as the fact that I was reading a book or seeing a movie. Or just reading something about someone who I know is a fan of King. And when it's been at its height, I've been planning trips to see King, doing interviews or experiencing the excitement when a new book arrives and you open that first page. But either way, King has and is very present in my life.

As I write this, I'm in one of the peak periods. I was in New York just a few weeks ago, where I saw Stephen and Owen read from *Sleeping Beauties* and got a chance to speak to them both backstage. I'm in various stages of editing five different editions of the books *Shining in the Dark*. In about a month, I'll be going to Bulgaria for the first time to promote *Shining in the Dark*, and a few months after that, I'll do an eight-stop, five-day tour in Sweden talking about Stephen King. It is a hectic time, but again, I love every second of it and wouldn't trade it for anything.

But it's not always easy to be a King fan. I have discovered that many of us King fans have the mind of a collector. And with King there is a lot to collect. You can collect every book in every version. You can collect all the movies, all the magazines that King has been published in, and so on. There is no end to what you can collect…other than the limitations of your wallet, because collecting King isn't cheap. And in the beginning, I collected everything I could get my hands on. When it was at its worst (yeah, I choose to call it worst) I even had a VHS tape where I collected trailers and teasers from TV (this was before those things were on the internet), as well as that text that ran at the end of the day, showing what was going to air tomorrow. Basically, the text said something like: "*The Shining*—8PM." I know it was crazy, but that was how much of a collector I was. I then decided that it's not possible to collect everything connected to King. At least not for me. Now I have a more (for me) healthy mindset to collecting King. I collect one book in each language King has been translated into and I collect movie props from King movies. But that's it.

But why the site, you might ask? Why do I spend so much time on Stephen King and his work? Well, it's easy. I love to read his books, and even if I didn't have the site, I would read all the books, and read all the information I could find about King and his books. I would still read it and enjoy it. The only extra step I do is to put it all on a website. And since I have done this for over twenty years, I have a routine that makes it quite easy to post an update or news about a book. But one of the reasons I still do it is because of all the new friends I've made over the years through the site: so many people who, like me, love to read, talk, and live King. And that is one of the biggest rewards. And it's a reward that never ends. I get new messages every day from people asking about King, commenting about King, or in some other way, "talking King" with me. That is one of the reasons I keep the site alive.

Another reason are all the fun things I have gotten to do thanks to the site. I have met King, I have interviewed him, and I have been able to edit a book, *Shining in the Dark*, which is full of stories from great authors. And let me tell you, editing a book is, in itself, the subject for an essay. Plus, every time I start my phone now, I see a photo of me and King. To me, that is a great treat and I feel very humble to have experienced all this. But what it all comes down to in the end, for me, is the excitement I get when I open a new King book and know that I have several hundred of unread pages in front of me. That is pure joy.

HOW TO RESEARCH AND WRITE A STEPHEN KING BIBLIOGRAPHY: A TALE FROM THE LITERARY TRENCHES

By Justin Brooks

Justin Brooks is the author of *Stephen King: A Primary Bibliography of the World's Most Popular Author* (and a revised second edition) and co-author of *Stephen King: The Non-Fiction* (with Rocky Wood). He is also the author of numerous articles on King. He lives in Richmond, Virginia, with his wife, son, and their two cats.

M y grandmother was a "list-maker" and so am I. Also, my mother is a collector and that's a category I also fall under. In the early '90s, my half-brother gifted me a whole stack of Stephen King mass market paperbacks after I expressed interest in King's work; I'd heard about the premise of the film adaptation of

Christine from another family member. At that time, I didn't have all of the master's books, although I did start buying additional titles to flesh out my brother's donation. This was a couple of years before the internet started to really take off or really even be available at all in rural Virginia. I'd gone to a local store with my parents and seen a couple of titles that, due to the fact that they were newer, were not listed in the "Also By" section of any of the books my brother had given to me. I decided to make my own, up-to-date list of all the books, so I wrote down those titles (I jotted down *Dolores Claiborne* as *Dolores Mailborne* for some stupid, eleven-year-old reason), so you may want to go back and check my work on Stephen King for errors! I took my piece of paper, the newest King book that I owned, another piece of paper, some white-out and an ink pen, and started making my own King checklist. I distinctly remember starting it at my parents' house and then taking it to my grandparents' house so I could continue to work on it as we watched the fourth of July fireworks in our small, heavily wooded town (shades of *The Tommyknockers*, anyone?). At any rate, this piece of paper was definitely the start of *Stephen King: A Primary Bibliography of the World's Most Popular Author*. This was literally the start of my 600-plus page bibliography. I literally carried around and re-copied this list until it eventually grew into the behemoth, the first edition of which was published in 2008.

At the age of twelve, while out to dinner with my parents, we saw a guy wearing a Stephen King t-shirt. My parents asked where he acquired said shirt and he told them from a store called Betts Bookstore in Bangor, Maine. For Christmas that year, I got an *Insomnia* t-shirt, but more importantly (and to my parents, somewhat bafflingly), I was more excited about the Betts Bookstore catalog that was included in the box. It spoke of a forthcoming novel called *Rose Madder*, which I naturally had to add to my list. But it also listed magazines, anthologies, and newspapers containing short stories and/or non-fiction pieces that did not appear in any of the proper King books on my list. This was opening up a whole new world to me. With the advent of the internet, after hours of searching, I found perhaps one or two websites that listed (in part) some of these "uncollected" and "unpublished" pieces.

A couple of years later, the internet allowed one to hook up with fellow King fans and "trade" photocopies of these rare works. It also made it easier to purchase copies of the magazines, books, and other publications that contained them from Betts Bookstore, Overlook Connection, eBay, and so forth. By this point, my list had been migrated to a Microsoft Word document on our home computer. It wasn't necessarily a checklist because I wanted to have something that nobody else had done before. Granted, there were a couple of other bibliographies dedicated solely to King that had been published at the time, but one problem was that they were as out-of-date as the "also by" list in a used King paperback! Naturally, at the pace that King writes, that is to be expected, but the more pressing concern was the fact that they missed vast swaths of pieces that should have been included. I understand that in pre- and early internet days, listing everything King had published was a much more difficult task, and to be honest, even today, I have trouble finding references for pieces that are rumored to exist.

At any rate, in 1999, a year before I was to go off to college, I decided I was going to flesh out the document by adding publisher, publishing location, date, and ISBN number. I didn't have any intention of turning it into a proper bibliography at this point and was simply thinking that the more detailed the entry, the better it would look. Because of my photocopy trading and independent research, especially in the area of tracking down "undiscovered" non-fiction pieces (and even some fiction), my work was noticed by my online friend, who had written some books on Stephen King. Rocky Wood, whom I'm sure many of the folks reading this book are aware of, or maybe even knew, offered to be my agent for the publication of my bibliography. To be honest, it really only required minimal effort on my part, as the document already existed with all of the information listed in an orderly fashion. I just had to come up with an index for all of the pieces.

At this point, I think it would be helpful to share what I think is a fun story about tracking down some truly "lost" King pieces. In the 1990s, Michael Collings listed four non-fiction pieces (published in 1988) where the title was unknown and the forum of publication was listed simply as *The Register* without any further information. One was on drunk driving, one about cocaine, one about Elvis Presley and one about tabloids. I searched for these for well over a dozen years. I contacted all of my sources and nobody had them. No reference book or article on King had any further information, although when I was re-reading a piece ("The Ultimate Catalogue") published in *Castle Rock: The Stephen King Newsletter*, I spied a small note that said it was a reprint from *The Register*. Eventually, I found out that *The Register* had been a small weekly newspaper published in Brewer, Maine. The idea of an online archive, or even an interlibrary loan for the microfilm copies of this newspaper, became laughable as I went on. There weren't even any references to the newspaper having existed on the internet, as far as I could tell. Don't believe me? Google "The Register" and "Stephen King" right now and you still won't get anything. Go ahead. I'll wait. I found out that this newspaper, before it went defunct, was run by King's brother-in-law, Christopher Spruce. I wrote to him, but did not receive any response. Even that information did not make it any easier to research. Still don't believe me? Google "The Register," "Brewer," and "Christopher Spruce." Throw "newspaper" in the mix and you still won't find anything.

To make a long story even longer, and possibly less interesting, I'll share how I ended up getting photocopies of these pieces. Some creative Googling (no, I don't remember the exact combination of words) led me to a document that appeared to be the resume of someone who had written for *The Register*. I e-mailed this person to see if they perhaps had copies of any of the newspapers in which they had published articles. I was told that they did not, but they directed me toward a local figure in town who might have them. I got in touch with this individual, who told me that they had just recently donated several garbage bags of old newspapers to the town's historical society. When I got in touch with the historical society, I found out it was only open by request and run by a retired transplant who volunteered there. I gave him the dates of the article (if I recall, one was incorrect) and, lo and behold, a couple of weeks later, I had photocopies of: "A New Cure for Old Drunks" (May 11, 1988), "Tabloid, Anyone?" (May 18, 1988), "America's Neglected Drug Problem" (May 25, 1988), "Yo, Elvis!" (June 1, 1988) and the original appearance of "The Ultimate Catalogue" (June 8, 1988). I even got a mention in the historical society's newsletter, but of course the real prize was having photocopies of the only King pieces I did not have in my collection and, moreso, having rescued them from being lost to the sands of time. There were no microfilm or digital archives of this newspaper and no index, online or otherwise, that would direct researchers to the Brewer Historical Society.

The story that I just related to the reader is one of many that I could tell about tracking down rare, lost, or unpublishedpieces. It may even distress a certain kind of person to know that, in many cases, King's office had no record of these pieces. We ended up providing our photocopies to *them*. Personally, I just feel that the work of artists (writers, musicians, painters), no matter how slight, should be preserved if at all possible. There are other examples of King pieces that his office had no record of and that, had they not been "rescued," would most likely be lost forever. Naturally, that happens outside of the King world, as well. Imagine the home tapes of one of your favorite artists being discarded, or the magnetic tape being damaged beyond repair by the heat of the attic. In the end, I'm just glad that my nerdy, childhood list-making was able to help the cause of the fellow King fanatic in some little way and, hopefully, it will help preserve and further disseminate a handful of items that may well have been lost forever.

"STEVE ROSE UP": RICK HAUTALA REMEMBERS HIS FIRST TIME

By Rick Hautala

They say we all remember our first time. Do you?

Rick Hautala went to college with Stephen King. "Steve Rose Up" is Rick's remembrance of the first time he read a Stephen King story. Anything else I could possibly say about the piece would only be superfluous to the essay itself, so I will shut up and allow Rick to recount for you his first time.

(Before I go, allow me to recommend the work of Mr. Hautala to you. No less than Stephen King himself blurbed Rick's first two novels Moondeath and Moonbog. Rick's other novels are Night Stone, Little Brothers, Winter Wake, and Dead Voices. Check him out.)

'm going to "date" myself, but I don't care. Anyone in my age group—that is, anyone who can no longer watch *thirtysomething* because of the age cut-off—has a few very sharp memories. We all know *exactly* where we were when we heard that President Kennedy had been assassinated. (I was in detention hall for goofing off in my sophomore French class.) We clearly remember when we heard the news that both Bobby Kennedy and Martin Luther King Jr. had been shot and killed. And, more recently, we have a perhaps too clear memory of where we were when we heard that John Lennon had been murdered. These memories are etched in our minds like harsh acid-bright lines. But for anyone who has enough of an interest in the work of Stephen King even to pick up a book titled *The Shape Under the Sheet: The Complete Stephen King Encyclopedia,* I'll bet there's one more event you can recall with a deep-bone shudder: the first time you experienced a story or novel by Stephen King.

Okay, maybe the exact time and place aren't there in your mind like the crackling voice of Walter Cronkite struggling to maintain his composure. You might not remember the time or day or the place precisely. Reading a novel or short story, after all, doesn't quite have the bombshell impact of hearing that someone you respected and admired has died. But I'll bet you haven't—and won't ever—forget how, as you first dove into Steve's work, you felt as if your whole sense of reality was being stretched and distorted like a long, sludgy string of taffy being pulled out to—and past—its limit.

Okay, so I've already hinted at my age; I'm just about as old as Stephen King. But there's a bit more to tell. You see, I was a freshman at the University of Maine in Orono in 1966, rooming on the third floor in a men's dormitory called Gannett Hall. (Most of the dorms at UMO are co-ed now. Damn! I always miss the fun!) Anyway, in the same dorm that same year, I think down on the second floor, was this other freshman. He was kinda strange looking, and he immediately stood out from the swirling mass of scared-looking freshmen (which I was) and cocky upperclassmen (which I guess I became) as we all crowded into the commons for our daily meals. This guy was...different; I saw that much right away.

Tall and, at least in my memory, hefty, he had thick black hair and wore eyeglasses that looked as thick as the bottom of a Coke bottle. He was always wearing faded jeans and a casual "frumpy"-looking shirt. In warmer weather, I seem to remember that he wore sandals or went barefoot. I have no idea when the beard first came because it, like the leaves on the trees in spring, seems to come and go overnight. Using the parlance of the 60s, he was "dressed down," like a Hippie, which was the "in" look at the time. If there were "designer jeans" back then, they sure as hell hadn't made it north of Boston. One thing I noticed about this guy *was* that he didn't even seem to be checking out the bevy of co-eds. Being a compulsive reader myself, I also noticed that he was always standing in the lunch line with his face and concentration lost in reading. What was he reading? Nope. Not some textbook or scholarly magazine; he always had a tattered, wild 'n crazy-looking science fiction paperback. In my memory, it seemed as though every day, seven days a week, he had a different book at each meal, morning, noon, and night. I remember thinking time and again: My God! That guy reads like a fiend!

Little did I know...

Somehow or other, I found out this guy's name was Steve King and that he was majoring in English. Somehow, that fit. Anyone who read that much, I figured, sure as hell wasn't majoring in Chemical Engineering or Forestry!

Fade out—

Fade in—a year later: my sophomore year. I had begun my college career as a Biology major with intentions of studying pre-med, so I thought. The problem was, I was a terrible student in biology and, especially, chemistry. (On the chemistry final, I scored a whopping twelve out of a possible 200 points.) I got onto the Dean's List both semesters of my first year at college all right, but it was the wrong Dean's list. It was a list of students who were t-h-i-s close to being asked to take a little vacation from school. With the specter of Vietnam breathing diesel fumes down my neck, I didn't think that promised me a very bright future. After barely hanging on for one more semester in biology, and figuring I'd always enjoyed reading, anyway (but certainly not three books a day!), I switched my major to English and began reading Shakespeare, Hawthorne, Hemingway, and the rest.

Also, for the first time, I became aware that the English majors were publishing a "literary" journal once every semester. The name seemed to change as often as the editor, but in the spring of 1968 (when Bobby Kennedy was unknowingly approaching the receiving end of a Saturday night special), the magazine was called *Ubris*. (A year or so later the title changed to *Onan* and, considering the level of most of the writing, that seemed damned appropriate.) I was writing my own stuff at the time, but I didn't have any confidence in my work, so I never submitted anything to the student magazine. I did, however, buy a copy each semester, and I read most of 'em, too...as bad as most of the fiction and poetry was.

"How bad was it?" I hear Ed McMahon ask. What is any college literary magazine like? It was full of half-baked character sketches trying to pass muster as short stories and rambling stream of semi-consciousness parading as poetry. I doubt student writing has changed much in the decades since then, but it was reading the first issue of *Ubris*, in the spring of 1968, that I came upon a little story entitled "Cain Rose Up." It started on page 33 and ended with a literal *bang* at the top of page 35. By the time that I finished reading that story, I knew I'd been nailed!

I'd just read my first Stephen King story!

Now I've never put a whole lot of faith in my critical abilities, even after earning an M.A. in English, but I knew one thing after I finished reading that story; this most definitely was not your run-of-the-mill student writing. I knew this story—and this King-fella—were somehow...different. In retrospect, I even remember wondering if maybe that story had been printed in a different typeface or in a different color ink because whatever it had going for it, it had the same "get-off-the-tracks-the-train's-comin'!" energy Steve brings to everything he writes. I don't think I was the only person back then in the spring of 1968 who started wondering what kind of mind could produce a story like this. But whereas I suspect most of the English department professors and students were freaked out by this piece and objected to its gruesome violence, I remember loving the *impact* of that story.

Everyone knows the story I'm talking about, right? The one where the kid finishes up his finals and then barricades himself in his dorm room, takes his rifle and scope, and methodically starts picking off people on the mall between the dorms. And maybe without even looking it up you remember that the woman's dorm across the way was called Carlton Memorial. (If you don't remember, I'm sure there's a reference to it somewhere here in *The Shape...*)

But you're wrong on this one; and if Steve Spignesi tells you it's Carlton Hall, then *he's* wrong, too!

I don't know what name Steve had in mind for the dorm from which the character Curt began firing. But I also know its real name.

It's Gannett Hall.

I knew from the way Steve described the scene outside Curt's dorm window that, sometime during his Freshman year, maybe many times, he'd been sitting by the window of his dorm room in Gannett Hall one floor below my own room and looking out across the mall to Androscoggin Hall. And at some moment during our freshman year, that wild imagination of his kicked into high gear. In a world where Texas Tower snipers and Lee Harvey Oswalds can shift the scales of reality in an instant that will make the evening news, Steve King, the sophomore English major, brought it all home to the University of Maine in Orono.

I love the story "Cain Rose Up" because, for the first time in my life, I *truly* experienced the magic of fiction making. Oh, sure—I'd read plenty of science fiction, fantasy, and horror stories, and I've loved a lot of 'em: Bradbury, Howard, Vonnegut, Burroughs, and Lovecraft in particular—but none of their stories ever hit me with the impact Steve's story had simply because, just a year before, I had been struggling to stay in college just like Curt so I wouldn't end up in Vietnam, where everyone seemed to be doing what Curt had done.

What Steve did, the magic he wove, was to take the intense pressure to stay in school that I and probably all but a handful of college freshmen feel, and make the horror of it *live*. Sure, he's done that lots of times since in dozens of novels, stories, and movies. Reading '*Salem's Lot* a few years later honest-to-God made me sleep with a light on for a week or two. But I'm sure, no matter how many times it's happened since, every avid King reader vividly remembers the first time Steve did it to 'em. I feel privileged to have "discovered" this man's work long before the rest of the world did, and I'm sure as hell glad he's still doing it to us!

Rick Hautala's 5 Favorite Stephen King Works

The Dead Zone
'*Salem's Lot*
The Body
Cujo
Misery

Copyright © 1990 Rick Hautala. Reprinted by permission.

POSTSCRIPT TO "STEVE ROSE UP"

By Holly Newstein Hautala

You've just read how Stephen King's writing affected his class-mate Rick Hautala in 1968 (and the rest of the world a bit lat-er). I remember reading *The Dead Zone,* and Rick coming into the bedroom and asking me why I looked so scared. I was clutching the book for dear life and couldn't read fast enough. Not many writers can engage me so fully in a story that I forget that it's "only a story."

What is not as well-known is that, after they both graduated from the University of Maine in Orono, Rick and Steve became friends. Steve was instrumental in getting Rick's first novel, *Moondeath,* noticed by agents and eventually published. They read each other's works-in-progress and got together just for fun. Before Steve bought his famous home in Bangor, he and Rick spent a day in Portland, looking at the mansions for sale on the Eastern Prom overlooking Portland Harbor.

By that time, Steve's fame was growing, and due to a perhaps ill-considered American Express TV commercial, he was being recognized on the street. Over a beer, Steve remarked that all he wanted was a place where he could be Steve, not "Stephen King." He finally decided on Bangor because it was comparatively remote, and close to Old Town and Tabitha King's family.

Early on, Steve gave Rick the first draft of *The Dark Tower* for him to read. Steve had scrounged some colored paper somewhere (he was still broke back then) to type the draft on. Rick kept the draft for several years, until Steve remarked to him one day, after the book had been published, that he couldn't find the first draft. Rick remembered that he had it—the colored paper made it even more memorable—and returned it to Steve.

The friendship eventually died, as friendships do. Steve did become "Stephen King," and moved in different circles than Rick did. Rick watched Steve's star rise with a mixture of admiration and envy, and with the rise of eBay and other auction sites, wondered how much he could have gotten had he kept the first draft of *The Dark Tower* and sold it. I'm just grateful he didn't throw it away…

THE KING OF HOLLYWOOD: THE 10 BEST STEPHEN KING FILM ADAPTATIONS

by Andrew J. Rausch

Andrew Rausch is a freelance film journalist, author, and celebrity interviewer. He has written two volumes on Stephen King (*The Stephen King Movie Quiz Book* and *The Wit & Wisdom of Stephen King*), with a third forthcoming from McFarland & Company. His writing has appeared in the unofficial Stephen King newsletter *Phantasmagoria*. He has written several works of fiction including the collection *Death Rattles* (which was inspired by and dedicated to Stephen King). He has also worked as a screenwriter, producer, and actor on numerous straight-to-video horror films.

I have been a fan of Stephen King's work for more than thirty years. I simultaneously discovered the novel *Carrie* and the film *Cat's Eye* when I was a twelve-year-old kid living in Podunk, Kansas. The former is great, the latter less so, but they were equally responsible for introducing me to Stephen King. No matter what your belief on the importance (or lack thereof) of King's cinematic output, especially lackluster fare like that particular film, you cannot deny that the man is equally associated with both literature and film. In fact, to the ever-increasing number of Americans who no longer read books, King is best known for the films. Not everyone has read a King book, but you can't throw a copy of one of his books into a crowded Wal-Mart or McDonald's without striking someone who has seen at least one of the man's many cinematic adaptations.

In the early 2000s, I set out to write a quiz book (inspired by Stephen Spignesi's *The Stephen King Quiz Book*) focusing on King's cinematic adaptations. It was then that I (and my coauthor R. D. Riley) became aware of just how few quality King films there were. To date, there are more than sixty King features in existence, with somewhere around twenty of them being at least decent. It's fairly easy to come up with five or six really solid King adaptations, but after that, things become sketchy rather quickly.

For his latest tome, my friend and mentor Stephen Spignesi has asked me to write an essay about the ten King films that I consider the best of the bunch. My background in film history and criticism, coupled with my having written extensively about King, made me ideally-suited for such a task. But you know what? Lists are subjective. Also, opinions are like assholes; everybody's got one. Both of these statements are completely accurate and applicable here, so you are hereby given full permission to take the following assertions with a proverbial grain of salt.

I hope to make this essay a little bit different from all those tiresome "top ten" lists going around. I'm going to present what I feel are the ten best King adaptations, but I'm not going to count them down in any real order. The truth is that all of these films are terrific and it could be argued that many of them are comparable in terms of quality. Because of this, there isn't going to be a definitive "number six" best movie or a "number four" best movie. Having co-written a book entitled *The 101 Scariest Movies Ever Made*, I'm as guilty as anyone for fashioning these silly lists. But I'm not going to do that here. So, if you believe the fourth and seventh films I mention are equally good, or if you believe they should be arranged in a certain way, feel free to make those adjustments in your head.

1408

- A movie on the outer edge of the "top ten" tier that managed to pleasantly surprise us is Mikael Hafstrom's 2007 offering *1408*. The film, adapted from the short story of the same title in *Everything's Eventual*, was written by Matt Greenberg and then later rewritten by Scott Alexander and Larry Karaszewski. Much of the adaptation's success is likely the result of Alexander and Karaszewski, the award-winning duo behind such hits as *The People vs. Larry Flynt*, *Ed Wood*, and *Man on the Moon*. In lesser hands, *1408* could easily have been just another dead-on-arrival, not-scary, clichéd, crappy, special-effects-laden ghost movie. But *1408* soars to unexpected heights. What was sort of a run-of-the-mill, good-but-not-great King story is transformed into something much more powerful here. This is what film adaptations are supposed to be—as good as, if not better, than the original source material. *1408* shows why excuses made for shoddy Dino De Laurentiis adaptations are simply that—excuses. Just because a story is fairly pedestrian doesn't mean it's destined to be an average to below-average film. This is why movies like *Graveyard Shift* or *The Mangler* didn't necessarily *have* to be as terrible as they were.
- Starring John Cusack and Samuel L. Jackson, Hafstrom's film effectively produces psychological tension à la Robert Wise's *The Haunting*, suggesting more than it actually shows. Its deft screenplay and superb direction constantly ratchet up the suspense and dread, making for an unforgettable and haunting thrill ride.

Both Cusack and Jackson have since turned in their fair shares of phoned-in, half-note performances (including another King adaptation, *Cell*), but here they both do terrific work.

- The film maintains the feel of King's work, but the filmmakers decided to alter the story's ending. In the original short story, Cusack's character, Mike Enslin, dies in a fire. In the film, however, Enslin survives. Both endings work well in their respective mediums, but Enslin's reprieve effectively serves as a happy and welcome conclusion to an otherwise dark story.

The Mist

- Another brilliant and, in my opinion, underrated King adaptation is Frank Darabont's *The Mist*, also released in 2007. The story of a group of strangers who find themselves under siege by mysterious creatures enveloped within a thick mist, the film is at its heart about the unseen evil found within everyday people. It's extremely reminiscent of *Lord of the Flies* in this way. It also makes a strong statement about the nature of religion and how this supposedly beautiful thing can be corrupted, misused, and misinterpreted to hurt and divide people.
- Darabont is no stranger to the work of King, this being his fourth interpretation of the author's work (I'm including his wonderful short *The Woman in the Room*), and here, as usual, he and King's voices sync perfectly. Darabont's direction is terrific, per usual, and the performances by the actors, particularly Thomas Jane, Marcia Gay Harden, and Andre Braugher, are pitch perfect.
- Just as the screenwriters of *1408* had decided to dramatically alter the ending of King's original source material, Darabont conceives a new conclusion here. However, instead of a happier ending, he has written something far more unhappy, creating something that is almost unspeakably dark. For my money, Darabont's ending is about as perfect a conclusion as one can

craft. It's perversely dark, but it makes sense in the context of the story. King himself was a fan of Darabont's reimagined ending, as well, remarking that horror movies don't need to have "*Pollyanna* endings." He's right, and if you look back at the author's short stories, you'll see that many of his tales have sad, dark, or tragic conclusions.

- If the film has any flaw worth commenting on, it is, for me, the hideously fake-looking CGI beasts that make a brief cameo beneath the opened garage door. But that's not enough to stop the movie from being a powerful one.

The Dead Zone

- The next movie on this list is David Cronenberg's 1982 offering *The Dead Zone*. Based on King's 1979 novel of the same title, screenwriting duties were handled deftly by Jeffrey Boam. (This is somewhat of a surprise considering the late Boam's tendency for mediocrity. *Funny Farm*, anyone?) After producer Dino De Laurentiis passed on a screenplay by King himself, said to be considerably darker in tone, it was decided that Boam would excise major portions of the novel's storyline.

- Cronenberg would seem to be an unlikely director for the psychological thriller as it's apparent that he doesn't "get" much of King's work. The director has said unflattering things regarding the quality and tone of the author's original unproduced screenplay, and has also remarked negatively about the lead character's name, which he found insufficient and overly-generic.

- For *The Dead Zone* to be effective, casting would be key. Cronenberg selected actor Christopher Walken in the lead role as schoolteacher-turned-psychic Johnny Smith. Walken's performances can be all over the map, ranging from the truly great (*The Deer Hunter*) to a terrible, painful-to-watch caricature of himself (roughly seventy-five percent of his filmography). Thankfully for us as viewers, Cronenberg mines a deliciously-multilayered performance from Walken, who gives one of the best and most memorable turns of his career.

- One of the major hurdles Cronenberg faced was casting a believable Greg Stillson. He needed an actor at the peak of his powers who could simultaneously display a charming facade with convincing allure, while also exuding a radiating energy that is pure evil. Martin Sheen, who had previously displayed impressive range on films like *Apocalypse Now* and *Badlands*, would prove to be casting perfection.

- Cronenberg displays a confident hand here behind the camera, doing a remarkable job in directing. The pacing stumbles momentarily here and there, but Cronenberg gets top-notch performances from his cast. At the end of the day, whether the director "got" King or not, he managed to craft an impressive representation of the author's work.

Carrie

- A discussion of the great King adaptations wouldn't be complete if we didn't mention *Carrie*, the first King adaptation, based on King's first published novel. The film would be helmed by an up-and-coming young filmmaker named Brian De Palma, who had already made a name for himself with stylish films like *Sisters* and *Phantom of the Paradise*. De Palma had been introduced to the novel by a mutual friend of he and King, and had immediately gone about obtaining the rights. De Palma then hired first-time scribe Lawrence D. Cohen to adapt the screenplay.

- Casting is always of the utmost importance in the production of any film, but the selection of the 17-year-old tormented outcast Carrie White had to be precise (as subsequent adaptations have proven). De Palma and casting director Harriet B. Helberg auditioned a number of young ingénues for the role, including Linda Blair and Melanie Griffith, eventually settling on Sissy Spacek.

This decision would ultimately prove to be the correct one as the young actress would deliver a masterful performance that fully embodies the essence of King's tortured character. Beyond Spacek, the entire cast is filled with top-notch performers like John Travolta, Piper Laurie, and Amy Irving.

- De Palma and Cohen made some alterations to the storyline as it originally appeared in the novel. Chief among those was a newly-concocted dream sequence in which the fallen Carrie White reaches out from beyond the grave to grab Sue Snell. The new scene worked extremely well, causing most audience members to scream and/or jump in their seats.

- The film was released to great acclaim and proved to be a major hit for United Artists, becoming one of the highest-grossing films of 1976. Its legacy is unquestionable as it has become iconic, its haunting pig's blood scene guaranteed to be referenced at prom time from now until infinity. It's also become a Halloween programming staple alongside films like *Halloween* and *The Exorcist*

The Green Mile

- The fifth film I have to mention here is another Frank Darabont powerhouse. This one, his second Stephen King prison movie, is *The Green Mile*. Based on King's 1996 serial novel, the already-iconic adaptation hits all the right notes. One big reason (but hardly the only one) that the film succeeds so well is because it's packed to the gills with virtuoso performances. Who will ever forget Tom Hanks' turn as prison officer Paul Edgecombe? Who can forget the late Michael Clarke Duncan's ridiculously-strong performance as jailhouse Jesus John Coffey? And let's not forget Doug Hutchison's once-in-a-lifetime performance as sadistic baddie Percy Wetmore. And that's hardly the end of it. Every single performance in this film is spot-on, with more undeniable turns by actors like David Morse, James

Cromwell, and Sam Rockwell, just to name a few. (You could discuss this film's dynamic performances all day long.)

- The film's running time is a tad long at 189 minutes, but one would be hard pressed to identify scenes which should have been left on the cutting room floor. Once again, King's writing is filtered through screenwriter/director Frank Darabont, capturing the feel of the author's work in a way that no other filmmaker does. Most of the truly successful film adaptations take significant liberties with the original source material in order to fit the needs of the medium, but with *The Green Mile*, Darabont has produced one of the most faithful King adaptations to date. That it translates so well is a testament to both King and Darabont, who are creative talents of the highest order.

- The resulting film was extremely well-received by critics and fans alike, and showered with accolades from just about every award-giving organization known to man. It received top honors from groups as varied as the Academy of Science Fiction, Fantasy and Horror Films and The People's Choice Awards. Perhaps most impressive, *The Green Mile* received four Academy Award nominations for Best Picture, Best Screenplay, Best Sound Mixing, and Best Supporting Actor for Duncan's unforgettable performance.

IT

- The year 2017 saw an abundance of fresh Stephen King adaptations with *The Dark Tower*, *1922*, *Gerald's Game*, and *It* (as well as new television series based on *Mr. Mercedes* and *The Mist*). Of all of these films, the one to make the biggest splash was director Andy Muschietti's *It*. With King's novel having already been adapted once in a mediocre, but well-remembered TV miniseries (well-remembered mainly because of Tim Curry), many questioned whether or not a new version of *It* could work. Most of the concerns centered around Pennywise and whether or not the new actor playing him would simply mimic Curry's performance. Those concerns would prove to be unfounded as Muschietti and actor Bill Skarsgård wisely decided to interpret the character in a completely fresh and equally (if not more) impressive way.

- Like the novel itself, the film excels in its ability to evoke feelings of familiarity and nostalgia. Recreating universal experiences through the use of archetypes is one of King's greatest strengths. The author has always had a unique ability to paint vivid pictures that seem to come straight from our own experiences, be they the relentlessly cruel attacks by cooler-than-thou juvenile delinquent bullies or the innocent "your mother" banter of adolescents who think they're being way more witty and adult than they actually are. King frequently manages to capture the essence of idealized youth similar to a Norman Rockwell painting, but in a way that is decidedly more authentic. Muschietti's film manages to channel the King childhood experience, just as *Stand By Me* had done. Even more impressive, Muschietti accomplishes this even while taking substantial liberties with King's original source material. The film relocates the novel's events, centered in 1957, to the 1980s. In doing so, the film reveals the universal truths of childhood.

- Muschietti's adaptation (written by Chase Palmer, Cary Fukunaga, and Gary Dauberman) is sublime in every way imaginable. Another wise deviation from King's novel was the filmmakers' decision to skip the awkward sewer orgy scene, and I would argue that the film is better for it. When I first read the novel, wonderful as it may be, that particular scene sort of stopped me dead, removing me from the action. It felt like a rare King misstep. "Am I really reading this? What is happening here?" I understand the reasoning for the scene in terms of story, but there are, as the film shows, other ways to convey the same things without pulling the audience's head out of the story.

- Muschietti and company make many alterations in this adaptation, and they're all pretty effective. The decision to focus the film solely on the childhood portion of King's story was a good one, as the novel in its entirety would be near impossible to adapt into a single feature-length film. (Now, hopefully, the forthcoming sequel does as good a job in translating the material.)

- But the film isn't just effective at recreating childhood scenarios. Like the trans-dimensional evil that is Pennywise, this film has real bite. One reason for this is Skarsgård's decision to completely avoid comparisons to Tim Curry by playing him as a feral, menacing beast. Skarsgård's Pennywise carries with him an aura of genuine danger. There's no sly comedic charm here, but instead a venomous creature whose sole purpose is to ravage and destroy without thought or mercy.

- Muschietti's skillful direction also works wonders, crafting a genuinely frightening motion picture brimming with tension and suspense. A lot of fright films come and go, many making a momentary mark on the horror landscape, but this one seems destined to hold a firm place in the hearts and minds of genre fans.

Misery

- The next film we need to discuss is Rob Reiner's 1990 adaptation of King's novel *Misery*. This was a novel that King was hesitant to sell the option to, citing the ever-increasing number of poor adaptations of his work. But when Rob Reiner, who had previously helmed the adaptation of King's coming-of-age novella *The Body* (as well as *Stand By Me*), came knocking, the author relented. Reiner quickly established himself as the right man for the job when he solicited Oscar-winning screenwriter William Goldman to adapt the novel.

- The lead role of romance novelist Paul Sheldon was offered to a bevy of actors including William Hurt, Robert Redford, and Richard Dreyfuss, but they all turned it down. Actor Warren

Beatty was attached to the project for a time, but wound up walking away. James Caan was then cast in the role, which at the time seemed questionable. Although the actor had given flawless performances in films like *The Godfather*, *Brian's Song*, and *Thief*, his best work seemed a full decade behind him. But Caan would ultimately have the last laugh, turning in a convincing performance as the increasingly-frustrated captive author.

- Unfortunately for Caan, however, his inspired performance would be overshadowed by that of his co-star, Kathy Bates. Bates, who had long been an effective-but-criminally-underused talent, absolutely shines as the demented Annie Wilkes, a nurse who claims to be Sheldon's biggest fan. Displaying warmth and sincerity in equal measures with menace and cruelty, the actress gives a once-in-a-lifetime performance, the Hannibal Lecter to Caan's Clarice. Bates does it all, showing a full range of emotions that go from a subdued simmer to a full-blown fever-pitched cacophony of fiery rage. As much suspense as Reiner manages to wring out of Goldman's screenplay, it is Bates' ability to make the audience wonder what's beneath the surface that makes *Misery* genuinely frightening. This film could not possibly have succeeded on the level it does with any other actress in this role. The casting of Bates by Reiner and company is exceptional, and Bates would ultimately win an Academy Award for her work.

- The supporting players are terrific, as well. In a film with a relatively small cast, *Misery* also features the impressive talents of Richard Farnsworth, Frances Sternhagen, Lauren Bacall, and J. T. Walsh. Frequent Coen brothers cameraman Barry Sonnenfeld, who would later go on to direct *Get Shorty* and *Men in Black*, also does impressive work here. Goldman's screenplay is first-rate and he does a commendable job in adapting King.

The Shining

- The next Stephen King adaptation is a controversial one, which King himself loathes. Yes, my friends, I'm talking about Stanley Kubrick's 1980 scare-fest *The Shining*. Widely acknowledged as one of the scariest films ever made, there are a great number of King fans who feel nothing but disdain for it. The story has been well-documented by this point, beginning with Kubrick's early-in-production boast he was going to make the scariest movie ever made. That absurd statement set the bar ridiculously high right from the git-go, and expectations could not have been higher. Some might argue that Kubrick succeeded in doing what he set out to do, while others refuse to acknowledge the film's effectiveness at all.

- Is *The Shining* frightening? If you are a person who is capable of being scared by a movie, then I would say yes, definitely, the film is frightening. Few films in the entire history of the medium (three or four at most) have ever accomplished this as effectively. The film's precisely-arranged set pieces, stark visuals, and hauntingly-simple score, create an unrivaled atmosphere of dread that is so thick one could almost cut it with a knife (or, in this case, an axe). Let me make this clear right now— anyone who disputes the film's effectiveness is simply an overly-dramatic King fan enjoying sour grapes.

- This is perhaps an understandable reaction when one considers that *The Shining* is an adaptation in name only. This film is not King's novel. It's just not. It shares the character names and the basic set-up of the novel, but that's about it. But that does not diminish the quality or effectiveness of the film itself. This is a great film, and even more to the point, it's a great *horror* film, whether the Annie Wilkes of King's fan base acknowledge it as such.

- Many of King's (and then those fans regurgitating) criticisms of the film are accurate. The two biggest flaws in the film as I see them are the casting of Jack Nicholson and then the casting of Shelly Duvall (and the overall handling of her character). While Jack Nicholson is an undeniably talented performer who does great work here, his casting is questionable. Nicholson, as he does in every picture, comes across as being crazy already. While that quality works for a character like *One Flew Over the Cuckoo Nest's* R. P. McMurphy, it's somewhat less perfect here. The entire point of *The Shining* is the gradual and shocking transformation of Jack Torrance from sane and (mostly) loving father to crazy-as-shit axe-wielding madman. But with Nicholson, there can be no effective visual breaking point. The problem with Shelly Duvall's casting is that Duvall comes ready-made to be a fragile, pathetic victim. In the novel, the Wendy character comes across as a strong woman and, even more importantly, normal. Nothing about either Jack Nicholson or Shelly Duvall comes across as a normal, everyday person. They're already caricatures before they even speak a word of dialogue. If Nicholson personifies the character of *Cuckoo's* McMurphy, then it can be said that Duvall equally personifies her *Popeye* character, Olive Oyl. Duvall comes across as a weak and sniveling victim from the start. In casting these performers, Kubrick does himself a bit of a disservice. They're fine, but their pre-established characterizations set unhelpful boundaries and expectations for the story.

- Despite these minor missteps, *The Shining* is a great film. Could it be even more effective? Yes, perhaps it could, but it's exceedingly potent as is. Is it a perfect film? No, but then what is? Even *Citizen Kane* can be said to have minor flaws. (If Kane dies alone, how does anyone know that his final utterance is "rosebud"? Apologists have since declared that Kane's majordomo was present at his death, but he sure isn't visible in that scene.) Again, no matter what anyone says about it, *The Shining* is widely recognized as a classic film and its iconic status cannot be disputed.

Stand By Me

- As I mentioned previously, *Misery* was Rob Reiner's second stab at adapting Stephen King. His first take on King's work was the 1986 film *Stand By Me*. Scripted by Bruce A. Evans and Raynold Gideon, the film tells the story of four prepubescent boys who trek through the woods in search of a dead schoolmate's body.

- Casting is an important part of making any film, but it was perhaps more important here as it can be extremely difficult finding child actors who are suitably charismatic and possess the talent to carry a motion picture. But Reiner and casting directors Janet Hirshenson and Jane Jenkins outdid themselves, managing to cast four astonishingly talented young performers with Wil Wheaton, River Phoenix, Corey Feldman, and Jerry O'Connell. In a 2011 NPR interview, Wheaton explained the genius of the casting, stating that each of the four boys was playing a character that was very similar to who they were in real life. The film's supporting cast, which features the likes of Kiefer Sutherland, John Cusack, and Richard Dreyfuss, is also outstanding.

- Similar to *It*, *Stand By Me* successfully captures the nostalgic tone of King's depictions of 1950s' childhood, effectively allowing younger viewers to experience what it was like as a young boy coming of age in the summer of 1959. Reiner, Evans, and Gideon (and King before them) manage to capture and bottle the essence of childhood camaraderie, when a premium is placed on friendship and we feel certain we will know these people for the rest of our lives. The writers also treat us to the adult Gordon LaChance's bittersweet and deadly-accurate realization that "friends come in and out of our lives like busboys in a restaurant." One need not be a boy or to have grown up in a small town in the 1950s, or even traveled to see a dead body, to relate to these experiences—one needs only to be human.

Like all great works of art, that authentic conveyance of universal truths and experiences is the film's grandest achievement.

- The fact that some of the finest King adaptations aren't in the horror genre is a testament to the author's substantial talent as a writer; not as a *horror* writer, but simply as a writer. As you know (or you wouldn't be reading a volume like this), the man can flat-out write with the best who ever lived.

The Shawshank Redemption

- Having said that, it should come as no surprise that *The Shawshank Redemption*, which is straight drama, is pretty much the *crème de la crème* of the King adaptations. Based on the 1982 *Different Seasons* novella, *Rita Hayworth and Shawshank Redemption*, the film tells the story of Andy Dufresne, a banker who is wrongly convicted and imprisoned for the murder of his wife and her lover.

- While King's original novella is high quality and an enjoyable read, it's not one of the author's most memorable works. (This is in no way a slight, but rather a testament to the sheer volume of quality work King has produced.) It is for this reason that *The Shawshank Redemption* is the rare cinematic adaptation that surpasses its original source material. *The Godfather* and *American Psycho* are other notable examples of this phenomenon. While the film succeeds in pretty much every aspect possible, writer/director Frank Darabont deserves the lion's share of credit for having the vision, talent, and drive to adapt the material in this manner. In *Rita Hayworth and Shawshank Redemption*, Darabont, who had previously adapted King's short story "The Woman in the Room," had the ability to recognize the immense potential the seemingly mundane story possessed.

- The casting, as always, is extremely important, but it isn't the primary reason *Shawshank* succeeds. The film's greatest strength is Darabont's screenwriting, which is far and away the greatest (thus

121

far) of the talented scribe's career. Darabont displays an uncanny knack here for knowing exactly what to excise from the novella, which characters and scenarios to amalgamate, and which new ingredients to add. In doing all of this, Darabont accomplishes what would seem to be impossible—he somehow manages to craft a film that not only captures the feel of King's distinct narrative voice and style, but actually seems to contain more of these things than the original King novella. Darabont amplifies these elements, making *Shawshank* the ultimate King story; it's more than just an adaptation of one novella, but a sort of stylized celebration of the author's entire *oeuvre*. The film can be seen as a display of both Darabont and King's greatest strengths, coming together in a duet that is so harmonic, it becomes impossible to distinguish one artist's voice from the other.

- The casting of Morgan Freeman as the character Red is interesting due to the character actually being an Irishman in the novella. The character's explanation of the nickname Red— "maybe it's because I'm Irish"—then became less of an explanation and more of a joke. Freeman's casting, as unorthodox as it initially seemed, would prove to be inspired, as he would deliver one of the all-time great performances as the man who could get you anything.

- For the role of Andy Dufresne, Darabont would approach a number of big-name actors including Tom Cruise, Tom Hanks, Kevin Costner, Gene Hackman, and Robert Duvall, all of whom passed on the project. Darabont eventually settled on Tim Robbins, who was less of a hot commodity at the time. This decision would pay dividends as Robbins turned in a multi-layered performance that displayed great range and precision.

- Roger Deakins' cinematography is as beautiful as anything you'll ever witness, and composer Thomas Newman's score does a superb job accompanying the film's many already emotional scenes without ever coming across as sappy or overly-manipulative.

- The film was released to rave reviews, but its initial box office returns were disappointing. *The Shawshank Redemption* ultimately received an astounding seven Academy Award nominations for Best Picture, Best Adapted Screenplay, Best Actor (Freeman), Best Cinematography, Best Editing, Best Sound Mixing, and Best Original Score. The film didn't take home any Oscars (*Forrest Gump* undeservedly won almost everything that year), but it would eventually gain a massive following, become a television staple, cement its place in pop culture iconography, be named to the American Film Institute's list of the 100 greatest American films, and spend many years ranked on the Internet Movie Database (IMDB) as the single best movie ever made.

- King's film work is very diverse. He has been extremely hands-on, he himself having directed the film *Maximum Overdrive* and also having written a handful of screenplays. And while none of those particular projects are on this list, his name appears on some truly fantastic films. While the filmmakers who crafted the adaptations play a substantial role in their creation and successes, they could not exist without King creating the stories in the first place. At the end of the day, Stephen King is one of the greatest American literary figures ever to publish, and as these films prove, he has left an indelible mark on the cinematic landscape, as well.

STEPHEN KING IS...

By Mick Garris

Mick Garris is the director of *Stephen King's Sleepwalkers, The Stand, Quicksilver Highway, The Shining, Riding the Bullet, Desperation,* and *Bag of Bones.*

Stephen King is still alive.
I don't think most of us realize how close that statement came to no longer being true. When King was hit by a van in June 1999, he came perilously near meeting his maker, and all of us would have been far poorer for it. Though he has shown incredible tenacity in mending—quicker and better than any of the medical masters could have predicted—we came too damned close to losing the master of a genre that has become his own.

I first met King as a fan at a bookstore signing back in the '70s. Who knew I would be lucky enough to direct the man's own screenplays of his finest works? Not me. Neither did I ever guess then that we'd become friends. But we have, and my life (and I'm not speaking professionally now, though that is true as well) is all the richer for it.

Few would guess what a happy, childlike, loyal and generous man the Big Guy is. I call him El Queso Grande, or La Grande Fromage, for he is, in many matters, the Big Cheese. He is hilariously funny, a great guy to spend time with, and his towering size belies the sweetness of his heart. When I first had a meeting with him on *Sleepwalkers*, it was at a diner in New York, not the Russian Tea Room. He showed up in busted out sneakers, and his knees were peeking out of the smiles of his jeans. He's the least affected rich guy you could know. Maybe it's because he still lives in Maine, not in mediacentric LA or NY. But I've a feeling that no matter where he resided, he'd still just be Steve.

Stephen King is a loving husband and father, a true family man, as well as a great writer. He's still alive, and we're all richer for it.

STEPHEN KING IS...

By Jay Holben

Jay Holben is the director of the short film *Paranoid*, based on Stephen King's poem, "Paranoid: A Chant." He is also the author of the acclaimed digital video textbook *A Shot in the Dark*.

Stephen King is *not* a Horror Writer.
Ghosties, ghoulies and things that go bump in the night—to the casual observer, these are the trappings of Stephen King.

If it makes you break out in gooseflesh, or leap like an Olympian pole-vaulter from the bathroom threshold into your bed in the dark of the night—it must be the work of Stephen King.

But these declarations are superficial and made without examination into the works of a writer whom I feel is one of the greatest observers of human behavior, and one of the most astute social commentators of our time.

To the unlucky masses that only know King's work from a casual impulse-buy at the supermarket checkout counter, or the latest weak film adaptation airing at 2 a.m. on their local superstation, King is synonymous with horror—but, in reality, his pen scratches so much deeper into the very nature of the human soul. King's true gift is not in conjuring up werewolves and vampires, but in capturing the essence of real people; complicated, honest characters who often find themselves in extraordinary—and yes—horrifying situations.

Many of King's greatest works don't even live in the neighborhood of horror—*The Long Walk* and *The Gunslinger* series are just two examples of unblemished non-horror writing. If we look deeper within the pages of King's prose, we find real people struggling with real problems and trying their desperate best to make their worlds right again. We find people who mirror our siblings, friends, and even ourselves. King manages to terrify his readers not so much with snarling beasts (although he's got his share) but more often by immersing the reader into the pages of the book and into their worst fears and insecurities about themselves. In his most potent tales, we find men like Jack Torrance and Louis Creed—men who are fighting tooth-and-nail to keep their families together. King brings us Ray Garraty (*The Long Walk*), Paul Sheldon (*Misery*), Jessie Burlingame (*Gerald's Game*), and Dolores Claiborne (*Dolores Claiborne*)—all very real people who are merely trying to make it through the day. They are all fighting against powers well beyond their comprehension, but we have all faced those moments. If you've ever spent a long night in a sterile hospital waiting room measuring breath after breath in anticipation of news of a loved one—you've lived a Stephen King story.

King's true mastery is capturing the essence of one person's tribulations and leading the reader on an often heart-wrenching journey to the eventual success—or demise—of that character. From time to time, King outdoes himself and will plunge readers not just into the mind of a tortured human, but also descend them deeply—and with extraordinary believability—into the tortured mind of a dying dog.

Although the proclaimed Master of Horror has openly embraced this title, such a simplistic label stops short of describing the true depth of Stephen King's work. More often than not, the humble scribe from Maine transcends the horror genre, and today's narrow-minded, pedestrian pedagogues will find their jaws agape as King's words live easily well beyond his years to be the greatly studied tomes of tomorrow's tortured souls.

STEPHEN KING IS...

By James Cole

James Cole began writing at an early age. In 1987, he co-wrote and directed the short film *The Last Rung on the Ladder*, based on the Stephen King story. He has contributed essays to the books *The Complete Stephen King Encyclopedia* (1991), *The Lost Work of Stephen King* (1998), and *The Essential Stephen King* (2001). He wrote the award-winning short film *The Night Before* in 2003.

S**tephen King is the writer who made me love to read.** I was always a good reader, blessed with parents who read to me as a youngster and teachers that helped me to read on my own. In school I couldn't wait for those Scholastic books to arrive—books about monster makeup or life in colonial times. Yet they always had illustrations. It wasn't until third grade that I first tackled books without pictures. These included James Blish's *Star Trek* adaptations and a cheesy mystery series, *Alfred Hitchcock and the Three Investigators*. Though I enjoyed them, it was always a struggle to finish.

Any book longer than one hundred pages intimidated me. And novels? They were for grownups. How could I get through three to five hundred pages of tiny typeface, let alone have the courage to start? By seventh grade I had to. My English teacher assigned Dickens' *Great Expectations*, a book that almost made me hate reading. I was convinced that all novels must be boring, so why bother?

Stephen King changed all that...with a little help from my dad.

My father was a voracious reader. His bookshelf was lined with dog-eared paperbacks, their spines bowed from being broken in so many places. One day a freshly read paperback with a black cover appeared on the shelf: *The Dead Zone*. Intrigued by the title, I read the back cover summary. A guy comes out of a coma with second sight? Cool! Yet as I fanned the pages, the sheer volume of words was frightening. Still, I sat down and read the first page. Then the second, then the third.

I couldn't stop. King's writing was the most descriptive, most visual style I had ever encountered. I could see what was happening in my head. Most important: I cared about the characters, felt like I knew them. I wanted to know what was going to happen to them even as I didn't want the story to end.

I later realized *The Dead Zone* was not my first encounter with King (I had read *The Shining* on vacation the previous summer), yet it was the first time reading felt easy. I was no longer conscious of the number of words or how many pages there were to go. The process of reading itself had changed, and I began to devour other books on the shelf: Clive Cussler. John Gardener. John D. MacDonald. Some were good reads, some great, some dull. Some I didn't even finish. But that didn't matter.

Thanks to Stephen King, I was no longer afraid to start.

"ALL THINGS KING: A STEPHEN KING FAN PAGE"

AN INTERVIEW WITH ANTHONY NORTHRUP: FOUNDER AND WEBMASTER OF THE FACEBOOK GROUP

Anthony Northrup, originally from Long Island, New York, has lived in Forest River, North Dakota for the last fifteen years. In 2012, he launched the Facebook group *All Things King*. He has had over 400 articles published, and has conducted over 200 interviews, including talks with thirty-two Stephen King "Dollar Baby" filmmakers. His wonderful wife Gena is his biggest supporter and the *All Things King* fan page is his way of recommending the great works of Stephen King to the world. He uses as the group's motto the warm words of Mother Abagail, "You are all welcome here!"

An enormous sociocultural indicator of the popularity and significance of an artist and his or her body of work is the scale of the "fandom" that springs up surrounding it. James Patterson is a hugely successful and popular author, but there aren't Patterson conventions, and Patterson action figures, and ceaseless Patterson film adaptations. Nor are there Patterson signed limited editions, and Patterson trivia quiz books, or Patterson authorized swords, a House Patterson ruled journal, and scores of books *about* his work. This dynamic does describe, however, the fandom community and universe that has emanated from the works of J.K. Rowling and her *Harry Potter* tomes, the whole *Star Trek* and *Star Wars* universes, George R. R. Martin's *Game of Thrones* and, of course, the work of our subject for today, Stephen Edwin King.

Anthony Northrup is the creator and webmaster of a 5,000-member strong Facebook group called "All Things King." It is a very active page, with lots of fun and interesting posts by Tony and his team, as well as posts by lots of King fans. I thank Tony for frequently featuring me on his page (his birthday tributes are legendary!), and for talking to me about ATK.

Stephen Spignesi: My first question is simple: what do you think there is about King that has resulted in the entire, enormous world of fan involvement and enthusiasm?

Anthony Northrup: King knows what scares us. He has proven this a thousand times over. I think the secret to this is that he knows what makes us feel safe, happy, and secure; he knows our comfort zones and he turns them into completely unexpected nightmares. He takes a dog, a car, a doll, a hotel—countless things that we know and love—and then he scares the hell out of us with those very same things. Deep down, we love to be scared. We crave those moments of fear-inspired adrenaline, but then once it's over we feel safe again. King's work generates that adrenaline and keeps it pumping. Before King, we really didn't have too many notables in the world of horror writers. Poe and Lovecraft led the pack, but when King came along, he broke the mold. He improved with age just like a fine wine and readers quickly became addicted, and inestimable numbers morphed into hard-core fans. People can't wait to see what he'll do next. What innocent, commonplace "thing" will he come up with and turn into a nightmare? I mean, think about it…do any of us look at clowns, crows, cars, or corn fields the same way after we've read King's works?

SS: How did your outstanding Facebook group "All Things King" come into being?

AN: About five years ago, I was fairly new to Facebook and the whole social media world. I'm a very "old soul" (I've been told that many times throughout my life: I miss records and VHS tapes), so Facebook was very different for me. My wife and friends showed me how to do things and find fan pages and so forth. I found a Stephen King fan page and really had a fun time. I posted a lot of very cool things, and people loved my posts. So, several Stephen King fans suggested I do my own fan page. It took some convincing, but I finally did it. Since then, I have had some great co-administrators, wonderful members, and it has opened some amazing doors for me, including hosting the Stephen King Dollar Baby Film fest twice at Crypticon Horror Con in Minnesota. I have scored interviews with actors, writers, and directors who worked on Stephen King films or wrote about King; I help promote any movie, or book, and many other things that are King related, and I've been blessed to meet some wonderful people. I have some great friends thanks to "All Things King." I also like to teach our members about King (his unpublished stories, lesser-known short stories, and really deep facts and trivia about his books, films, and the man himself—info the average or new fan might not know). Our page is full of fun facts, trivia, games, contests, Breaking News, and conversations about all things Stephen King. We have been doing it for five years now as of August 19th—and yes, I picked that date on purpose.

SS: You and your crew obviously put a huge amount of work into "All Things King." What is your schedule like in terms of working on the page? How often do you work on it? Every day? How many hours? What's your routine when you set out to work on the page? Do you have Admins? Do you respond to comments first? Do you post art and info first? Give us a peek behind the ATK curtain.

AN: Working on "All Things King" is not easy. For five years, people from around the world have come to our page. Close to 5,000 members visit to see what we have to say about Stephen King. It is mind-boggling sometimes, and often overwhelming as well. We are honored and humbled by it. We have members who were with us since the beginning five years ago.

My schedule for ATK is basically whenever I get free time. I work on it mostly in the evenings, and I always post something, oftentimes an "On This Stephen King Date" moment. I tried taking on the page by myself in the beginning, but between work and life, it was tough, so I brought on board Co-Administrators to help me out. They have scheduled days that they post when I'm not around. I have had different Co-Ads over the years, but currently I have a very solid and amazing staff. My wife, Gena; Hans Von Wirth (a long-time friend who lives in Germany); and Amber Pace, a long-time friend, mother, and wife, who lives in Wyoming. I couldn't ask for better companions. Or as we call ourselves; "*Ka-tet*." The hours I spend on ATK depends. Sometimes it's a few minutes, sometimes hours!

The two toughest parts of running the site are, first, downloading all the pictures and graphics needed for each post. Posts are usually games, trivia, "Did You Know?", and other fun things. I check the page daily to make sure all is well, that there are no dramas going on, and to make sure everyone is having a good time. I answer members' questions, make my own comments to posts, but mostly I'm always pulling together graphics and pictures ready for the next day of posting. The main challenge of ATK is coming up with ideas. After five years, it is *not* easy coming up with new and fun things to post. During those five years, I've covered every possible angle of anything and everything Stephen King has done, in every category. We've broken his works down and talked about them, found amazing details that are new info to many fans. We also post the latest news about his son, Joe Hill, and his books.

People think running a fan page is easy. It's not. It is fun, but it is a *lot of work*. It pays off, though, because we are making thousands of fans happy and the emails and messages I get from our members make it all worthwhile. There are some amazing people out there and if we can bring a little happiness into their lives, then we've done our job and done it well.

Stephen King ✔
@StephenKing

Follow

Anyone who has to call himself a
genius...isn't.

9:09 AM - 6 Jan 2018

8,945 Retweets **32,997** Likes

SS: How strict are you about limiting posts and discussions to "All Things King"? For example, when King tweets about Trump, do you allow comments about Trump when they have nothing to do with King or King's comments?

AN: As a professional and respectable fan page, we do have to have rules. Some of those rules are such things as: *no* hot topics. This includes politics (mostly), no profanity, no disrespect to ethnicities, partner preference. We just like to keep all drama off the page because this is not the place to talk about hot topics and [we] prefer to keep them at bay. We want nothing but a "fun zone" for all our members. We are a diverse group, therefore, we have a zero tolerance policy for inflammatory or contentious topics. We get all age groups and genders—essentially, people from all walks of life and age groups, so we keep it a welcoming place.

We do have occasions when members will post a tweet from King about Trump, but it comes down. We just don't need a long thread of hate and political debates among members and we learned long ago it causes major problems, so we don't dare let that happen again. We just want the basics: King's books, other works, films, biographical stuff, and news of up-and-coming books and projects. It's simple, fun, and drama free. ATK doesn't take political sides regardless if it comes from King or not.

SS: As someone on the front lines of King fandom, what are you seeing in terms of SK fans' interest in the work of Joe Hill and Owen King? Is there more interest when King collaborates with his sons? Or is there serious interest in general?

AN: There are definitely SK fans who keep up with the King family and already know about Joe Hill and Owen King and what new projects they are working on or coming out with.

A *lot* of King fans are becoming Joe Hill fans as time goes on. Joe is an amazing writer and not *just* because he is his dad's son, but because he really can tell a tale. A lot of people say this regarding

Joe's writing: "He reminds me of Stephen King's early works." And it's true. Joe has done something King has done, and that is to scare me! I don't scare easy. Joe's *NOS4A2* is great fun and really scared the heck outta me! He is getting better and better and the *Locke & Key* graphic novel is amazing!

I can tell you this, coming from, as you described, the front-lines: SK fans have *all* agreed on two things regarding Joe Hill: 1. Heaven forbid something happens to Sai King, or after he passes on, they have all said they *will* continue reading and collecting Joe's works as they feel the torch has then been passed on; and 2. *All* Stephen King fans that I have spoken with have agreed that Joe *should* write more *Dark Tower* stories if something happens to his father. They feel Joe could capture that magic his dad created and also add his own unique touch to it.

Owen doesn't have as large a body of work as his brother. I've read *Double Feature* and that's it, so I and many others are curious to see him open his wings and fly (regarding writing) with his new book, *Sleeping Beauties*, [written] with his dad. I'm looking forward to it enormously. King has collaborated with other writers and those books turned out to be hits, so I'm sure *Sleeping Beauties* will, too. I would like to see more from Owen.

These are conversations we've had on ATK many times and it is nice to hear various opinions on the subject.

SS: Last question: If you could have a sit-down with Stephen King and ask him anything you wanted, and he promised to answer truthfully, what would you ask and why?

AN: That's a tough one. I've had discussions on ATK about this in the past. You hear the same answers all the time: "Where do you get your ideas?" Well, I wouldn't ask that. It would be hard for me to ask him *just one* because I have a ton to ask and even just talk about. I would tell him that I lived in the town where *Silver Bullet* was filmed, that I've been across the bridge in *Maximum Overdrive* tons of times when I lived in North Carolina, and that I've interviewed some of the same people who filmed or starred in his films. I'd also tell him about my hosting two Dollar Baby Film Fests and, of course, I'd talk about ATK and the five years running it.

But to stick to the question at hand, I would ask him three things: (1) If you could go back in time and save Kennedy (*11-22-63*) would you do it?, (2) Will we ever see Roland and his ka-tet in a new book again?, and (3) The fans are a dedicated bunch. Their devotion includes everything from the long lines they wait in at book signings, building huge book and memorabilia collections, having tattoos of characters from your books on their bodies, social media fan pages, to those who have gone through tough times and your books have gotten them through those tough times. So, my question would be: Sai King, what are your true feelings and thoughts about Stephen King fans? (And I do *not* mean the Annie Wilkes of the world!)

SS: Good questions, Sai Tony. Thanks for being in *Stephen King, American Master*!

TWO STEPHEN KING ONE-OF-A-KIND ITEMS: *THE STORY OF A KING IN WHITE SATIN*

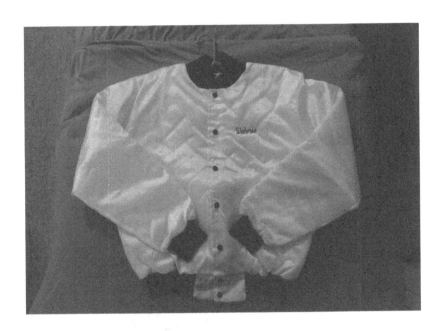

AN INTERVIEW WITH VALERIE BARNES

Valerie Barnes has been a Stephen King fan since she was ten years old, but frankly, the word "fan" doesn't even come close to the depth of her fondness for the work of Stephen King. She's a superfan and I have a photo of Valerie and Stephen King together on my wall and my website. There is no photo of me and Stephen King on my wall or my website.

She has researched King's life for the writing of a possible biography at some point, and for years she spent weekends in Bangor, often shopping at Betts' Bookstore for collectibles and limited editions, and visiting the King-related sites. She was a charter member of the Stephen King E-Mailers group (SKEMERs) before she even had a computer, and once sold three of her King limited editions to buy a Kia.

This interview tells the story of a jacket. Well, two jackets, actually. Two custom-made "Rock Bottom Remainders" white satin jackets. One has "Stephen" embroidered on the front, and one has "Valerie" embroidered on the front.

Val had them made for herself and King in appreciation for his work, and for the enjoyment she had reaped from reading his work for decades.

Valerie Barnes says Stephen King once slept here and also wrote about this house at 1543 West Broad St., Stratford, in his latest, "Hearts in Atlantis" (Scribner, $28).

Photo by Melanie Stengel ©New Haven Register Used by permission.

Stephen Spignesi: Where'd the idea to have a jacket made for Stephen King come from?

Valerie Barnes: I wanted to do something just to thank him for all the years of entertainment his writing had provided me, and countless others, of course. My initial thought was to send him a Red Sox jacket but I wanted to do something a little more unique, something that he'd remember, but also something practical that he might be able to use. And I remembered the Rock Bottom Remainders (King's band) t-shirts that they would sell during the concerts, but they never had jackets, so I thought that would be a good idea.

SS: It is actually *quite* a good idea. How does one go about having such a thing made?

VB: Initially, I found some good images of the drawing that were on the t-shirt, and I took them to the Arctic Sports Shop in Bridgeport, Connecticut. They were known for doing lots of school jackets for high schools. I knew it would have to be a custom-made item, and since it was custom-made, I was able to pick the fabric, the colors, the snaps, and so forth. I went with black and white because I wanted it to match the t-shirts that the band had made. When I showed the guy the image that I wanted to have embroidered on the back of the jacket, he was shocked. He immediately realized how intricate the design was and knew it would be very expensive.

SS: How expensive?

VB: Once I told him cost was no object because it was for Stephen King, he then asked me how many I wanted to do. I told him two. One for Stephen and one for me. He then quoted me a ballpark figure of close to a thousand dollars for the two jackets. He also told me that the design would require 50,000 stitches.

SS: What was your reaction when you heard what a big project it was going to be? Did you hesitate about having it done?

VB: Not at all! I said I don't care how much it costs or how long it takes, I want it done. It's for Stephen King, so just do it.

SS: How long did it take?

VB: First, they had to sew the jackets, and then they had to do the embroidery, so it took about three weeks for the whole job. And the final cost was $750. Frankly, I was thrilled that it was less than a thousand bucks. It didn't really matter, but less is always better.

SS: Once you had the jackets, then what did you do?

VB: On my next trip up to Bangor, I visited Stu Tinker at Bett's Bookstore and showed him the jacket. I told him I was thinking of having it delivered to King, but Stu said I needed to bring it myself right to the house. He said it was too cool to just show up in a FedEx box. So off I went to Stephen King's house on West Broadway.

SS: What was that like?

VB: A little nerve-wracking. I sat in my car in front of his house for about twenty minutes, trying to marshal the nerve to set foot on Stephen King's private property. I eventually got out of the car, walked up to the front door, and rang the doorbell, as I'm looking up at security cameras.

SS: Did someone answer the door?

VB: No. Even though I rang the bell two or three times, no one ever answered the door.

SS: What'd you do then?

VB: I know this sounds a little stalkery, but I sat in my car for about an hour, waiting for someone to show up. Eventually a minivan pulled into the driveway. The woman that got out looked a lot like Tabitha, but it turned out it wasn't her. It was her sister Stephanie.

SS: Did you dare to go up to her?

VB: Oh, yeah! I got out of the car and yelled out, "Excuse me! You got a minute?" She then said, "Yeah. Can I help you?" And as she got closer to me I said, "I'm sorry. I thought you were Tabitha 'cause you look an awful lot like her." And that's when she told me she was Stephanie, her sister.

SS: What happened next?

VB: I said, "I have a gift for Steve," and she told me that they were at the house in Center Lovell for the summer. And I said, "That's okay, can I leave it with you?" And she said, "Well, it depends on what it is." And I said, "It's a jacket I had made for him."

SS: What was her reaction?

VB: She asked to see it, so I went and got it out of the back seat of my car. I showed it to her and her eyes bugged out of her head. "This is awesome," she said. "Yeah, I'll take it and I'll leave it right on his desk." She asked me how he'd know who it was from, and when I told her I didn't really care that he knew it was from me, I just wanted him to have it, she then insisted that I write a letter so he would know that I was the one who gave it to him. I said I didn't think a letter would get through to him, and she told me how to send it so he'd definitely get it.

SS: And did he?

VB: He certainly did. I got a Thank You note from his assistant telling me that he loved the jacket and was very grateful.

SS: So you never got to talk to him about the jacket?

VB: Oh, yeah! I did!

SS: How'd that happen?

VB: A couple of months after I left the jacket with Stephanie, King was involved in the "Reading Stephen King" conference at his alma mater, the University of Maine in Orono. I was at the conference and also attended the banquet dinner that night. No one knew Stephen King was going to be at the dinner and people were surprised when he walked in. Once the food was served, I mustered the courage to go up to him.

SS: You interrupted his dinner?

VB: I sure did. I knelt down right next to his chair as he was putting a forkful of salad into his mouth. He was incredibly gracious. He put down his fork, held out his hand, and said, "Hi, I'm Stephen King." So we shook hands and I said, "Hi, my name is Valerie and I am so sorry for interrupting your dinner, but I just wanted to be sure you got this"—and held up my own Rock Bottom Remainders jacket—"and that it fit you okay."

SS: What was his reaction?

VB: He said, "Oh, yes! I did get it and it fits perfectly! In fact, I almost wore it tonight but it's too mild out, so I didn't need a jacket."

SS: And then what happened?

VB: I then made a joke about how it's a good thing he didn't wear it because if I had seen him walk in with it on, I probably would have fainted. He laughed, and I then said, "Well, I'm so glad it fits and again, I'm sorry I interrupted and I'll let you get back to your dinner." And he said, "Oh, no, thank *you*." And I went back to my own table.

PART II

The Creepy Corpus

Ex-CAMPUS writer hits the big time

A former columnist for the *Maine Campus* and an UMO graduate made his debut on the big-money literary scene, the Campus learned last week.

Stephen E. King, author of a popular *Campus* column of the late sixties, "King's Garbage Truck," learned last March that Doubleday & Co., Inc. purchased the hardcover rights to his novel, "Carrie," for $2,500 plus royalties on sales.

Doubleday expects to publish the hardcover version of the novel, which tells the story of a high school girl with telekinetic powers (ability to sprirtually cause objects to move), next January.

King jumped into the big-money bracket last week however, when he learned from Doubleday that New American Library purchased the paperback rights to "Carrie" for a reported $4000,000. King has been guaranteed 50 percent of that figure, plus royalties on sales.

The paperback edition is expected to be published sometime early in

Steve King

1975.

Currently an English instructor at Hampden Academy, King is a 1970 graduate of UMO, holding a B.S. in Education. Prior to the sale of "Carrie," he published several short stories in *Cavalier* and *Adam* magazines.

It's probably wrong to believe there can be any limit to the horror which the human mind can experience....And the most terrifying question of all may be just how much horror the human mind can stand and still maintain a wakeful, staring, unrelenting sanity.

Pet Sematary

I.
THE NOVELS

Stephen King is a very prolific novelist. He doesn't get just a bookshelf in fans' homes; he gets an entire bookcase. Or three. Stephen King "shelfies" are especially popular on Stephen King Facebook groups.

Stephen King at his high school prom.

Carrie (1974)

"Carrie White may be picked on by her classmates, but she has a gift…"

- *Carrie* was originally a short story that King threw away. It was rescued from the trash by his wife, Tabitha. "I did three single-spaced pages of a first draft, then crumpled them up in disgust and threw them away," King wrote in *On Writing*.
- In "On Becoming a Brand Name," King wrote, "The story had so many strikes against it from the very beginning that it never should have been written at all. The first problem had occurred about an hour after I sat down and began writing. I decided I couldn't write it at all. I was in a totally foreign environment—a girls' shower room—and writing about teenage girls. I felt completely at sea."
- Continuing a fun tradition in his writing, Stephen King himself makes two cameo appearances in *Carrie*, his first published novel. (Well, two personas of Stephen King.) One of Carrie's teachers was "Edwin King," and Stephen King's middle name is Edwin; and the folk singer who performed at the Ewen High School prom (the Black Prom) was John Swithen. "John Swithen" was the pseudonym Stephen King used in 1972 to publish (in *Cavalier* magazine) his crime short story "The Fifth Quarter."
- The 1976 film adaptation of *Carrie* starring Sissy Spacek, Piper Laurie, Amy Irving, William Katt, Nancy Allen, and John Travolta is one of the most beloved film versions of any of Stephen King's stories.
- In 1988, *Carrie: The Musical* starring Betty Buckley and Linzi Hateley opened on Broadway. It was directed by Terry Hands and the book was by Lawrence D. Cohen, who had written the screenplay to the Brian De Palma screen adaptation of the novel. (He also wrote the original *IT* miniseries.) Music was by Michael Gore with lyrics by Dean Pitchford. It closed after five

performances, but was revived off-Broadway in 2012 where it was much more warmly received. Since then, it has been staged in Seattle and Manila in 2013, and Los Angeles and London in 2015.

Essential Stephen King ranking: **20**

The 1898 Shiloh Chapel in Durham, Maine, King's inspiration for the Marsten House. Photo by Valerie Barnes ©2017 All rights reserved.

'Salem's Lot (1975)

"Ben Mears has returned to Jerusalem's Lot..."

- This is King's classic vampire novel, essentially a modern-day *Dracula*.
- King's original title for *'Salem's Lot* was Second Coming.
- King's childhood friend Chris Chesley tells the story of having dinner with King and Tabitha and discussing Bram Stoker's *Dracula*. They mused about whether or not it was possible for Dracula to exist in modern times, i.e., Dracula in the frozen foods section of a grocery store? This inspired King to take a swing at writing a novel in which a vampire exists in contemporary America. In "On Becoming a Brand Name," King recalls the dinner: "The dinner conversation that night was a speculation on what might happen if Dracula returned today, not to London with its 'teeming millions' (as Stoker puts it with such purely Victorian complacency), but to rural America....I began to turn the idea over in my mind, and it began to coalesce into a possible novel. I thought it would make a good one, if I could create a fictional town with enough prosaic reality about it to offset the comic-book menace of a bunch of vampires."
- King told the same story during his lecture at the Billerica Library, which is reprinted in *Secret Windows*: "With *'Salem's Lot*, I was teaching *Dracula* in high school....We were talking about it with a friend one night at supper and I said, 'This is the magic question. What would happen if Dracula came back today?' And my wife said, 'Well, he'd land at Port Authority in New York and get run over by a taxicab and that'd be the end of him.' And then this friend of mine said, 'But suppose he came back to a little town somewhere inland in Maine. You know, you go through some of those little towns and everybody could be dead and you'd never know it.'"

154

- King once gave serious thought to writing a sequel to *'Salem's Lot*. In a 1982 interview with *Fangoria* magazine, King actually revealed how such a sequel would begin: "I think about a sequel a lot. I even know who would be in it and how it would launch...it's Father Callahan. I know where he is....He went to New York City and from New York he drifted across the country and he landed in Detroit. He's in the inner city and he's running a soup kitchen for alcoholics...and he's been attacked a couple of times and...people think he's crazy. He doesn't wear the turned-around collar anymore, but he's...trying to get right with God. So one day this guy comes in. He's dying and he says, 'I have to talk to you, Father Callahan.' And Callahan says, 'I'm not a Father anymore and how did you know that?' [As the guy dies], the last thing he says as he grabs Callahan by the shirt and pulls him down into this mist of beer and whiskey and puke...is, 'It's not over in the Lot, yet.' Then he drops dead."
- In *On Writing*, King describes *'Salem's Lot* as "a peculiar combination of *Peyton Place* and *Dracula*."

Essential Stephen King ranking: **8**

Rage (written as Richard Bachman) (1977)

(Dear Readers: Please note that this particular synopsis contains spoilers. Considering the limited availability of the novel, it is included here for King fans who may never get their hands on a copy. If you have not read Rage *and you do foresee the day when you will find and read a copy, then eschew the reading of this synopsis.)*

- **Wikipedia synopsis of *Rage*:** Charlie Decker, a Maine high school senior, is called to a meeting with his principal about a previous incident in which he struck his chemistry teacher with a pipe wrench, leading to the teacher's hospitalization and Charlie's suspension. For unknown reasons, Charlie subjects the principal to a series of insulting remarks, resulting in his expulsion. Charlie storms out of the office and retrieves a pistol from his locker, then sets the contents of his locker on fire. He then returns to his classroom and fatally shoots his algebra teacher. The fire triggers an alarm, but Charlie forces his classmates to stay in the room, killing another teacher when he attempts to enter. As the other students and teachers evacuate the school, the police and media arrive at the scene. Over the following four hours, Charlie toys with various authority figures who attempt to negotiate with him, including the principal, the school psychologist, and the local police chief. Charlie gives them certain commands, threatening to kill students if they do not comply. Charlie also admits to his hostages that he does not know what has compelled him to commit his deeds, believing he will regret them when the situation is over. As his fellow students start identifying with Charlie, he unwittingly turns his class into a sort of psychotherapy group, causing his schoolmates to semi-voluntarily tell embarrassing secrets regarding themselves and each other. Interspersed throughout are narrative flashbacks to Charlie's troubled childhood, particularly his tumultuous relationship with his abusive father. Several notable incidents include a violent disagreement between two female students and a police sniper's attempt to shoot Charlie through the heart. However, Charlie survives due to the bullet's striking his locker's combination lock, which he had earlier placed in the breast pocket of his shirt. Charlie finally comes to the realization that only one student is really being held against his will: a seeming "Big Man On Campus" named Ted Jones, who is harboring his own secrets. Ted realizes this and attempts to escape the classroom, but the other students brutally assault him, driving him into a battered catatonic state. At 1:00 p.m., Charlie releases the students, but Ted is unable to move under his own power and remains. When the police chief enters the classroom, the now-unarmed Charlie moves as if to shoot him, attempting suicide by cop. The chief shoots Charlie, but he survives and is found not guilty by reason of insanity and committed to a psychiatric hospital in Augusta, Maine until he can answer for his actions. The final chapters contain an inter-office memo concerning Ted's treatment and prognosis at the hospital where he is now a patient, and a letter from one of Charlie's friends describing assorted developments in the students' lives during the months following this incident. The story ends with Charlie addressing the reader: "That's the end. I have to turn off the light now. Good night."

- King's original title for *Rage*, his first "Richard Bachman" novel, was *Getting It On*.
- *Rage* is about a high school hostage situation and shooting.
- After a series of school shootings in the 1980s and 1990s, King decided he wasn't comfortable with the book remaining in print.
- *Rage* is still available in older editions as used books, but it is officially out of print with the publisher.

- King cited the December 1997 shooting by Michael Carneal, 14, in Kentucky as the tipping point for his decision to pull the book from print. Carneal killed three and wounded five people of a prayer group with a Ruger MK II semi-automatic pistol and it was later discovered that he had a copy of the Bachman omnibus (which has *Rage* in it) in his locker.

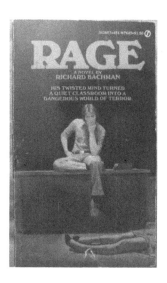

- In his keynote address at the Vermont Library Conference's Annual Meeting on May 26, 1999, King said, "The Carneal incident was enough for me. I asked my publisher to take the damned thing out of print. They concurred."
- King also addressed *Rage* in his 2013 essay "Guns":

> "I didn't pull *Rage* from publication because the law demanded it; I was protected under the First Amendment, and the law *couldn't* demand it. I pulled it because in my judgment it might be hurting people, and that made it the responsible thing to do. Assault weapons will remain readily available to crazy people until the powerful pro-gun forces in this country decide to

do a similar turnaround. They must accept responsibility, recognizing that responsibility is not the same as culpability. They need to say, 'We support these measures not because the law demands we support them, but because it's the sensible thing.'"

- In a BBC documentary on Stephen King that aired in the United States on December 19, 1999 on The Learning Channel, King said, "I've written a lot of books about teenagers who are pushed to violent acts. But with *Rage*, it's almost a blueprint in terms of saying, 'This is how it could be done.' And when it started to happen...particularly, there was a shooting thing in Paducah, Kentucky, where three kids were killed in a prayer group...and the kid who did it, that book was in his locker. And I said, that's it for me; that book's off the market. Not that they won't find something else...I don't think that any kid was driven to an act of violence by a Metallica record, or by a Marilyn Manson CD, or by a Stephen King novel, but I do think those things can act as accelerants."

- The "Cherokee Nose Job," vividly described by Charlie in the novel, actually was used by the Plains Indians, including the Cherokees, Choctaws, Chickasaws, Creeks, and Seminoles. In Chapter 13 of his book *Commerce of the Prairies*, Josiah Gregg writes, "Adultery is punished by cutting off both the nose and ears of the adulteress, but the husband has a right to say if the law shall be executed. In fact, he is generally the executioner, and that often without trial."

- A stage adaptation of *Rage* written by Robert B. Parker and starring Parker's son Daniel as Charlie Decker debuted at The Blackburn Theater in Gloucester, Massachusetts on March 30, 1989.

Essential Stephen King ranking: **31**

The Shining (1977)

"Jack Torrance's new job at the Overlook Hotel is the perfect chance for a fresh start…"

- *The Shining* is one of King's most loved, acclaimed, and literary novels. He was twenty-nine when he wrote it.
- In a March 1979 interview with Mel Allen in *Yankee* magazine, King talked about writing the novel's bathtub scene: "When I was writing *The Shining* there was a scene I was terrified of having to face writing. Writing is a pretty intense act of visualization. I won't say it's magic, but it's pretty close to magic. There was this woman in the tub, dead and bloated for years, and she gets up and starts to come for the boy who can't get the door open…The closer I got to having to write it, the more I worried about it. I didn't want to have to face that unspeakable thing in the tub, any more than the boy did. Two or three nights running, before I got to that section, I dreamed there was a nuclear explosion on the lake where we lived. The mushroom cloud turned into a huge red bird that was coming for me, but when I finished with the scene, it was gone."
- In the mid-1970s, King and his wife Tabitha checked into the Stanley Hotel in Estes Park, Colorado—exactly when the hotel was preparing to close for the season. King and his wife ended up essentially alone in the hotel (along with a skeleton crew—sorry) and since King's mind works the way it does, the story of the Torrances came to him and he decided to write it down. Many of the elements of the novel—the fire hose, the long corridors, the ballroom—are derived from King's stay at the Stanley.
- King's use of "redrum" as a totemic portent sent to Danny by his alter ego Tony is very clever and has become an oft-cited part of the culture.

- *The Shining* was Stephen King's first bestseller.
- *The Shining* is about as literarily significant as it gets. It is one of those rare books *about which* a book—*The Shining Reader* by Dr. Tony Magistrale—has been written. The undeniable gravitas of the novel has also spawned some fairly serious literary critique, including such essays as "The Redrum of Time: A Meditation on Francisco Goya's 'Saturn Devouring His Children' and Stephen King's *The Shining*" by Greg Weller, and "The Red Death's Sway: Setting and Character in Poe's 'The Mask of the Red Death' and King's *The Shining*" by Leonard Mustazza.
- Stanley Kubrick's film adaptation of the novel is one of the most loved, hated, controversial, and micro-analyzed cinematic versions of a King work ever created. In the novel, Jack dies a martyr, sacrificing himself (and the Overlook Hotel) for his family; in the film, he dies a raging psychopath intent on murdering his family. Kubrick completely reversed Jack's motivation and conclusion. and only reluctantly (when Grady lets Jack out of the cupboard) acknowledged the supernatural component of the hotel's influence on Jack."

Essential Stephen King ranking: **3**

The Long Walk (written as Richard Bachman) (1978)

"Against the wishes of his mother, sixteen-year-old Ray Garraty is about to compete in... The Long Walk... "

- *The Long Walk* is one of King's most psychologically dense novels and it is one of his tales which most compellingly communicates the individual terrors, insecurities, and weaknesses of its characters.

- *The Long Walk* contains many clues that it was actually written by Stephen King instead of Richard Bachman. These include references to Pownal and Bangor, Maine; mention in the text of a "gunslinger"; dedications to long-time King associates Burt Hatlen, Jim Bishop, and Ted Holmes; and a mention of King favorites Edgar Allan Poe and Ray Bradbury. Additionally, there is a foreshadowing of the "playing elevator" scene in *The Shining* when Ray Garraty remembers his father picking him up and swinging him wildly, and even an "RF" character, Roger Fenum, who was the fiftieth boy to go down.

- Jay Holben (see his essay in this volume), the director of *Paranoid* (the 2000 short film adaptation of King's chilling poem, "Paranoid: A Chant") concluded his film with the following onscreen quotation: "And when the hand touched his shoulder again, he somehow found the strength to run." That quote is the final line of *The Long Walk*.

- Runners and walkers consider a four-miles-per-hour pace to be "very brisk."

Essential Stephen King ranking: **28**

The Stand (1978)

"A patient escapes from a biological testing facility, unknowingly carrying a deadly weapon: a mutated strain of super-flu that will wipe out 99 percent of the world's population within a few weeks..."

- *The Stand* has consistently been the fans' favorite Stephen King novel.

- When I wrote *The Essential Stephen King*, I ranked *It* as King's greatest work and put *The Stand* at number two. I stand by my decision, but I quickly learned that *The Stand* is the fans' most beloved King novel. Some readers suggested my first and second ranking should be reversed, but I still think King's magnum opus is *It*. (And I say that knowing full well that, in the classic sense of the definition of magnum opus, it would probably be *The Dark Tower* series, but I went with single volumes for my ranking.)

- When Stephen King completed writing *The Stand* in 1977, he did not have the marketability he does now. Today, King can publish two hardcovers at once (*Desperation* and *The Regulators*); six individual novellas in a row (*The Green Mile*); a novel and novella available only on the internet (*Riding the Bullet* and *The Plant*), and everything sells. Everything sells. Publishers don't balk anymore or fear Stephen King overexposure. Back in 1977, it was a different story. King was required to cut almost 150,000 words from the manuscript of *The Stand* (bringing it down to around 400,000 words) before Doubleday would publish it. King reissued the novel with the cut material restored (plus some minor editorial changes) in 1990 as *The Stand: The Complete & Uncut Edition*. (See my *Complete Stephen King Encyclopedia* for details on the restored characters and scenes.)

- In a March 1979 interview with Mel Allen in *Yankee* magazine, King talked about the genesis and writing of *The Stand*: "I wrote 'A dark man with no face' and then glanced up and saw that grisly little motto again: 'Once in every generation a plague will fall among them.' And that was that. I spent the next two years writing an apparently endless book called *The Stand*. It got to the point where I began describing it to friends as my own little Vietnam, because I kept telling myself that in another hundred pages or so, I would begin to see the light at the end of the tunnel."

- King has always been intrigued by the question of the existence or presence of an empirical evil in the affairs of mankind, and Randall Flagg (and many of his "RF" characters throughout King's entire canon) is the manifestation of this primal evil reality. In *The Stand*, we first meet Mr. Flagg and learn that not only is he legion, but that he is indestructible (as the coda to the uncut edition of *The Stand* unequivocally tells us).

- In his 2016 essay "Five to One, One in Five" in *Hearts in Suspension*, King writes that his poem "Harrison State Park '68" was "a precursor to *The Stand*."

Essential Stephen King ranking: **2**

The Dead Zone (1979)

"When Johnny Smith was six-years-old, head trauma caused by a bad ice-skating accident left him with…hunches…"

- *The Dead Zone* is a political/paranormal thriller.
- Many readers believe that Stephen King predicted the persona and presidency of Donald Trump with the character of Greg Stillson in this novel. King has been extremely vocal and negative about Trump, mainly via Twitter, to the point that Trump blocked King after some of his tweets.
- In an April 1, 2017 essay for the UK *Guardian*—"Stephen King on Donald Trump: 'How do such men rise? First as a joke'"—he talked about the comparison between Greg Stillson and Donald Trump: "I had written about such men before. In *The Dead Zone*, Greg Stillson is a door-to-door Bible salesman with a gift of gab, a ready wit and the common touch. He is laughed at when he runs for mayor in his small New England town, but he wins. He is laughed at when he runs for the House of Representatives (part of his platform is a promise to rocket America's trash into outer space), but he wins again. When Johnny Smith, the novel's precognitive hero, shakes his hand, he realizes that some day Stillson is going to laugh and joke his way into the White House, where he will start world war three."
- During the period when Johnny was in his coma, Sarah Bracknell lived in Veazie, Maine on Flagg Street.
- In a July 1984 interview with David Sherman in *Fangoria* magazine, King talked about *The Dead Zone*: "What always happens for me—with a book—is that you frame the idea of the book or the 'what if.' And little by little, characters will take shape. Generally as a result of a secondary decision about the plot….In the case of *The Dead Zone*, it was simply what

if a man was able to have this ability to see the future? What if you were to explore that idea in the book, if he was just an ordinary guy that could really do it? The secondary thing was the visualization of this guy taking a test paper from a student, and saying, 'You gotta go home right away. Your house is burning down.' That never actually appears in the book, but it set the thing of him as a teacher; there were some other decisions that were made, and then it was time to pick the book up and begin to go."

Essential Stephen King ranking: **4**

Firestarter (1980)

"Andy McGee and Vicky Tomlinson were once college students...volun-teering as test subjects for an experiment orchestrated by the clandestine government organization known as The Shop..."

- The main character in *Firestarter*, Charlie McGee, can start fires with her mind.
- When Charlie's mother was pregnant with her, her parents participated in government experiments that resulted in her having pyrotechnic abilities.
- *Firestarter* is Stephen King at his most paranoid, and the novel can be thematically linked with King's 1985 poem, "Paranoid: A Chant" in which a narrator believes he is being surveilled for some horrible, nefarious reason.
- In *Firestarter*, one of The Shop's clinical psychologists/psycho-therapists is named Doctor Patrick Hockstetter. In King's 1986 novel *IT*, we are told that a Derry resident named Patrick Hockstetter disappeared in 1958. (Eddie Kaspbrak does dream that he sees Hockstetter's decomposing body, but it is only a dream and by novel's end, Hockstetter is still missing.) Is it possible that these two Patrick Hockstetters are the same character? If this theory is correct, Patrick Hockstetter vanished from Derry in 1958 when he was approximately eleven years old and surfaced twenty or so years later as a Shop doctor, and King used *IT* to reveal Hockstetter's back story, powerfully linking the two tales. Some readers believe the two characters' names are merely a coincidence. My thinking is that "Patrick Hockstetter" is a pretty specific name to coincidentally use twice.
- In an interview with Douglas E. Winter in *Stephen King: The Art of Darkness*, King talked about what he considered the "most horrifying" scene in the book: "To me, the most horrifying scene in the book is the outright terrorism that goes on in

a lunchroom when The Shop is looking for Andy and Charlie; this Shop agent terrorizes first a waitress and then a short-order cook—it's an awful piece of work. To suggest that there aren't guys like that who are actually getting their salaries from the taxpayers is to claim that there aren't guys like Gordon Liddy who ever worked for the CIA. And they love their work, man. They love their fucking work."

- A film adaptation of *Firestarter* came out in 1984 starring David Keith, Drew Barrymore, Heather Locklear, and Martin Sheen. It was directed by Mark L. Lester from a screenplay by Stanley Mann.
- A new film adaptation of *Firestarter* was announced in April 2017, to be directed by Akiva Goldsman.

Essential Stephen King ranking: **19**

Roadwork (initially as Richard Bachman) (1980)

"It's all coming to an end for Barton Dawes...."

- *Roadwork* was written a year after King's mother had died of cancer and, initially, he considered it the worst of his Bachman books because it was "trying to find some answers to the conundrum of human pain."
- King later reassessed the book and said he considered it his favorite of the early Bachman books.
- Barton Dawes remembers shooting a jay with a new rifle when he was twelve and not killing it. When he approached it, he saw the beak "opening and closing." In *Desperation*, Audrey tells the same story, of shooting a jay when she was twelve, not killing it, and the beak slowly "opening and closing."
- The question posed in *Roadwork* is: "How much can one person take before snapping?" Dawes lost his young son to cancer, his wife to divorce, and the city, for no good reason, has plans to take his house, and the laundry where he works for an unnecessary highway extension.
- Like most Bachman books, *Roadwork* does not have a happy ending.
- As of this writing, there have been no film adaptations of *Roadwork*, either as a feature film or as a Dollar Baby.

Cujo (1981)

"Cujo used to be a big friendly dog, lovable and loyal to his trinity (THE MAN, THE WOMAN, and THE BOY)…and always did his best to not be a BAD DOG…."

- It is impossible to know how many "Cujo" jokes have been made in TV shows and movies since this book and movie came out. Is there a dog in a scene? In many cases, it will be referred to as "Cujo" at some point. It always gets a laugh. And it's always a cheap laugh. (It's too easy.)

- In *On Writing*, King wrote of *Cujo*, "At the end of my adventures I was drinking a case of 16-ounce tallboys a night, and there's one novel, *Cujo*, that I barely remember writing at all. I don't say that with pride or shame, only with a vague sense of sorrow and loss. I like that book. I wish I could remember enjoying the good parts as I put them down on the page."

- At one point in *Cujo*, Donna Trenton recalls that "Cujo" was the name of one of the members of the radical terrorist group the Symbionese Liberation Army, the organization that kidnapped Patty Hearst. King has, from time to time, talked about a novel he began writing in 1974 called *The House on Value Street*, which was about the SLA's kidnapping of Patty Hearst. That novel metamorphosed into *The Stand*.

- In a 1982 interview with Douglas E. Winter in *Stephen King: The Art of Darkness*, King talked about an incident that planted the seeds of *Cujo*: "I took the bike out there, and I just barely made it. And this huge Saint Bernard came out of the barn, growling. Then this guy came out and, I mean, he was Joe Camber—he looked like one of those guys out of *Deliverance*. And I was retreating, and wishing that I was not on my motorcycle, when the guy said, 'Don't worry. He don't bite.' And so I reached out to pet him, and the dog started to go for me. And the guy walked over and said, 'Down Gonzo,' or whatever the dog's name was, and gave him this huge whack on the rump, and the dog yelped and sat down….The guy said, 'Gonzo never done that before. I guess he don't like your face.'"

- A film version of *Cujo* came out in 1983 starring Dee Wallace, Danny Pintauro, Daniel Hugh Kelly, Christopher Stone, and Ed Lauter. It was directed by Lewis Teague from a screenplay by Don Carlos Dunaway and Lauren Currier.

Essential Stephen King ranking: **16**

The Running Man (initially as Richard Bachman) (1981)

"Ben Richards is a desperate man…"

- Stephen King wrote this novel in a weekend. (It can take some fans more time than that to *read* it.)
- Ben Richards has to survive thirty days without being captured to win one million New Dollars. If he's caught, he'll be killed. And he can kill anyone trying to capture him.
- King likes this Bachman novel. In "Why I Was Bachman," the introduction to the October 1985 New American Library omnibus edition of *The Bachman Books*, he said, "*The Running Man*…may be the best of them all because it's nothing but story—it moves with the goofy speed of a silent movie, and anything which is not story is cheerfully thrown over the side."
- In a spooky precognitive finale, [**Spoiler Alert**] Ben Richards hijacks a plane and flies it into the tallest building in New York: "Heeling over slightly, the Lockheed struck the Games Building dead on, three quarters of the way up. Its tanks were still better than a quarter full. Its speed was slightly over five hundred miles an hour. The explosion was tremendous, lighting up the night like the wrath of God, and it rained fire twenty blocks away."
- King mentions both Harding and Derry in *The Running Man*. Harding is the setting for King's unpublished "race riot" novel *Sword in the Darkness*; Derry is the setting for *IT*, *Insomnia*, *Dreamcatcher*, and other King works.
- Like the rest of the Bachman tales, *The Running Man* paints a bleak picture of our future and ends on a defiantly pessimistic note. This dark sensibility is why Ace Books initially rejected the novel, telling King they were not interested in science fiction that dealt with "negative utopias."

- In August 2000, a Berlin-based company inaugurated a game called RealityRun, which the creators acknowledged was based on Stephen King's novel *The Running Man*. The main difference, of course, was that the contestant only lost the game, not his life, if he was not able to remain on the run for twenty-four days. The first contestant was "captured" in seven days by a German woman. She won the ten-thousand-dollar grand prize that the contestant would have garnered had he been able to elude recognition and identification for the entire twenty-four days. The other difference between the book and the game is that viewers monitored the runner on realityrun.com—instead of on television.

- A film version of *The Running Man* came out in 1987 starring Arnold Schwarzenegger and Maria Conchita Alonso. It was directed by Paul Michael Glaser from a screenplay by Steven E. de Souza. The movie is a lame and unfaithful adaptation, but still notable for its interesting casting, including: former pro wrestler Jesse Ventura, Mick Fleetwood of Fleetwood Mac, Frank Zappa's son Dweezil, and *Family Feud* host Richard Dawson. Considering the talent involved, this film should have been better than it is. King spoke out about this film in the January 2001 issue of the magazine *WRITERS' Journal*: "I didn't care for the way they made *The Running Man* very much. It was not very much like my book, and I liked that book a lot. I relate it to a period of my life that I enjoyed, and I remember the writing of it with great affection. I didn't like the movie, but I kept my mouth shut. Now the movie's gone, but the book rules."

Essential Stephen King ranking: 41

THE DARK TOWER SYNOPSES

A Note About the Dark Tower Series: *As a gesture of literary respect (as well as a nod to the vagaries of word count and the number of pages in this book), we decided not to attempt to reduce this masterpiece to bullet points. However, to provide some spoiler-free details about the books, and to acclimate new readers to the complete story, below are the official synopses of each book from www.stephenking.com.*

The Dark Tower I: The Gunslinger (1982)
- The first book of King's *Dark Tower* series.

"'The man in black fled across the desert, and the gunslinger followed.' So begins Book I of Stephen King's iconic fantasy series, *The Dark Tower*. Part sci-fi novel, part futuristic dystopia, part spaghetti Western, and part high fantasy vision, *The Gunslinger* tells the story of Roland Deschain, Mid-World's last gunslinger, who is tracking an enigmatic magician known only as the man in black. Following his quarry across the demon-infested Mohaine Desert, Roland confronts a mad preacher woman and her murderous flock, holds palaver with a speaking demon, and finally befriends a young boy from our world named Jake Chambers. Jake joins Roland on his quest, but while Roland travels with his young companion Jake, the man in black travels with Roland's soul in his pocket."

The Gunslinger begins with a line that fits Stephen King's own description of an opener that works, a great hooker: "The man in black fled across the desert and the gunslinger followed." (See King's nonfiction essay, "Great Hookers I Have Known" in his collection *Se-*

cret Windows for more on what makes a killer opening sentence.)

Essential Stephen King ranking: **10** (whole series)

The Dark Tower: The Gunslinger (Revised) (2003)

- This is a rewritten version of the original novel (which was a collection of short stories and not really a novel). This version provides more narrative cohesion. The original version is officially out of print, but available from used book sellers.

The Dark Tower II: The Drawing of the Three (1987)

- The second volume of King's *Dark Tower* series.

"After his final confrontation with the Man in Black in a remote mountain Golgotha, an exhausted Roland awakes on the beach of the Western Sea and is immediately attacked by a shoreline monster known as a lobstrosity. Roland kills the clawed creature, but not before it bites off two of his fingers and half of one big toe. Fighting off the delirium brought on by the lobstrosity's poison, Roland forces himself along the beach where he discovers three freestanding doorways that lead into our world. The first opens onto New York, 1987, and the mind of a heroin addict called Eddie Dean. The second leads to 1964 and the divided personality of Odetta Holmes/Detta Walker, an African American woman who has lost the bottom half of her legs but gained a second, psychotic self. The third door leads to 1977 and the mind of a psychopath called The Pusher, the very criminal responsible for Odetta's injuries. Roland's task is to make Eddie and Odetta into gunslingers before raging Detta destroys them all, and before the Pusher can continue his bloody killing spree."

The Dark Tower III: The Waste Lands (1991)
• The third volume of King's *Dark Tower* series.

"Several months have passed, and Roland's two new tet-mates have become proficient gunslingers. Eddie Dean has given up heroin, and Odetta's two selves have joined, becoming the stronger and more balanced personality of Susannah Dean. But while battling The Pusher in 1977 New York, Roland altered ka by saving the life of Jake Chambers, a boy who—in Roland's where and when—has already died. Now Roland and Jake exist in different worlds, but they are joined by the same madness: the paradox of double memories. Roland, Susannah, and Eddie must draw Jake into Mid-World then follow the Path of the Beam all the way to the Dark Tower. But nothing is easy in Mid-World. Along the way our tet stumbles into the ruined city of Lud, and are caught between the warring gangs of the Pubes and the Grays. The only way out of Lud is to wake Blaine the Mono, an insane train that has a passion for riddling, and for suicidal journeys."

The Dark Tower IV: Wizard and Glass (1997)
• The fourth volume of King's *Dark Tower* series.

"Roland, Eddie, Susannah, Jake, and Jake's pet bumbler survive Blaine the Mono's final crash, only to find themselves stranded in an alternate version of Topeka, Kansas, one that has been ravaged by the superflu virus. While following the deserted I-70 toward a distant glass palace, they hear the atonal squalling of a thinny, a place where the fabric of existence has almost entirely worn away. While camping near the edge of the thinny, Roland tells his ka-tet a story about another thinny, one that he encountered when he was little more than a boy. Over the course of one long magical night, Roland transports us to the Mid-World of long-ago and a seaside town called Hambry, where Roland fell in love with a girl named Susan Delgado, and where he and his old tet-mates Alain and Cuthbert battled the forces of John Farson, the harrier who—with a little help from a seeing sphere called Maerlyn's Grapefruit—ignited Mid-World's final war."

The Dark Tower V: Wolves of the Calla (2003)

- The fifth volume of King's *Dark Tower* series.

"Roland and his tet have just returned to the path of the Beam when they discover that they are being followed by a group of inexperienced trackers. The trackers are from the town of Calla Bryn Sturgis, and they desperately need the help of gunslingers. Once every generation, a band of masked riders known as the Wolves gallop out of the dark land of Thunderclap to steal one half of all the twins born in the Callas. When the children are returned, they are roont, or mentally and physically ruined. In less than a month, the Wolves will raid again. In exchange for Roland's aid, Father Callahan—a priest originally from our world—offers to give Roland a powerful but evil seeing sphere, a sinister globe called Black Thirteen which he has hidden below the floorboards of his church. Not only must Roland and his tet discover a way to defeat the invincible Wolves, but they must also return to New York so that they can save our world's incarnation of the Dark Tower from the machinations of the evil Sombra Corporation."

The Dark Tower VI: Song of Susannah (2004)

• The sixth volume of King's *Dark Tower* series

"The Wolves have been defeated, but our tet faces yet another catastrophe. Susannah Dean's body has been usurped by a demon named Mia who wants to use Susannah's mortal form to bear a demon child. Stealing Black Thirteen, Mia has traveled through the Unfound Door to 1999 New York where she plans to give birth to her chap, a child born of two mothers and two fathers who will grow up to be Roland's nemesis. With the help of the time-traveling Manni, Roland and Eddie plan to follow Susannah while Father Callahan and Jake will find Calvin Tower, owner of the vacant lot where a magical rose grows: a rose that must be saved at all costs. But despite our ka-tet's intentions, ka has its own plans. Jake, Callahan, and Jake's bumbler companion are transported to New York to follow Susannah, while Eddie and Roland are tumbled into East Stoneham, Maine, where they are greeted by Eddie's old enemy, the gangster Balazar. But it isn't just bullets that Roland and Eddie must brave. Soon they will meet their maker, in the form of a young author named Stephen King."

The Dark Tower VII: The Dark Tower (2004)

• The final volume of King's *Dark Tower* series.

"At the outset of the final installment of our saga, Roland's ka-tet is scattered across several different wheres and whens. Susannah Dean (still in the clutches of the demon Mia) is in End-World's Fedic Dogan: a chamber of horrors where magic and technology can be merged and where a monstrous half-human child can be brought forth into the world. Eddie Dean and Roland Deschain are in Maine, 1977, searching for the site of otherworldly walk-in activity, and a possible doorway back to Mid-World. Jake Chambers, Father Callahan, and the bumbler Oy are battling vampires and low men in New York's Dixie Pig Restaurant, circa 1999, a place where long pig is definitely on the menu. As soon as our tet reunites, they must journey to the headquarters of Thunderclap's Wolves in order to discover exactly why the Crimson King's minions have been culling the brains of young children for twin-telepathy enzymes. The answer is more horrible than they realized, and bears directly upon Roland's quest to reach the Dark Tower."

The Dark Tower: The Wind Through the Keyhole (2012)

"Although it is officially the eighth book of the *Dark Tower* saga, Stephen King likes to call *The Wind Through the Keyhole* book 4.5 of the series, since it takes place after our tet escapes the Green Palace at the end of *Wizard and Glass*, and before they reach Calla Bryn Sturgis, setting for *Wolves of the Calla*. *The Wind Through the Keyhole* is a story within a story within a story. At the outset, Roland and his American tet are traveling toward the River Whye in Mid-World. A great storm, called a Starkblast, is about to blow. While our tet is sheltering from the storm, Roland tells a story about his younger days, when he and his tet-mate Jamie De-Curry were sent to Debaria to investigate reports of a skin-man, a kind of dangerous shape-changer. While trying to comfort a young boy named Bill Streeter—the only survivor of a particularly brutal attack by the skin-man, and Roland's only witness to the crime—Roland recounts yet another story. This time it is a sinister fairytale drawn from the book *Magic Tales of Eld*. The three stories are woven together by the freezing, howling winds of the Starkblast."

The Little Sisters of Eluria

- This Dark Tower spin-off story first appeared in the 1998 anthology Legends.

"'The Little Sisters of Eluria' is a prequel to the first volume of the *Dark Tower* saga. Roland's beloved city of Gilead has fallen to the Good Man's forces, and the Gunslingers have been slaughtered at the Battle of Jericho Hill. Roland is now a lone wanderer, searching for the trail of the elusive sorcerer known as the Man in Black. On a hot day during the season of Full Earth, Roland enters a deserted town in the Desatoya Mountains. The town is called Eluria, and it is empty except for a lame dog, a drowned boy, and the eerie sound of tinkling silver bells. As Roland searches for the town's missing inhabitants, he is attacked by the slow mutants known as the Green Folk. Our unconscious hero is rescued by an itinerant band of female healers who call themselves the Little Sisters of Eluria. But Roland's rescuers are not what they seem, and our gunslinger must fight their narcotic potions to stay awake, and alive."

A REVIEW OF *THE DARK TOWER* MOVIE

The Dark Tower is not the movie that Stephen King, the *Dark Tower* epic, or Stephen King fans deserve. It is, at the same time, a reductionist spin on, and a purported continuation of King's story and characters that, unfortunately, diminishes the gravitas of the *Dark Tower* mythology. It's Jimmy Fallon and the Roots playing "Call Me Maybe" on toy instruments. It's recognizable as the song, but it's clearly a "less than" rendering of what became a pop classic. *The Dark Tower* movie is also like saying you're making an omelet for four people, but only using one egg and making up the difference with white rice.

They say it's a sequel. Okay. But where in the movie is it established that it is a sequel to an existing story? And how would viewers who have never read a *Dark Tower* book know that this isn't from the *Dark Tower* novels? At the very beginning of the movie, "Based on the *Dark Tower* novels" appears on the screen. Say what? It is, thus, a failure as a sequel and a failure as an adaptation. And it's certainly not part of the Stephen King canon because it was not written by Sai King himself.

Sure, the movie has characters we know (some, but where's Susannah? Eddie? Oy? Blaine?), and scenarios we don't (the Breakers are kids? Roland's motivation is revenge?), but overall it proves it's probably not a good idea to "adapt" or claim to write a sequel to a seven-volume series and condense it into ninety-five minutes. It sounds ludicrous to even verbalize the idea. *The Dark Tower* should have been given the *Lord of the Rings* multiple film treatment, or the HBO *Game of Thrones* multiple episodes and multiple seasons treatment.

So, with that all being said, I'll now say this: I did like it! It was fun! I enjoyed watching it. And I've come to the conclusion that the only way for Stephen King fans to watch *The Dark Tower* movie without stroking out is to forget that the books exist. Context is everything, so go into it with the idea that it's a free-standing fantasy thriller. Otherwise, it'll drive you nuts.

In conclusion, here's the best exchange in the movie. Roland and Jake are at a food cart on a New York street in Keystone Earth:

Roland: What is this?

Jake: A hot dog.

Roland: Savages. (*Takes a bite*) What breed?

Pet Sematary (1983)

"When the Creeds move into a beautiful old house in rural Maine, it all seems too good to be true..."

- *Pet Sematary* has been described by many readers and critics as the most frightening book Stephen King has written.
- *Pet Sematary* is the novel Stephen King felt was too horrific to publish. In fact, when he finished it in 1979, he put it in a drawer and refused to offer it for publication. As fulfillment of a contract with Doubleday, though, King eventually relented and allowed publication in 1983, but he refused to participate in the promotion of the book.
- In an interview with Douglas E. Winter in *Stephen King: The Art of Darkness*, King talked about the genesis of the idea for *Pet Sematary*: "When ideas come, they don't arrive with trumpets. They are quiet—there is no drama involved. I can remember crossing the road, and thinking that the cat had been killed in the road...and [I thought], what if a kid died in that road? And we had had this experience with Owen running toward the road, where I had just grabbed him and pulled him back. And the two things just came together—on one side of this two-lane highway was the idea of what if the cat came back, and on the other side of the highway was what if the kid came back—so that when I reached the other side, I had been galvanized by the idea, but not in any melodramatic way. I knew immediately that it was a novel."
- A film version of *Pet Sematary* came out in 1989 starring Dale Midkiff, Fred Gwynne, Denise Crosby, Brad Greenquist, Michael Lombard, and Miko Hughes. It was directed by Mary Lambert from a screenplay by Stephen King.

Essential Stephen King ranking: **9**

Christine (1983)

"It's love at first sight for high school student Arnie Cunningham...
when he...spot[s] the dilapidated 1958 red-and-white
Plymouth Fury for sale..."

- A haunted car.
- In "Has Success Spoiled Stephen King? Naaah," by Pat Cadigan, Marty Ketchum, and Arnie Fenner in the Winter 1982 issue of *Shayol* magazine, Stephen King said, "*Christine* [is] the first horror novel I've done, I think, since *The Shining*. That's all I'm going to say about it. Except it's scary. It's fun, too. It's maybe not my best book—it's kind of like a high school confidential. It's great from that angle."
- In an interview in the February 1984 issue of *Twilight Zone* magazine, Randy Lofficier asked King, "Why was *Christine* written using two different narrative styles?" King replied, "Because I got in a box. That's really the only reason. It almost killed the book...Dennis was supposed to tell the whole story. But then he got in a football accident and was in the hospital while things were going on that he couldn't see. For a long time I tried to narrate the second part in terms of what he was hearing hearsay evidence, almost like depositions—but that didn't work. I tried to do it a number of ways, and finally I said, 'Let's cut through it. The only way to do this is to do it in the third person.'"
- In the novel, it is said that Christine the car was a four-door model. The first mention of this is in the chapter "First Views" when King writes, "He tried the back door on the passenger side, and it came open with a scream." However, Plymouth never made a four-door 1958 Plymouth Fury. They were all two-door. (They changed the car to a two-door model for the John Carpenter movie version.) Also, although all 1958 Plym-

outh Furys were manufactured in ivory color, in *Christine*, King states that Christine was custom ordered in Ford red.

Essential Stephen King ranking: **39**

The Talisman (1984)

"Why had twelve-year-old Jack Sawyer's mother frantically moved the two of them from Rodeo Drive to a New York City apartment to the Alhambra?"

- *The Talisman* was co-written with Peter Straub.
- Stephen King's enormous popularity and worldwide fame was not allowed to overshadow the fact that *The Talisman* was a collaborative project and that its two authors each contributed to the book on an equal basis. The title page lists the two authors in alphabetical order; the copyright does likewise. The most blatant indication of the deliberate insistence that the two authors receive equal billing, though, is on the front and rear covers of the hardcover. The front of the book jacket has Stephen King on the top and Peter Straub on the bottom; the rear of the jacket has Peter Straub on the top and Stephen King on the bottom.
- In an interview with Douglas E. Winter in *Stephen King: The Art of Darkness*, King talked about collaborating on *The Talisman* with Peter Straub: "We both agreed that it would be nice to make the book seamless—it shouldn't seem like a game to readers to try to figure out who wrote what…When I worked on my half of the copy editing, I went through large chunks of the manuscript unsure myself who had written what…"
- In September 2017, Steven Spielberg, who has been working on an adaptation of *The Talisman* since 1984, issued a statement revealing that the project was still in development. He

used the phrase, "our upcoming projects, *The Talisman* and *The Wand.*"

Essential Stephen King ranking: **12**

Thinner (originally as "Richard Bachman")(1984)

"Attorney Billy Halleck seriously enjoys living his life of upper-class excess..."

- *Thinner* was the book that revealed King's "Richard Bachman" pseudonym to the world.
- *Thinner* was originally published as a "Richard Bachman" book, but when the news broke that Bachman was King, NAL released all remaining and new copies of the book with a cardboard wrapper that said "Stephen King writing as Richard Bachman."
- The man who discovered in 1985 that "Richard Bachman" was a Stephen King alias was Stephen P. Brown, a freelance writer who also worked in a bookstore. After being convinced that the "Richard Bachman" novels he had read had actually been written by Stephen King, he did some research. He visited the Library of Congress and checked the copyright records for the four paperback Bachman novels—*Rage* (1977), *The Long Walk* (1979), *Roadwork* (1981), and *The Running Man* (1982). He discovered that three of the Bachman books had been copyrighted in the name of Kirby McCauley, who just so happened to be Stephen King's literary agent. That alone could have raised suspicions, but the beans, as they say, were spilled when Brown checked the copyright record for *Rage*. That book's copyright was in the name of Stephen King. Brown wrote King a letter (this was in the pre-email, snail mail days) explaining what he had discovered. In an April 9, 1985 article in *The Washington*

Post, Stephen Brown told what happened next: "[O]ne day, the phone rang. 'Steve Brown? This is Steve King. Okay, you know I'm Bachman, I know I'm Bachman, what are we going to do about it? Let's talk.'"

- In *Thinner*, Richard Ginelli, an Italian organized crime boss, owns a restaurant called The Three Brothers. In King's serial novel, *The Plant*, a character named Richard Ginelli owns a restaurant called The Four Fathers. This is yet another clue that *Thinner* was written by Stephen King—but the only readers who would have noticed it were the lucky few who were receiving King's *Plant* Christmas mailings when *Thinner* was published. When King began offering the individual chapters of *The Plant* for sale on his website in 2000, King fans instantly noticed the Ginelli connection the day Chapter Three (the first time Ginelli is mentioned in *The Plant*) was posted on King's site.

- In an interview with Douglas E. Winter in *Stephen King: The Art of Darkness*, King said of the idea for *Thinner*: "After I started really losing weight, I couldn't help but feel attached to it. There's a line in the book about how our version of reality depends a lot on how we see our physical size. I began to think about just what would happen if someone who began to lose weight found he couldn't stop."

Essential Stephen King ranking: **45**

Cycle of the Werewolf (1985)

"A werewolf is stalking Tarker's Mills and only young, wheelchair-bound Marty Coslaw suspects the truth..."

- King's "werewolf" novella.
- In the "Foreword" to *Silver Bullet*, the volume containing the original *Cycle of the Werewolf* novella and King's *Silver Bullet*

screenplay, King wrote, "My wife, Tabby, reminded me that a year where all the full moons fell on holidays would be a mad year indeed. I agreed, but invoked creative license. 'I think your license should be revoked for speeding, dear,' she said, and wandered off to make us all something to eat."

- The hero of *Cycle of the Werewolf* is Marty Coslaw, a ten-year-old boy who is paralyzed and confined to a wheelchair. King has often created heroic characters who are physically disabled in one way or another, from stuttering Bill Denbrough in *IT* to Duddits in *Dreamcatcher*, who has Down's syndrome. *Cycle's* Marty Coslaw is part of that fraternity and he admirably ignores his handicap and [**Spoiler Alert**] triumphs over the werewolf.

- In *Cycle of the Werewolf*, *Today* show weatherman Willard Scott tells his viewers that a foot of snow fell in the Canadian Rockies on September 21st, which is Stephen King's birthday.

- A film version of *Cycle of the Werewolf* was released in 1985 as *Silver Bullet*, aka *Stephen King's Silver Bullet*. It starred Gary Busey, Everett McGill, Corey Haim, Megan Follows, and Terry O'Quinn. It was directed by Daniel Attias from a screenplay by Stephen King.

Essential Stephen King ranking: **61**

IT (1986)

"Welcome to Derry, Maine…a place as hauntingly familiar as your own hometown. Only in Derry the haunting is real…"

- Stephen King's magnum opus. (Note: Some consider the *Dark Tower* series King's magnum opus and that is a valid judgement. I prefer to assign that accolade to a single volume, *IT*.)
- Stephen King's middle name is "Edwin," and in *IT*, there is a character named "Eddie King," described as "a bearded man

whose spectacles were almost as fat as his gut." Eddie King was one of the guys playing poker in the Sleepy Silver Dollar the day Claude Heroux went nuts and killed everyone in the game. Eddie King's demise was particularly grisly. When Claude began his rampage, Eddie tried to flee, but ended up falling out of his chair and landing flat on his back on the floor. Claude straddled King (who was screaming to Claude that he had just gotten married a month ago) and buried an axe in Eddie King's ample belly. Claude then wiggled the axe out, and swung again, this time putting an end to Eddie's screaming, and to Eddie. "Claude Heroux wasn't done with him, however; he began to chop King up like kindling-wood."

- In his essay "How *IT* Happened," King said, "Sometime in the summer of 1981 I realized that I had to write about the troll under the bridge or leave him—IT—forever. Part of me cried to let it go. But part of me cried for the chance; did more than cry; it demanded. I remember sitting on the porch, smoking, asking myself if I had really gotten old enough to be afraid to try, to just jump in and drive fast. I got up off the porch, went into my study, cranked up some rock 'n' roll, and started to write the book. I knew it would be long, but I didn't know how long. I found myself remembering that part of *The Hobbit* where Bilbo Baggins marvels at how way may lead on to way; you may leave your front door and think you are only strolling down your front walk, but at the end of your walk is the street, and you may turn left or you may turn right, but either way there will be another street, another avenue, and roads, and highways, and a whole world." [Note: King was thirty-four when he started writing *IT*; he was thirty-eight when he finished it.]

- The 2017 film adaptation (Part One of a two-part series) of *IT* scored the second biggest weekend opening for a horror film. *IT* is currently number one for highest-grossing horror film of all time. On January 12, 2018, *Deadline Hollywood* announced that the film had reached a box office gross of 700.2 million dollars worldwide.

Essential Stephen King ranking: **1**

The Eyes of the Dragon (1987)

"Once, in a kingdom called Delain, there was a king with two sons…"

- Stephen King wrote *The Eyes of the Dragon* for his daughter Naomi.
- *The Eyes of the Dragon* is dedicated to Naomi King and also to King's "great friend" Peter Straub's son, Ben.
- On the dust jacket flap copy of the hardcover edition of *The Eyes of the Dragon*, King wrote, "I respected my daughter enough then—and now—to try and give her my best…and that includes a refusal to 'talk down.' Or put another way, I did her the courtesy of writing for myself as well as for her."
- In *The Eyes of the Dragon*, our friend Flagg owns a paperweight made of obsidian, which, at the time, was the hardest rock known. This is revealing, since obsidian, which is really natural glass with a hardness of only five (diamond, the hardest gem, is a ten), is formed only in areas of volcanic activity and is actually volcanic lava that cooled too quickly. This means that it is possible that, at some point, there had to have been volcanoes in or near Delain (or that Flagg had traveled in areas with volcanic activity), and that opal, peridot, onyx, aquamarine, emerald, topaz, cat's eye, ruby, sapphire, and, of course, diamond (all of which have hardness ratings higher than five), had not yet been discovered.
- An animated adaptation of *The Eyes of the Dragon*, with a forty-five million dollar budget, was scheduled for completion in

early 2001 and release in late 2001 or early 2002. The project was abandoned after the rights lapsed in 2000.

- In 2012, the cable channel Syfy announced that they were developing several projects for potential television adaptations, one of which was *The Eyes of the Dragon*.

Essential Stephen King ranking: **18**

Misery (1987)

"Paul Sheldon is a bestselling novelist who has finally met his number one fan. Her name is Annie Wilkes…"

- *Misery* is the novel that was inspired by certain experiences King had had with fans. Like any good fabulist, he extrapolated the persona of certain "intense" fans to create the one and only Annie Wilkes.
- The Dedication of *Misery* reads, "To Jim and Stephanie Leonard, who know why. Boy, do they." At the time, Stephanie was the editor of *Castle Rock: The Stephen King Newsletter* and dealt with King's fan mail on a regular basis. Read into that what you will.
- In an October 31, 2014 interview with *Rolling Stone*, King said, "*Misery* is a book about cocaine. Annie Wilkes is cocaine. She was my number-one fan."
- In a 1998 interview with journalist Peter Conrad, quoted in *On Writing*, King said, "I wrote most of *Misery* by hand, sitting at Kipling's desk in Brown's Hotel in London…Then I found out he died at the desk. That spooked me, so I quit the hotel."
- King originally planned on publishing *Misery* as a "Richard Bachman" novel.

Essential Stephen King ranking: **7**

This exchange is from a 1998 interview with journalist Ben Rawortit

Q: And have you had any bad experiences with a "Number One Fan" yourself?

Stephen King: I haven't directly, but my wife has. There was a guy who broke into our house when she was home alone. It was about six o'clock in the morning, and she had just got up when she heard glass breaking downstairs.

Q: And she went down to investigate?

SK: Yes.

Q: What did he look like?

SK: He looked like Charles Manson with long hair, and he had a rucksack in his hands. He said that he was my biggest fan. Then he stopped suddenly and said he actually hated me because I'd stolen the novel Misery from his aunt. Then he held up the rucksack and said that he had a bomb and was going to blow her up.

Q: Jesus! What did your wife do?

SK: She ran out in her bare feet and nightgown, man! The police came round and he was still there. It turned out that all he had in the bag was a load of pencils and paperclips in a box.

Q: What was up with him, then?

SK: It turned out he was from Texas. His aunt was a nurse who'd been fired from some hospital, and he made a connection with the nurse in Misery.

The Tommyknockers (1987)

"On a beautiful June day, while walking deep in the woods...Bobbi Anderson quite literally stumbles over her own destiny..."

- One of King's blatant science fiction novels. Others include *11/22/63* (time travel), *Dreamcatcher* (aliens), *Firestarter* (pyrokinesis), *Carrie* (telekinesis), and *Under the Dome* (force field). **Note**: Genres overlap, especially when it comes to King's work, but when a sci-fi superpower or elements are dominant in a story, we'll call it science fiction. King's sci-fi short stories and novellas include "The Jaunt," "Word Processor of the Gods," "Obits," "I Am the Doorway," "Beachworld," *The Mist*, *The Langoliers*, "The End of the Whole Mess," *The Sun Dog*, and others.
- In an October 31, 2014 interview with *Rolling Stone*, King said, "*The Tommyknockers* is an awful book. That was the last one I wrote before I cleaned up my act. And I've thought about it a lot lately and said to myself, 'There's really a good book in here, underneath all the sort of spurious energy that cocaine provides, and I ought to go back.' The book is about 700 pages long, and I'm thinking, 'There's probably a good 350-page novel in there.'"

Essential Stephen King ranking: **72**

The Dark Half (1989)

"After thirteen years of international bestseller stardom with his works of violent crime fiction, author George Stark is officially declared dead..."

- *The Dark Half* is seen by many as King writing about having a pseudonym—Richard Bachman—that was discovered. But, of course, with an added "Stephen King" element.

- The nightmarish premise of *The Dark Half* is the "What if?" question: What if a writer's pseudonym refused to stay dead?
- *The Dark Half*'s character of Wilhelmina Burks (Rawlie DeLesseps' girlfriend) may be an homage to an earlier King character named Wilma Northrup. Wilma Northrup first appeared in July 1979 (in *Gallery* magazine) in Stephen King's short story "The Crate." Wilma later appeared in King's 1982 film *Creepshow*, which included a King-scripted adaptation of "The Crate." In both versions of the story, Wilma Northrup told people, "Just call me Billie. Everyone does." The first time Wilhelmina Burks is mentioned in *The Dark Half*, she is described as "The one who goes around blaring, 'Just call me Billie, everyone does.'"
- In an interview in the November/December 1989 issue of Waldenbooks' magazine *W•B*, King commented on the genesis of *The Dark Half*: "I started to play with the idea of multiple personalities and then I read somewhere, probably in the case of the twin doctors that the film *Dead Ringers* was based on, that sometimes twins are imperfectly absorbed in the womb and I thought, 'Now wait a minute. What if this guy is the ghost of a twin that never existed?' After that, I was able to wrap the whole book around that spine and it made everything a lot more coherent."
- In the "Notes" to *Nightmares & Dreamscapes*, King wrote that *The Dark Half* was originally an almost completed novel called *Machine's Way*, written by Richard Bachman's pseudonym George Stark.
- *The Dark Half* has one of the great openings of a Stephen King novel. In the Prologue, the young Thad Beaumont has brain surgery and an eye is found peering out of his gray matter, causing nurse Hilary to flee screaming from the operating room. The operating surgeon, Doctor Pritchard, nonchalantly

says, "I want that silly cunt that ran out of here fired. Make a note, please."

- A film version of *The Dark Half* was released in 1993 starring Timothy Hutton, Amy Madigan, Michael Rooker, and Julie Harris. It was directed by George A. Romero from Romero's own screenplay adaptation of the novel.

Essential Stephen King ranking: **22**

THE DARK HALF PHONE NUMBER STORY

By Gerald Winters

When Stephen King was writing *The Dark Half* in 1989, he came to the part of the story where Sheriff Alan Pangborn needed to speak with a Doctor Pritchard in Wyoming, the doctor that had treated a suspect of his when he was a child—Thad Beaumont. Alan left a message on his answering machine, requesting that he call him back as soon as possible, as it was an urgent matter. The message included "Please call me collect at the Orono State Police Barracks—207-866-2121. Thank you."

Stephen King knew he was writing about a police station in his nearby Orono, Maine, so why not get the real number, which is exactly what he did. It was there in the phone book in bold type. What happened after the book was published was anything other than expected.

Constant Readers from all over the world started to call the number, and why not, it was in Stephen King's book, plain as black and white. Could there be a coded message to surprise callers, or a mystery person that was just curious if anyone would call? No, it was the Orono State Police, and specifically Dan Lawrence, the dispatcher.

Dan fielded calls from Montana, Florida, California, and as far away as Japan, the UK, and Australia. Why not, it's only an international call to their favorite author's home state. Many callers told Dan they would be vacationing in Maine in the summer of 1990, and asked whether they could visit him for his autograph. Finding the humor in this situation, Dan located the passage in Mr. King's latest novel and sure enough, he saw his number on page 210 (Chapter 16).

Dan felt the need to write a letter to the editor at *Bangor Daily News*, but like Mr. King, he never realized the chain of events that would transpire from that simple act. He got a chance to visit his favorite author's office and receive an inscription in his personal copy. Mr. King apologized for his oversight, and true to his word, he changed the number in the later printing of the paperback.

Gerald Winters is the proprietor of Gerald Winters and Son booksellers in Bangor, Maine.

The Stand: The Complete & Uncut Edition (1990)

- In May 1990, Doubleday released the uncut edition of *The Stand*, restoring approximately 150,000 words that were cut from the original 1978 edition.
- *The New York Times*, in its review of the uncut edition by Robert Kiely, a professor of English at Harvard, provided an all-time truly memorable line from a book review: "Hundreds of pages of text are devoted to vignettes—some poignant, nearly all disgusting—of Americans in all regions and walks of life being stopped in the tracks of their ordinary existence by the dread and incurable disease."
- It's the additional characters and scenes in the uncut edition that make it a much richer experience. Some examples: We learned that Flagg had communicated with Nadine Cross when she was in her teens: the scene where he talks to her via a Ouija Board is terrifying; also, the scene of Frannie Goldsmith's confrontation with her mother over her pregnancy is incredibly powerful. King describes the living room as filled with "segments of time in a dry age."
- My *Complete Stephen King Encyclopedia* has six two-column pages of additional characters in the uncut edition.
- In 1994, ABC aired *Stephen King's The Stand* as a miniseries starring Gary Sinise, Molly Ringwald, Jamey Sheridan, Ruby Dee, Miguel Ferrer, and many others. It was directed by Mick Garris from a screenplay by Stephen King. The opening of the movie, in which Captain Trips escapes the lab, is set to Blue Oyster Cult's "Don't Fear the Reaper" and is one of the greatest opening sequences of all time.

Essential Stephen King ranking: **2**

Needful Things (1991)

"The town of Castle Rock, Maine has seen its fair share of oddities over the years, but nothing is a peculiar as the little curio shop that's just opened for business...."

- *Needful Things* was promoted as the "last Castle Rock story." It turned out not to be.
- In an August 9, 1998 UK interview with Peter Conrad, King said, "Everything's for sale, and the only price is your immortal soul. I thought [*Needful Things*] was fucking hilarious!"
- In the coda to *Needful Things*, Leland Gaunt opens a new store, Answered Prayers, in Junction City, Iowa, which is the home of Ardelia Lortz and the Library Policeman.

Essential Stephen King ranking: **24**

Gerald's Game (1992)

"Once again, Jessie Burlingame has been talked into submitting to her husband Gerald's kinky sex games..."

- The first of King's three "abused woman"-themed novels: *Gerald's Game, Dolores Claiborne,* and *Rose Madder.*
- In a 2006 interview with *The Paris Review*, King described the research process for *Gerald's Game*: "*Gerald's Game* [is] about only one person, Jessie, who's been handcuffed naked to her bed. The little things all get so big—the glass of water, and her trying to get the shelf above the bed to tip up so she can escape. Going into that book, I remember thinking that Jessie would have been some sort of gymnast at school, and at the end of it she would simply put her feet back over her head, over the bedstead, and wind up standing up. About forty pages into

writing it, I said to myself, I'd better see if this works. So I got my son—I think it was Joe because he's the more limber of the two boys—and I took him into our bedroom. I tied him with scarves to the bedposts. My wife came in and said, 'What are you doing?' And I said, 'I'm doing an experiment, never mind.' Joe tried to do it, but he couldn't. He said, 'My joints don't work that way.' …And the only thing you can do at that point is say, 'Well, I could make her double-jointed.' Then you go, 'Yeah, right, that's not fair.'"

- A film adaptation of *Gerald's Game* was released on September 29, 2017 on Netflix. It starred Carla Gugino and Bruce Greenwood. It was directed by Mike Flanagan from a screenplay by Flanagan and Jeff Howard.

- After watching an early cut of the film, King tweeted the following:

 **Stephen King** ✓
@StephenKing

Saw a rough cut of Mike Flanagan's GERALD'S GAME yesterday. Horrifying, hypnotic, terrific. It's gonna freak you out.

7:28 PM - Feb 10, 2017

♡ 442   ↲ 1,008   ♡ 7,320   ⓘ

- In a January 1, 2018 interview with *Cinemablend*, Flanagan said the next Stephen King novel he would like to adapt would be either *Doctor Sleep* or *Lisey's Story*. He said:

- [T]he ones I'd want to do the most are *Doctor Sleep* and *Lisey's Story*. In both cases, it's because I identify with the protagonists so much. *Lisey's Story* is a stunning piece of work, a beautiful exploration of marriage. And who wouldn't want to venture back into the world of Danny Torrance?

- At the end of January 2018, Warner Bros. confirmed that Flanagan would indeed be directing the *Doctor Sleep* film. Flanagan said he'd rewrite the script that was originally written by Akiva Goldsman.

Essential Stephen King ranking: **25**

Dolores Claiborne (1993)

"When Vera Donovan…dies suddenly in her home, suspicion is immediately cast on her housekeeper and caretaker, Dolores Claiborne…."

- The second of King's three "abused woman"-themed novels: *Gerald's Game*, *Dolores Claiborne*, and *Rose Madder*.
- *Dolores Claiborne* is told entirely in the first-person voice of Dolores Claiborne St. George.
- In a December 1992 interview with *USA Today* to promote *Dolores Claiborne*, King said, "Don't say that I'm stretching my range or that I've left horror behind. I'm just trying to find things I haven't done, to stay alive creatively."
- *Dolores Claiborne* and *Gerald's Game* were written "in tandem," so to speak, and were intended to be a two-volume set called *In the Path of the Eclipse*. Here's how they are connected: As Dolores, on Little Tall Island, is waiting for Joe to die during the July 20, 1963 eclipse, she experiences a psychic bond with young Jessie Burlingame of *Gerald's Game*, as Jessie's father is sexually molesting her. King does not fully explain the connection, but it obviously has something to do with the fact that Dolores's daughter Selena was similarly abused by her father, Joe.
- A film version of *Dolores Claiborne* was released in 1995 and starred Kathy Bates and Jennifer Jason Leigh. It was directed by Taylor Hackford from a screenplay by Tony Gilroy.

Essential Stephen King ranking: **15**

Insomnia (1994)

*"Ralph Roberts never expected to live out his remaining golden years
mourning the death of his beloved wife...."*

- *Insomnia* is a "Dark Tower" novel in the sense that the novel was given to Roland by Moses Carver in *The Dark Tower,* but Roland threw it away.
- *Insomnia* is dedicated to King's wife Tabby, and also to musician Al Kooper. Kooper was one of the professional "ringers" who toured with King's band The Rock Bottom Remainders and who participated in their band-written book *Mid-Life Confidential.*
- The original hardcover edition was published with two different covers. One had "Insomnia" in red and "Stephen King" in white; the other had the colors reversed.
- In 1994, *Insomnia* was nominated for a Bram Stoker Award for Best Novel but *Dead in the Water* by Nancy Holder won that year.

Essential Stephen King ranking: **11**

The Regulators (initially as Richard Bachman) (1995)

*"It's a gorgeous midsummer afternoon along Poplar Street in the peaceful
suburbia of Wentworth, Ohio..."*

- King said the epiphany as to how to write *The Regulators* came one day while backing out of his driveway: "The idea was to take characters from *Desperation* and put them into *The Regulators.* In some cases, I thought, they could play the same people; in others, they would change; in neither would they do the same things or react in the same ways, because the different stories would dictate different courses of action. It would be, I thought, like the members of a repertory company acting in two different ways."

Essential Stephen King ranking: **52**

Rose Madder (1995)

"After surviving fourteen years of hell in a violently abusive marriage, Rosie Daniels finally summons the courage to flee for her life...."

- The third of King's three "abused woman"-themed novels: *Gerald's Game*, *Dolores Claiborne*, and *Rose Madder.*
- In *Rose Madder*, King introduces us to the character of Norman Daniels, an abusive cop who thinks nothing of beating and torturing not only his criminal suspects, but also his meekly subservient wife, Rosie. In *The Stephen King Universe*, King authorities Stanley Wiater, Christopher Golden, and Hank Wagner state with certainty that "*Rose Madder* stands as King's most unflinching look at abuse."
- The character of Wendy Yarrow, who is reincarnated into the world of Rosie's painting as Dorcas and who acts as a mentor to Rosie, may be an homage to King's wife Tabitha. Check out the biblical verse Acts 9:36 (KJV): "Now there was at Joppa a certain disciple named Tabitha, which by interpretation is called Dorcas: this woman was full of good works and almsdeeds which she did."
- *Rose Madder* got a starred review (the highest) in the May 1995 issue of *Publishers Weekly*, in which they said, "Relentlessly paced and brilliantly orchestrated, this cat-and-mouse game of a novel is one of King's most engrossing and topical horror stories. At the center of the action is heroine Rose McClendon, a battered wife who starts life anew by leaving her police of-

ficer husband, a consummately cruel man depicted by King as a paragon of evil. Crowded with character and incident, the novel builds to a nearly apocalyptic conclusion that combines the best of King's long novels—the breadth and vision of *The Stand*, for example—with the focused plot and careful psychological portraiture of *Dolores Claiborne*. The story of Rose's joyous growth from tortured wife (her persecution gruesomely but realistically portrayed) to independent woman alternates with the terrifying details of her husband's deliberate pursuit to create unflagging tension. The book is a phantasmagorical roller-coaster ride, peopled by a broad array of indelibly characterized men and women and fueled by an air of danger that is immediate and overwhelming."

- IMDB.com reports that a film version of the novel is in development.

Essential Stephen King ranking: **17**

Desperation (1996)

"[P]olice officer Collie Entragian, chief law enforcement for the small mining town of Desperation, Nevada, appears to be completely insane...."

- *Desperation* is what has come to be known as "classic King" (or "Klassic King," as some way-too-clever journalists might suggest); the Stephen King of *The Stand* and *The Shining* and *'Salem's Lot*, and even *IT*. It is a sprawling tale of a band of... pilgrims?...who come face-to-face with a minion of a possibly eternal evil and who must depend on the wisdom and God-centeredness of a young boy who just may have a direct line to the Big Guy himself.
- Considering the spiritual/metaphysical bent to some of King's more thoughtful works (including *The Green Mile, Desperation,*

and *The Girl Who Loved Tom Gordon*), his comments on religion in his March 5, 1999 letter to reviewers that was included with review copies of *The Girl Who Loved Tom Gordon* are especially interesting. "I have been writing about God—the possibility of God and the consequences for humans if God does exist—for twenty years now, ever since *The Stand*. I have no interest in preaching or in organized religion, and no patience with zealots who claim to have the one true pipeline to the Big Guy..."

- In a November 17, 1988 interview with Janet Beaulieu, King talked about his perception of good and evil: "Above all else, I'm interested in good and evil. And I'm interested in the question about whether or not there are powers of good and powers of evil that exist outside ourselves. I think that the concept of evil is something that's in the human heart. The goodness in the human heart is probably more interesting, psychologically, but in terms of myth, the idea that there are forces of evil and forces of good outside, and because I was raised in a fairly strict religious home, not hard-shelled Baptist or anything like that, I tend to coalesce those concepts around God symbols and devil symbols, and I put them in my work."

Essential Stephen King ranking: **13**

The Green Mile

"Welcome to Cold Mountain Penitentiary, home to the Depression-worn men of E Block..."

Part 1. *The Two Dead Girls* (March 1996)
Part 2. *The Mouse on the Mile* (April 1996)
Part 3. *Coffey's Hands* (May 1996)
Part 4. *The Bad Death of Eduard Delacroix* (June 1996)

Part 5. *Night Journey* (July 1996)
Part 6. *Coffey on the Mile* (August 1996)

- In the Introduction to the single-volume edition of *The Green Mile*, King talked about the writing of the serial novel: "I wrote like a madman, trying to keep up with the crazy publishing schedule and at the same time trying to craft the book so that each part would have its own mini-climax, hoping that everything would fit, and knowing I'd be hung if it didn't."
- At one point, there was a rumor going around that Tom Hanks was slated to play the John Coffey role in the film. Tyson Blue explains this in an excerpt from his book, *The Making of the Green Mile*:

  While rumors on the Internet and other sources had at least some rational basis, one went so far as to suggest that [Hanks] had even wanted to play John Coffey(!), the rationale being that he enjoyed taking roles which gave him a chance to expand the horizons of his acting. Hanks could easily understand how these rumors could begin. "That's the other thing that's really miraculous about this story is that they're all good roles," he said. "It's that kind of ensemble piece. You know, the only thing that makes me Number One on the call sheet is that Paul's the narrator! Other than that, all the guys have great parts. I certainly would have jumped at the chance to play, say, Wild Bill, or even Percy, although I'm not short enough to be Percy. It's such a key thing."

Essential Stephen King ranking: **5**

Bag of Bones (September 1998)

"Four years after the sudden death of his wife, bestselling novelist Mike Noonan is still grieving...."

- *Bag of Bones* was the novel that marked King's departure from Viking for his new publishing home, Scribner.
- *Bag of Bones* was inspired by and is an homage to Daphne du Maurier's novel *Rebecca*.
- King said, "*Bag of Bones* contains everything I know about marriage, lust, and ghosts."
- *Bag of Bones* was Stephen King's first authentic ghost story since *Pet Sematary*. It revisits Castle Rock and Derry (the setting of *IT, Insomnia,* and *Dreamcatcher*), and centers on a bestselling writer's grief over his wife's death, a tragedy which is somehow related to some strange doings at their summer lakeside place, known as Sara Laughs, in western Maine.
- *Bag of Bones* boasts an ancient curse, dazzling sequences of mind-boggling and horrifying paranormal activity, as well as a couple of the most memorable villains with which King has ever blessed us.
- In King's May 1998 letter to reviewers of *Hearts in Atlantis*, included with review copies of the book, King wrote about *Bag of Bones*: "I hope *Bag of Bones* gave you at least one sleepless night. Sorry 'bout that; it's just the way I am. It gave me one or two, and ever since writing it I'm nervous about going down into the cellar—part of me keeps expecting the door to slam, the light to go out, and the knocking to start. But for me, at least, that's also part of the fun. If that makes me sick, hey, don't call the doctor."
- In *The Stephen King Universe*, the authors write, "Simply stated, [*Bag of Bones*] ranks amongst the four or five best novels the author has written in his entire career."

- The title of the novel comes from something British author Thomas Hardy (a King favorite) reportedly once said: "Compared to the dullest human being actually walking about on the face of the earth and casting his shadow there, the most brilliantly drawn character in a novel is but a bag of bones." King's final reference to Hardy's remark (of several in the novel) occurs in the book's second-to-last paragraph when he writes, "Thomas Hardy, who supposedly said that the most brilliantly drawn character in a novel is but a bag of bones, stopped writing novels himself after finishing *Jude the Obscure* and while he was at the height of his narrative genius."

Essential Stephen King ranking: **6**

The Girl Who Loved Tom Gordon (1999)

"During a six-mile hike on the Maine-New Hampshire branch of the Appalachian Trail, nine-year-old Trisha McFarland… wanders off by herself…"

- *The Girl Who Loved Tom Gordon* may have been inspired by William Blake's two connected poems, "The Little Girl Lost" and "The Little Girl Found." King has also said that for this novel, he wanted to write *Hansel and Gretel* without Hansel.
- In "The Little Girl Lost," the young girl (the Trisha McFarland character in *Tom Gordon*) is named Lyca. She is seven years old and ends up lost in a "desert wild." Like Trish, Lyca "wander'd long," slept under a tree, "while the beasts of prey,/Come from caverns deep,/View'd the maid asleep." Also, there is a scene in the poem where Lyca watches the moon rise, echoing a similar scene in *Tom Gordon*.
- Blake's companion poem to "Little Girl Lost" is "The Little Girl Found." It contains a scene in which Lyca is found and

carried in the arms of her rescuer ("In his arms he bore/Her, arm'd with sorrow sore"). This scene is similar to the scene in *The Girl Who Loved Tom Gordon*, in which Travis Herrick carries Trisha out of the woods ("She wanted to tell him she was glad to be carried, glad to be rescued...").

- In the "Author's Postscript" to this novel, King tells us that even though Tom Gordon the baseball player is real, the Tom Gordon in the novel is fictional. King then makes a revealing comment about the nature of fame and his own celebrity: "The impression fans have of people who have achieved some degree of celebrity are always fictional, as I can attest of my own personal experience."

- In a March 5, 1999 letter to reviewers, King wrote, "My heroine (Trisha) would be a child of divorce living with her mother and maintaining a meaningful connection with her father mostly through their mutual love of baseball and the Boston Red Sox. Lost in the woods, she'd find herself imagining that her favorite Red Sox player was with her, keeping her company and guiding her through the terrible situation in which she found herself. Tom Gordon, #36, would be that player. Gordon is a real pitcher for the Red Sox; without his consent I wouldn't have wanted to publish the book. He did give it, for which I am deeply grateful.... *The Girl Who Loved Tom Gordon* isn't about Tom Gordon or baseball, and not really about love, either. It's about survival, and God, and it's about God's opposite as well. Because Trisha isn't alone in her wanderings. There is something else in the woods— the God of the Lost is how she comes to think of it—and in time she'll have to face it."

- Director George A. Romero was attached to write and direct a film adaptation of *The Girl Who Loved Tom Gordon* as early as 2001, but the project stalled in 2005. Romero died in 2017.

- In 2004, the "Little Simon" imprint of Simon & Schuster published a pop-up edition of *The Girl Who Loved Tom Gordon*. It was fourteen pages with elaborate pop-up depictions of scenes from throughout the story.

Essential Stephen King ranking: **32**

Dreamcatcher (2001)

"Twenty-five years ago, in their haunted hometown of Derry, Maine, four boys bravely stood together..."

- King originally titled this novel *Cancer* but changed it on the urging of his wife, novelist Tabitha King, who refused to refer to it by that title.
- In a live AOL chat on September 19, 2000, King said, "*Dreamcatcher* [has] got a little bit of that *Stand* vibe...My accident changed everything. Not all those changes are bad. But it's a little easier to see the small shit in life for what it is after you've almost gotten the gate."
- One interesting point that can be discussed without giving anything away is that, in *Dreamcatcher*, a victim of an automobile accident reveals that he learned after his recovery that he had died in the ambulance and had needed to be shocked with cardiac paddles to resuscitate his heartbeat. This begs the question, "Is this fictional incident a way for Stephen King to reveal something none of his fans knew?"
- A film version of *Dreamcatcher* was released in 2003. It starred Morgan Freeman, Thomas Jane, Jason Lee, Damian Lewis, Timothy Olyphant, Tom Sizemore, and Donnie Wahlberg. It was directed by Lawrence Kasdan from a screenplay by William Goldman and Kasdan.

Essential Stephen King ranking: **26**

Black House (2001)

"Twenty years ago, a boy named Jack Sawyer traveled to a parallel universe called the Territories to save his mother and her Territories 'Twinner' from an agonizing death…"

- *Black House* was written by Stephen King and Peter Straub and is a sequel to *The Talisman*.
- *Black House* was nominated for a 2001 Bram Stoker Award. It lost to Neil Gaiman's *American Gods*.
- The cannibalistic serial killer known as The Fisherman in *Black House* is based on real-world serial killer Albert Fish. The Fisherman is aware of the real Fish and intentionally emulates his "style," so to speak.
- There are crossover elements in *Black House* that connect it to the *Dark Tower* series, including the Crimson King, opopanax, and Twinners.
- From a *Publishers Weekly* review of *Black House:*

  The book abounds with literary allusions, many to the King-verse, and readers not familiar with King's work and particularly with *The Talisman* may feel disoriented, especially at first. But there's so much here to revel in, from expertly executed sequences of terror, awe or passion—the novel is a deep reservoir of genuine emotion—to some of the most wonderful characters to spring from a page in years, to a story whose energy is so high and craft so accomplished that most readers will wish it ran twice its great length. What is probably the most anticipated novel of the year turns out to be…a high point in both the King and Straub canons.

- *Black House* is reportedly the second book of the Jack Sawyer Trilogy and King has acknowledged his and Straub's plans to write the third.
- Regarding the third book, King said the following in an interview with Lilja's Library:

  Jack is hurt, goes over to the Territories and the way things are left is that he'll be OK if he's over there on the other side but if he comes back to our world he will sicken and die in short order so of course you have to put him in some sort of situation where he has to come back and then the clock is ticking.

From A Buick 8 (2002)

"Since 1979, the state police of Troop D in rural Pennsylvania have kept a secret in the shed out behind the barracks..."

- *From A Buick 8's* title came from a Bob Dylan song called "From a Buick 6."
- Is the Buick 8 related to Christine? Not likely, since Christine was most assuredly born and raised in the U.S. of A, and the Buick 8 was...definitely not.
- *From A Buick 8* is a horror novel, but one with a strong science fiction element. The Buick 8 is not a car, and it could very well be a portal to another...what? Planet? Dimension? It's actually [**Spoiler Alert**] a fake car: nothing in it is real, and it can heal itself. Can it be destroyed? Should it be destroyed? It has killed, after all.
- Tobe Hooper was attached to direct a film adaptation of the novel, but financing stalled the project. Hooper died in 2017.

The Colorado Kid (2005)

"Vince Teague and Dave Bowie are the sole operators of The Weekly Islander, a small Maine newspaper… When intern Stephanie asks if they've ever come across a real unexplained mystery… they tell her the story of 'The Colorado Kid.'"

- Gotta love a story that boasts an editor named David Bowie.
- Two old-school newspaper guys and a young intern work to solve the mystery of the Colorado Kid, a Colorado man whose body was found in 1980 on the Maine island of Moose Lookit.
- A TV series (somewhat) based on the novel premiered on the Syfy channel in 2009 called *Haven*. It ran for five seasons.

Cell (2006)

"Clayton Riddell…just landed a deal that might finally enable him to make art instead of teaching it…but all those good feelings about the future change in a hurry…[due to] The Pulse.…"

- A science fiction novel about evil cell phones. The Pulse, a signal transmitted to every cell phone in the world, turns users into ravenous, killer zombies.
- A film adaptation of *Cell* was released in 2016 starring John Cusack and Samuel L. Jackson. It was directed by Tod Williams from a screenplay by Stephen King.
- **Spoiler from Stephen King, via Lilja's Library**: "Based on the information given in the final third of *Cell*—I'm thinking about the reversion back toward the norm of the later phone crazies—it seems pretty obvious to me that things turned out well for Clay's son, Johnny. I don't need to tell you this, do I?"

Lisey's Story (2006)

"Lisey lost her husband Scott after a twenty-five-year marriage of profound and sometimes frightening intimacy..."

- In a 2007 interview with Lilja's Library, King stated that he considered *Lisey's Story* his best book.
- In an October 31, 2014 interview with *Rolling Stone*, King was asked, "If you had to pick your best book, what would it be?" His response: *"Lisey's Story.* That one felt like an important book to me because it was about marriage, and I'd never written about that. I wanted to talk about two things: One is the secret world that people build inside a marriage, and the other was that even in that intimate world, there's still things that we don't know about each other."

Blaze (as Richard Bachman) (2007)

*"*Blaze *is the story of Clayton Blaisdell, Jr.—of the crimes committed against him and the crimes he commits..."*

- In an interview with Lilja's Library, King talked about *Blaze*: "I have been thinking about [*Blaze*] off and on for a while and every time I would think about it...you know I did the early books as Richard Bachman books and this is going to be a Bachman because it came from the same time. It was written right before *Carrie* and finally I thought to myself...the reason I've never done it was because, in my memory at least, it was a tearjerker of a book, you know it was kind of sentimental and just kind of....every now and then I think of what Oscar Wilde said about *The Little Match Girl*. He said that it's impossible to read about the little match girl without weeping tears of laughter and...you know something that is so sad it's actually funny."

- *Blaze* tells the story of an abused, mentally-challenged, three-hundred-pound man, Clayton Blaisdell, Jr.—who kidnaps an infant and holds him hostage.
- *Blaze* is King's homage to John Steinbeck's *Of Mice and Men*, a novella he has referred to several times in his writings. King describes *Blaze* as a "literary imitation." The character of Clayton (aka Blaze) is similar to Lennie in the Steinbeck novella.
- King said of the original manuscript that "some of the pages of *Blaze* had been typed on the reverse side of milk-bills."
- As Kevin Quigley puts it in a review of *Blaze* on his Charnel House website, "this being a Bachman book, a happy ending isn't really in the offing." And a happy ending is not what the reader gets.

Duma Key (2008)

"A terrible construction site accident takes Edgar Freemantle's right arm and scrambles his memory and his mind..."

- Stephen King's first "Florida" novel.
- Edgar Freemantle is a loser, specifically of his wife and his right arm. Wracked with depression and suicidal thoughts, he rents a beach house on Duma Key, a small island off the coast of Florida. It is there that he begins to paint. And it is then Edgar learns that, like Michael Anderson and his obituaries in the short story "Obits," his paintings have powers. What he paints, happens. And then an evil entity known as Perse (really the Greek goddess Persephone) manifests to seek revenge on the Alzheimer's-afflicted co-owner of Duma Key, Elizabeth Eastlake. Then, chaos ensues, which may or may not result in the total destruction of Duma Key.
- A film version of *Duma Key* is in development.

Under the Dome (2009)

"On a beautiful fall day, the small town of Chester's Mill, Maine, is suddenly and inexplicably sealed off from the rest of the world by an invisible force field…"

- In an April 1, 2017 essay for the UK *Guardian* titled "Stephen King on Donald Trump: 'How do such men rise? First as a joke,'" King compared *Under the Dome*'s Jim Rennie to Donald Trump: "Big Jim Rennie in *Under The Dome* is cut from the same cloth. He's a car salesman (selling being a key requirement for the successful politician), who is the head selectman in the small town of Chester's Mill, when a dome comes down and cuts the community off from the world. He's a crook, a cozener and a sociopath, the worst possible choice in a time of crisis, but he's got a folksy, straight-from-the-shoulder delivery that people relate to. The fact that he's incompetent at best and downright malevolent at worst doesn't matter."
- The *Under the Dome* TV series ran on CBS from June 24, 2013 through September 10, 2015. The series was developed by Brian K. Vaughan. It starred Mike Vogel, Rachel Lefevre, Alexander Koch, Marg Helgenberger (she was also in *The Tommyknockers* film), and Dean Norris (he was also in *The Lawnmower Man* (the one King sued over)).
- In the *Under the Dome* episode "Awakening," the character Big Jim lays his hand on a bible on the top shelf of his locker. Next to the bible is a black pork pie hat like the one Walter White wore in *Breaking Bad*. Dean Norris played Hank Schrader in *Breaking Bad*.

11/22/63 (2011)

*"Jake Epping is a thirty-five-year-old high school English teacher
in Lisbon Falls, Maine, who makes extra money teaching adults
in the GED program..."*

- *11/22/63* is Stephen King's alternate history novel about the JFK assassination. What would have happened if someone had been able to go back in time and kill Lee Harvey Oswald before he killed John F. Kennedy? We find out in this novel, and it's nowhere near what one might expect.
- In an interview promoting *11/22/63*, King talked about the research he did to write the book. He said he read a stack of books as tall as he was (I'm paraphrasing) to fully understand the assassination and time period of *11/22/63*.

Doctor Sleep (2013)

*"On highways across America, a tribe of people called the True Knot
travel in search of sustenance..."*

- *Doctor Sleep* is the sequel to King's 1977 novel *The Shining*.
- Danny Torrance and Dick Hallorann are still feeling the after-effects of their experiences at the Overlook. Danny works in a hospice, is an alcoholic (like papa Jack), has a psychic cat, and the two can sense when people are going to die.
- The True Knot consume "steam." Steam is a psychic effluence that is produced when people feel pain. This premise sets up a truly nasty premise.
- A film version of the novel is currently in development with Akiva Goldsman (*A Beautiful Mind*) writing the script.

Joyland (2013)

"Set in a small-town North Carolina amusement park in 1973, Joyland tells the story of the summer in which college student Devin Jones comes to work as a carny and confronts the legacy of a vicious murder..."

- Tonally (and this is only one reader's opinion), *Joyland* feels a bit like *Doctor Sleep*.
- A film version of *Joyland* to be written and directed by Tate Taylor (*Winter's Bone*) is currently in development hell.

Mr. Mercedes (2014)

Stephen King ✔
@StephenKing

🔵 Follow

Donald Trump blocked me on Twitter. I am hereby blocking him from seeing IT or MR. MERCEDES. No clowns for you, Donald. Go float yourself.

9:55 PM - Aug 24, 2017

💬 4,822   🔁 62,663   ♡ 212,133

"In a high-suspense race against time, three of the most unlikely heroes Stephen King has ever created try to stop a lone killer from blowing up thousands..."

- The first book in the Bill Hodges trilogy.
- A TV series adaptation of *Mr. Mercedes* debuted on the Audience channel in August 2017. It was renewed for a second season to debut in 2018.

Revival (2014)

"The new minister came to Harlow, Maine, when Jamie Morton was a boy doing battle with his toy army men on the front lawn..."

- *Revival* is Stephen King's "Lovecraftian" novel, i.e., a novel containing elements written in the style of H. P. Lovecraft.
- The final third of this novel is some of the scariest stuff King has ever written.

Finders Keepers (2015)

"'Wake up, genius.' So announces deranged fan Morris Bellamy to iconic author John Rothstein..."

- The second book in the Bill Hodges trilogy.
- *Finders Keepers* is about the murder of a famous writer named John Rothstein.

End of Watch (2016)

"For nearly six years, in Room 217 of the Lakes Region Traumatic Brain Injury Clinic, Brady Hartsfield has been in a persistent vegetative state..."

- *End of Watch* is the third book in the Bill Hodges trilogy.
- Is Detective Hodges doomed? Pancreatic cancer is often merciless. After his diagnosis, he works to solve a murder case he never closed...before it's too late?

Charlie the Choo Choo (as Beryl Evans) (2016)

"Engineer Bob has a secret: His train engine, Charlie the Choo Choo, is alive...and also his best friend..."

- King's publisher announced that this book is for ages five and up, and grades preschool and up.
- "Beryl Evans" showed up at the 2016 Comic-Con to sign copies of *Charlie*. No one seemed to care that she had written the book in 1942 and was killed many years ago in another dimension. (Evans, of course, is the pseudonym King used to wrote *Charlie the Choo-Choo*. Actress Allison Davies played Beryl at the convention.)

Sleeping Beauties (2017)

Stephen Spignesi [l] and Owen King. Photo by James Cole
©2016 Used by permission.

"[W]hat might happen if women disappeared from the world of men?"

- *Sleeping Beauties* was co-written by Stephen King and his son Owen King, author of the 2005 collection *We're All In This Together*, the 2008 collection *Who Can Save Us Now?: Brand-New Superheroes and Their Amazing (Short) Stories*, the 2013 novel *Double Feature*, the 2015 comic *Intro to Alien Invasion* (co-written with Mark Jude Poirier), and the screenplay *Fade Away*, co-written with his brother Joe Hill, which is being developed as a TV series.

- In a September 25, 2017 co-interview with Owen for *Entertainment Weekly*, King said, "To be asked by Owen to collaborate on a book was the greatest thing in the world. You see these signs that say Smith & Son's hardware or stuff. So, sons do follow in their father's footsteps. But in a specialized area of one of the arts? It was very gratifying to me."

- As research for the book, King and Owen visited a women's prison in New Hampshire. Speaking of the visit, King told *Entertainment Weekly* that "Any of those fantasy movies where you have a prison filled with these gorgeous women with great hair, we found out that wasn't the case. A lot of the women there just seemed to be working through their time and not very happy about it, but doing what they have to do. We tried to put that in the book and make that prison as realistic as possible. I'm sure that a lot of people who staff women's prisons will say we got this wrong and we got that wrong, but I'm hoping that we got the flavor right."

Stephen King ✓
@StephenKing

(Follow) ∨

I and both of my sons are together on the NY Times bestseller list, SLEEPING BEAUTIES at #4 and Joe's STRANGE WEATHER at #9. Awesome!

6:34 PM - 1 Nov 2017

- In the same interview, Owen also commented on the visit to the prison: "We wanted to respect people's experiences. It's something that we cared a lot about getting right as much as we possibly could, and of course, fiction takes its own path, but we tried to stay true, even though the book is a fable."

- In April 2017, the entertainment company Anonymous Content purchased the TV rights to the novel.
- In November 2017, BuzzFeed asked famous writers which book they were most grateful for that year. This was Stephen King's response:

  The book I'm most grateful for this year is *Sleeping Beauties*. I ordinarily wouldn't say that about a book I had a part in creating, but a man doesn't get a chance to collaborate with one of his children very often, or to find himself hardly able to keep up with that grown child's brilliant work. We also had a chance to go on tour together, and since we both have our own families and concerns, that was a rare opportunity.

- Fyi, James Patterson was grateful for J.K. Rowling's *Harry Potter* series; Joyce Carol Oates was grateful for James Joyce's *Ulysses*; R. L. Stine was grateful for Carl Hiaasen's *Razor Girl*; Chuck Palahniuk was grateful for Denis Johnson's *Jesus' Son*; and T. C. Boyle was grateful for *Essays After Eighty* by Donald Hall (one of my all-time favorite books).
- In December 2017, Owen King wrote a note that was sent out to everyone on the Simon & Schuster mailing list, which read:

Dear Reader,

I've been enormously gratified by the response to *Sleeping Beauties*, the novel that I wrote with my father, Stephen King. Wow!

A little surprised by some of the reactions, too. Who knew that so many people were so queasy about moths? They're just crackly, papery, little fluttering insects who are hardly ever a threat to anyone except on those rare occasions when a vengeful fairy commands them to attack! Pull yourselves together!

For us, the experience of writing this novel was a delight. We love moths. We love vengeful fairies. We love getting together to spin out a story for all of you wonderful readers. Sleep is overrated. Let's stay up all night and flip some pages, shall we?

Happy Holidays,
Owen King

AN INTERVIEW WITH OWEN KING AND STEPHEN KING
ABOUT *SLEEPING BEAUTIES*

Owen King: The idea for *Sleeping Beauties* was pretty random. In our family we do a lot of pitching of ideas to each other. I had the idea and I said, "Well, what about a story about the world where all the women have fallen asleep." And my dad said, "That's an awesome idea," and I said, "Great, go write it." [SK laughs] And he said, "No, no, you have to write it." But eventually we settled on writing it together.

Stephen King: To me, when Owen pitched that idea, we were…I don't know if we were on the phone or we were texting back and forth, but he said, "What about if all the women fell asleep?" and I immediately started to think of all the ramifications that were possible. And I said, "Y'know, we really ought to write this." Then Owen said to me, "What if we did it as a limited TV show?" A TV series like nine or ten episodes. So we started to do a screenplay. We actually did a pilot.

OK: And we did a second episode as well.

SK: Owen just kind of said, "Whoa, wait, wait, wait. We gotta do this as a book." [To Owen] "Right?"

OK: It was an exciting TV series…I felt hemmed in, in terms of the characterizations and the one-hour pacing. I wanted to do more with the characters and I felt like it should be a book before it was a show.

SK: Yeah. When we read the book it's hard for us to remember who wrote what. Owen rewrote me and I rewrote Owen and the thing is, when we finished this process, we were still friends.

OK: Yeah.

SK: We still got along, we were still taking each other's calls, which is a great thing. But it's wonderful to be asked to collaborate with your son. What I didn't know was how good it was gonna be and what the… y'know, kind of the unique blending of your sensibility and mine.

OK: Right, that sort of third voice. But that's why we rewrote each other because we ended up with this third voice that's both of us.

SK: Yeah.

Access the full video interview on StephenKing.com

The Outsider (May 2018)

"An unspeakable crime. A confounding investigation…"

- King first revealed the title of this novel in an August 9, 2017 interview with *USA Today*.
- At the Naperville, Illinois *Sleeping Beauties* book signing with Owen King on October 1, 2017, an attendee reported to Hans Lilja of Lilja's Library that King said *The Outsider* was about a southwest gentleman committing some murders, and that there would be a character readers would recognize.

STEPHEN SPIGNESI ON *THE OUTSIDER*

One of my favorite TV series is HBO's *The Night Of*. It's an 8-episode series that was supposed to star James Gandolfini, but he had only shot the first episode at the time of his death. Gandolfini's role was taken over by John Turturro and his performance garnered him nominations for an Emmy, a Golden Globe, and a SAG Award. The series itself won an American Film Institute Award for Best Television Series, and, again, was nominated for an Emmy and a Golden Globe for Best Series.

The Night Of was written by Richard Price and I tell you all this to introduce this brief look at Stephen King's novel *The Outsider*.

Richard Price—whose credits also include *Clockers, Sea of Love, The Deuce,* and *The Wanderers*—has signed on to write a ten-episode adaptation of *The Outsider* and, to me, it's as if King wrote another prison story and Frank Darabont signed on to adapt and direct it. The writing of *The Night Of* is extraordinary, and, thus, I suspect Price's adaptation of *The Outsider* may very well end up in the upper echelon of King adaptations.

But enough about the series. The novel is our topic for today. I think it will be difficult to write a comprehensive review without descending into the Realm of Spoilers, but we'll give it our best shot.

What is *The Outsider*? It's a murder mystery, a police procedural, a supernatural extravaganza, and a compelling human drama. And it is categorically superb. It has a *Revival/Dark Half* feel to it at times, and it brings back one of King's most appealing female characters, the damaged PI Holly Gibney.

The plot is sublime: A beloved Little League coach is arrested for killing an 11-year-old boy. They have more evidence against him than Carter has liver pills. But videotape emerges of him somewhere else at the time of the murder. Videotape that is incontrovertible. Not to mention the dozens of eyewitnesses who saw him in the aforementioned somewhere else. But someone can't be in two places at the same time, can they? (Here's where we can imagine Sai King rubbing his hands together at his computer, laughing conspiratorially, and whispering, "We'll just see about that.")

The novel can be described as having three acts, but not really. It's actually broken into several titled sections, and the whole story takes place over a few days in July, There are, however, three distinct story beats: the aftermath of the murder, the pursuit of the evidence, and the resolution in which the "outsider" of the title is revealed. It's very cinematic. And very fast-paced.

Any more would give stuff away. So let me conclude by saying *The Outsider* is a terrific novel, one of King's best, and I'm confident it will make an amazing TV series. And, regarding possible awards for the forthcoming series, it will not surprise me if a cave wins Best Supporting Actor at some point.

If dogs could fly, nobody would go out without an umbrella.

Stephen King
September 4, 2017 Tweet

II.
THE SHORT STORY COLLECTIONS

Stephen King is a master of the short story. He calls them "a kiss in the dark." Here is a look at the six collections he's published over the years.

I. *Night Shift* (1978)
Jerusalem's Lot
- This story first appeared in *Night Shift*.
- The story takes place in the town of Jerusalem's Lot, the same locale as in *'Salem's Lot*.
- The story—and the history of Jerusalem's Lot, rats, vampires, and all—is told through a series of letters from Charles Boone to Bones.
- Boone describes the discovery of a book, *De Vermis Mysteriis*, or *Mysteries of the Worm*. This book was created by writer Robert Bloch and used by H. P. Lovecraft in his Cthulhu stories. King's including it in "Jerusalem's Lot" is clearly an homage to the two great writers and influences.
- King would revisit Lovecraftian mythos and style in his 2014 novel *Revival*.
- "Jerusalem's Lot" is one of the stories illustrated by artist Glenn Chadbourne for King's *Secretary of Dreams* graphic comic series.

Graveyard Shift

- This story first appeared in the October 1970 issue of *Cavalier* magazine.

- In *Danse Macabre*, King talked about this story and his initial intention to "self-plagiarize" the rat scene for *'Salem's Lot*: "Rats are nasty little buggers, aren't they? I wrote and published a rat story called 'Graveyard Shift' in *Cavalier* magazine four years prior to *'Salem's Lot*—it was, in fact, the third story I ever published—and I was uneasy about the similarity between the rats under the old mill in 'Graveyard Shift' and those in the basement of the boarding house in *'Salem's Lot*. As writers near the end of a book, I suspect they cope with weariness in all sorts of ways—and my response as I neared the end of *'Salem's Lot* was to indulge in this bit of self-plagiarism."

- In his June 1983 interview in *Playboy* magazine, King talked about his lack of success in using the rat scene twice: "In the first draft of *'Salem's Lot*, I had a scene in which Jimmy Cody, the local doctor, is devoured in a boardinghouse basement by a horde of rats summoned from the town dump by the leader of the vampires. They swarm all over him like a writhing, furry carpet, biting and clawing, and when he tries to scream a warning to his companion upstairs, one of them scurries into his open mouth and squirms there as it gnaws out his tongue. I loved the scene, but my editor made it clear that no way would Doubleday publish something like that, and I came around eventually and impaled poor Jimmy on knives. But, shit, it just wasn't the same."

- The name of the main character in this story, Hall (no first name is given), has the same surname as King's longtime childhood friends, the Hall brothers, Douglas, and the twins Dean and Dana.

- "Graveyard Shift" is a very early story by King (his third published; he was in his early twenties when he wrote it) and it is one of his all-time best.
- The narrative in "Graveyard Shift" is succinct and controlled in the way it unfolds and the resolute "then this happened, then this happened" pace adds to the impact of the truly horrific scenarios depicted in the story.
- King has always admired—and practiced—the "story rules all" touchstone of storytelling. In *The Mist,* he uses what is probably the single best opening of all time: "This is what happened"; although in *Secret Windows,* King admits that he "borrowed" that from Douglas Fairbairn's novel *Shoot.*
- *Stephen King's Graveyard Shift* was released as a feature film in 1990. It starred David Andrews, Kelly Wolf, Stephen Macht, and Brad Dourif. It was directed by Ralph S. Singleton from a screenplay by John Esposito.

Essential Stephen King ranking: **78**

Night Surf

- This story first appeared in the Spring 1969 issue of *Ubris.*
- "Night Surf" takes place in the same universe as *The Stand.*
- "Night Surf" has the first appearance of the plague "Captain Trips," also known as A6.
- "Night Surf" incudes a mention of Harrison State Park. The previous year, 1968, King had published the poem "Harrison State Park '68" in *Ubris* magazine. In the short story, King writes:

When I was a kid my mother used to take us kids to Harrison State Park and there was a fun house with a big clown face on the front and you walked in through the mouth.

- The clown, of course, would appear later as a symbol of horror in *IT*, as Pennywise the Clown, and in King's film *Maximum Overdrive*, in which the front of a killer truck has a huge clown face.

I Am the Doorway

- This story first appeared in the March 1971 issue of *Cavalier* magazine.
- "I Am the Doorway" was the story chosen as the source for the cover illustration for the Signet paperback edition of *Night Shift*. The cover drawing by Don Brautigam shows a right hand half wrapped (half unwrapped, actually) in gauze; the top half of the hand reveals eight beautiful blue eyes scattered across the fingers and palm.
- "I Am the Doorway" was written in 1971, a year after the Russian unmanned spacecraft *Venera-7* landed on Venus and transmitted data from the surface of the planet back to Earth.
- A deep-space astronaut named Arthur returns from a mission to Venus "infected" with creatures who burrow up through the skin of his fingers and grow eyes with which they view our world. The crippled and wheelchair-bound Arthur (he was seriously injured during re-entry) is the "doorway" for these creatures, who can control his body at will and make him kill at their command.
- IMDB.com lists four *I Am the Doorway* short films (2015, 2016, 2017 and 2018) and one *I Am the Doorway* film in development.

Essential Stephen King ranking: **85**

The Mangler

- This story first appeared in the December 1972 issue of *Cavalier* magazine.

- The Hadley-Watson Model-6 Speed Ironer and Folder is possessed by a demon that was summoned when a virgin's blood accidentally splashed into its workings. (Of course.) It is up to Officer John Hunton to stop the machine's grisly attacks (which involves pulling humans into its rollers and gears) and make the Blue Ribbon Laundry safe again for wet sheets (and people).

- When Stephen King graduated from the University of Maine in 1970, he discovered to his dismay that his "B.A. was worth absolutely nothing." Unable to find work as a teacher, King took a job in an industrial laundry (the New Franklin Laundry in Bangor). His experiences working there—coupled with a dynamic and inventive imagination— inspired and informed this terrifying short story. As King said in a 1999 BBC profile, "The first thing I am is a husband; the second thing I am is a father; the third thing that I am is, I'm a man of my place and my time and my community. And I have to be all those things first because if I want to be a writer, everything trickles down." "The Mangler" is stark evidence of this: Everything trickles down.

- In "The Mangler," King lists the ingredients needed to summon a demon. They are: the blood of a virgin, graveyard dirt, belladonna, bat's blood, night moss, horse's hoof, and eye of toad. In the story, the mangler came to life from Sherry Ouelette's blood and E-Z Gel tablets, which contained a derivative of belladonna.

In a 1998 interview with journalist Ben Rawortit, King discussed the real-world mangler:

Stephen King: I worked in a laundry while I was writing for men's magazines.

Q: Was working in the laundry weird?

SK: There was a guy who worked there who fell into the pressing machine, or "mangler," as you call it. He was over the machine dusting off the beams when he just lost his balance and fell.

Q: And the machine ate his hands?

SK: Yeah, it swallowed his arms. So he had two hooks where his hands used to be.

Q: Must have been tricky doing up his laces...

SK: True. And he always wore a white shirt and a tie. We used to wonder how he got that tie knotted so perfectly. He used to go to the bathroom and run one hook under the hot tap and one under the cold, then he'd creep up behind you and put the hooks on your neck. That was his little joke.

- **Personal Story**: I never worked in a laundry, but I did work in a dry cleaner's for a few years when I was young. Without a doubt, some of those washers and pressing machines were scary. We used one machine called The Puffer, which was a headless and armless human torso that spurted steam when you stepped on a pedal. The Puffer was used to eliminate wrinkles on jackets and blouses that didn't have a crease. When the torso was "dressed" with a blouse and then the pedal was stepped on, the blouse filled up with steam in a second, and its arms waved around like some kind of possessed headless demon shuddering in agony. If you were standing nearby, you would get whacked in the head by a flapping, steam-filled arm.
- The film *The Mangler* was released in 1995. It starred Robert Englund, Ted Levine, and Vanessa Pike. It was directed by Tobe Hooper from a screenplay by Tobe Hooper, Stephen Brooks, and Peter Welbeck [Harry Alan Towers].

Essential Stephen King ranking: **79**

The Boogeyman
- This story first appeared in the March 1973 issue of *Cavalier* magazine.
- Lester Billings visits Dr. Harper, a psychiatrist. Lester is convinced that a boogeyman has killed his three children, but that he himself, their own father, was the one ultimately responsible for their deaths. Why? Because he always knew his children were being stalked by the boogeyman, but never did anything to protect them.
- At one point in the story, Billings relates a dream in which he talks about an old *Tales from the Crypt* comic book story, in which a woman drowns her husband in a quarry, but he comes back "all rotted and black-green." This *Crypt* story inspired King's *Creepshow* tale "Something To Tide You Over," except

that Leslie Nielsen (the jilted husband in the story) buries Ted Danson up to his neck on a beach and lets the tide do his dirty work. Ted comes back later, "all rotted and black-green," to exact a watery revenge.

- Stephen King has twice described himself as a boogeyman. In a 1991 article he wrote for *Entertainment Weekly* magazine called "How I Created *Golden Years*," King wrote, "At some point between *'Salem's Lot*, my second book, and *The Dead Zone*, my sixth, I became America's Best-Loved Bogeyman." King authority George Beahm later paid homage to King's remark in the title of his own 1998 book, *Stephen King: America's Best-Loved Boogeyman*. Earlier, in "Straight Up Midnight: An Introductory Note" from his novella collection *Four Past Midnight*, King wrote, "When this book is published in 1990, I will have been sixteen years in the business of make-believe. Halfway through those years, long after I had become, by some process I still do not fully understand, America's literary boogeyman, I published a book called *Different Seasons*." One other interesting item regarding "The Boogeyman": In the story, King mentions Frankenstein, The Wolfman, and The Mummy, all of whom make cameo appearances in *IT*.
- In "The Boogeyman," we're told that Lester had once taken his kids to Savin Rock in West Haven, Connecticut. This was a hugely popular amusement park that was torn down. King once lived in Stratford, Connecticut and probably also visited Savin Rock with its Laughing Lady (she scared the shit out of me), roller coaster, bumper cars, and food stands.
- In 1982, the short film *The Boogeyman* was released as part of the *Night Shift Collection, Vol. 2*. It was directed by Jeffrey C. Schiro from his own teleplay adaptation.

Essential Stephen King ranking: **71**

Gray Matter

- This story first appeared in the October 1973 issue of *Cavalier* magazine.
- This is an archetypal horror story in the sense that it uses the tropes and narrative of classic horror: A guy drinks a bad can of beer and transforms into a giant, oozing slime-slug that eats dead cats and doubles in size on a regular basis.
- The character of Henry Parmalee, proprietor of the Nite-Owl, summed up this tale trenchantly: "I'm not saying there's any truth in it, but I am saying that there's things in the corners of the world that would drive a man insane to look 'em right in the face."
- "Gray Matter" was first published in 1973 when King was twenty-six, and contains one of King's first uses of a giant spider as a monster figure. (*IT* would come in 1986, thirteen years later). In "Gray Matter," the story is told of a Bangor Public Works Department worker named George Kelso who quit his job after descending into a sewer pipe and coming upon a "spider as big as a good-sized dog setting in a web full of kittens..."
- "Gray Matter" is another story set in King's hometown of Bangor. A character named George Kelso is mentioned in the story, but it isn't said whether he is related to the voted-out-of-office Sheriff Carl Kelso from *The Dead Zone*.

Essential Stephen King ranking: **56**

Battleground

- This story first appeared in the September 1972 issue of *Cavalier* magazine.
- Toy soldiers come alive and wage battle in a guy's apartment—with real artillery. Is that a great premise or what?
- The G. I. Joe Vietnam Footlocker delivered to Renshaw included the following artillery and troops:

- ○ 20 Infantrymen
- ○ 10 Helicopters
- ○ 20 BAR Men
- ○ 2 Bazooka Men
- ○ 2 Medics
- ○ 4 Jeeps
- ○ 1 Rocket-Launcher
- ○ 20 Surface-to-Air "Twister" Missiles
- ○ 1 Scale-Model Thermonuclear Weapon
- A one-hour film was made of this short story as an episode of the 2006 *Nightmares & Dreamscapes* TV series. The script was by Richard Christian Matheson and contained not one word of dialogue.

Trucks

- This story first appeared in the June 1973 issue of *Cavalier* magazine.
- "Trucks" is another "fear of technology"-themed story from Stephen King. The narrative "what if?" question is "What if machines came alive?" (Well, hell, in 1997, Skynet gained consciousness, right? King was definitely a harbinger with these types of stories.)
- In the story, the trucks sent the following message to the people in the truck stop by blowing Morse code with their horns: "Someone must pump fuel. Someone will not be harmed. All fuel must be pumped. This shall be done now. Now someone will pump fuel."
- "Trucks" has one of Stephen King's greatest last lines: The narrator sees two planes flying over the truck stop and thinks, "I wish I could believe there are people in them."
- Stephen King adapted this short story into the 1986 film *Maximum Overdrive*, his directorial debut.

Sometimes They Come Back

- This story first appeared in the March 1974 issue of *Cavalier* magazine.

- When the character Jim is nine, his 12-year-old brother Wayne is murdered by a gang of greasers. The murder haunts Jim throughout his life.

- "Sometimes They Come Back" is a Stratford, Connecticut story. One street mentioned is Barnum Avenue, which I know well and visit often. Also, Jim and Wayne were on their way to the Stratford Library when they were murdered. I have given my "Stephen King: The Art of Darkness" illustrated lecture at that very library, which has as its director my friend Katie McFadden.

- Jim dreams of his brother's death and specifically mentions that they were walking down Broad Street headed for the library when they were ambushed. The dedication of *Cujo* reads, "This book is for my brother, David, who held my hand crossing West Broad Street, and who taught me how to make skyhooks out of old coat hangers. The trick was so damned good I just never stopped. I love you, David."

- When "new students" start appearing in the high school English class he teaches, Jim begins to realize that, yes, sometimes they come back.

- Jim's mission is to rid the world of the resurrected demonic greasers once and for all…before he himself is killed.

- This story was made into a TV movie in 1991 starring Tim Matheson as Jim.

Strawberry Spring

- This story first appeared in the Fall 1968 issue of the University of Maine literary magazine *Ubris*, when King was a twenty-two-year-old student at the school. A substantially revised version was later published in the men's magazines *Cavalier* and

Gent, and ultimately collected in *Night Shift* and elsewhere. (If you're interested in the differences between the *Ubris* version and the later *Night Shift* version, see my *Complete Stephen King Encyclopedia,* in which I provide a "Strawberry Spring" concordance and complete details on the people, places, and things of the story, with separate entries for the *Ubris* version of the story when it differed from the later revised version.)

- A serial killer is murdering women on the campus of New Sharon Teachers' College. The story of the terrible "strawberry spring" (a false spring) of 1968 is told seven or so years later by a narrator who, we later learn, may have been the one responsible for the murders.

- The atmosphere and tone of this story perfectly evoke not only the weird, otherworldly feel of the fog-laden strawberry spring itself, but also that of the sociocultural climate of a college campus in the late 1960s: "The jukebox played 'Love is Blue' that year," King writes. "It played 'Hey Jude' endlessly. It played 'Scarborough Fair.'"

- One especially nice touch in the story is King's use of a *Lord of the Rings* metaphor. After the narrator exits the campus eatery called The Grinder and walks into the damp and all-encompassing fog, he muses that "You half expected to see Gollum or Frodo and Sam go hurrying past." With this simple image, King evokes all the magic and dark wonder of J. R. R. Tolkien's Middle Earth and places us squarely in the ambiance of its environs.

- "Strawberry Spring" powerfully evokes the Jack the Ripper mythology (even mentioning Jack in the text) with King effectively creating his own homegrown version of the elusive serial killer.

- Adding to this story's appeal are the little touches, such as when the narrator is stopped by the State Police on campus and asked to show an ID. "I was clever," he tells us. "I showed him the one without the fangs." As the story progresses, we realize he wasn't joking. "Strawberry Spring" is one of King's more stylistic stories and hints at the voice he would resurrect for *Hearts in Atlantis*.

- Several short films have been made of "Strawberry Spring," but as of this writing, no feature-length adaptations have been announced.

Essential Stephen King ranking: **47**

The Ledge

- This story first appeared in the July 1976 issue of *Penthouse* magazine.
- Narrator Stan Norris is having an affair with crime boss Cressner's wife. (Not a good idea.) Upon discovery, Cressner plants heroin in Norris's care and makes him a wager: successfully walk around the five-inch ledge of Cressner's building, forty-three stories up, and he'll get his freedom, Cressner's wife, and twenty thousand dollars. Otherwise, he'll go to jail for forty years for heroin possession.
- **[Spoiler Alert]** Norris succeeds, Cressner welches by telling Norris where Marcia Cressner was buried, and Norris sends Cressner out onto the ledge.
- A short film adaptation of this story was included as a segment of the 1985 film *Cat's Eye*. The film was directed by Lewis Teague from a screenplay by Stephen King.

The Lawnmower Man

- This story first appeared in the May 1975 issue of *Cavalier* magazine.
- The December 1981 issue of *Bizarre Adventures* magazine featured a comic adaptation of this story. The text was by King and the artwork was by Walter Simonson. The story was very close

to the original text version, except in a few instances where King changed characters' names or created a name, like naming the lawnmower man "Karras" and the Smith's cat "Shasta."

- In the *Bizarre Adventures* version, the mother of the boy who used to cut Harold's lawn before he went off to college was "Mrs. Stark." In *The Dark Half,* "George Stark" is the pseudonym Thad Beaumont used for his mystery novels.

- In 1992, New Line Cinema released the film *Stephen King's The Lawnmower Man* starring Jeff Fahey, Pierce Brosnan, and Jenny Wright. It was directed by Brett Leonard from Leonard's own screenplay. This film was a virtual reality sci-fi story that bore little to no resemblance to Stephen King's short story, yet they were promoting it as *Stephen King's The Lawnmower Man.* King sued and won. The court issued an injunction preventing New Line from using King's name to sell the film, and awarded King $2.5 million in damages. In 1993, King got suspicious about whether or not the studio was complying with the court order and hired private investigators to visit video stores and determine if the copies no longer had his name on them. They did have his name on them and King went back to court. New Line was found in contempt of court and King was awarded $10,000 a day for each day the violating video was still available. King was also awarded all the profit from the video release. King's lawyer Peter Herbert said, "Stephen is thrilled and feels he's been vindicated."

Quitters, Inc.

- This story's first publication was in *Night Shift.*
- "Quitters, Inc." is a traditional "What if?" story. What if a "Quit Smoking" company resorted to physical abuse, torture, and even death to get people to quit smoking? Classic.

- This story is satirical, but King, with a straight face, pulls out all the stops to structure the increasing levels of abuse a failing client will have to endure.
- The Quitters, Inc. "Stop Smoking Program for Dick Morrison" consisted of the following steps:
  - **1st Offense**: The "quitter's" wife, Cindy Morrison, is put in a room with an electrified floor.
  - **2nd Offense**: Dick is placed in the electrified room.
  - **3rd Offense**: Dick and Cindy are placed in the room together.
  - **4th Offense**: Alvin, Dick and Cindy's mentally challenged son, is beaten.
  - **5th Offense**: Dick and Cindy are placed in the room together, his son is beaten again, and Cindy is beaten.
  - **Steps 6, 7, and 8**: More trips to the electrified room, more serious beatings.
  - **Step 9**: Alvin's arms are broken.
  - **Step 10**: Dick is executed.
- Dick's Bill from Quitters, Inc. was five thousand dollars and fifty cents. It was for one treatment (2,500 dollars), one counselor (2,500 dollars), and fifty cents for electricity.
- A short film adaptation of this story was included as a segment of the 1985 film *Cat's Eye*. The film was directed by Lewis Teague from a screenplay by Stephen King.

I Know What You Need

- This story first appeared in the September 1976 issue of *Cosmopolitan* magazine.
- The demonic book *The Necronomicon* mentioned in King's story does not exist. Horror writer H. P. Lovecraft invented it in 1927 in an essay. Here is an excerpt from Lovecraft's discussion of the "diabolic" *Necronomicon*:

  Composed by Abdul Alhazred, a mad poet of Sanaá, in Yemen, who is said to have flourished during the period of the Ommiade caliphs, circa 700 A.D. He visited the ruins of Babylon and the subterranean secrets of Memphis and spent ten years alone in the great southern desert of Arabia—the Roba el Khaliyeh or "Empty Space" of the ancients—and "Dahna" or "Crimson" desert of the modern Arabs, which is held to be inhabited by protective evil spirits and monsters of death. Of this desert many strange and unbelievable marvels are told by those who pretend to have penetrated it. In his last years Alhazred dwelt in Damascus, where *The Necronomicon* (Al Azif) was written, and of his final death or disappearance (738 A.D.) many terrible and conflicting things are told.

- In "I Know What You Need," a short, skinny weirdo—Ed Hamner—who doesn't wash his hair too often and who wears mismatched socks, approaches Liz Rogan one evening in the library as she's desperately cramming for her Sociology final. The first thing Edward Jackson Hamner Junior says to Liz is "I know what you need," and it turns out he's not kidding. After some hesitation on Liz's part to get involved with this guy, she eventually gives in and Ed provides her with a verbatim transcript of last year's Sociology final exam. With this kind of help, she scores a ninety-seven on her test, guaranteeing her scholarship for the following year. As is typical in a Stephen King tale, trouble soon ensues for Liz, and her loved ones and friends.

- In *The Stephen King Universe*, the authors note the following: "The powers of Ed Hamner in 'I Know What You Need' are quite similar to those of the main character of a classic *The Twilight Zone* TV series episode which might have inspired King. Its title? 'What You Need.'"

Essential Stephen King ranking: **87**

Children of the Corn

- This story first appeared in the March 1977 issue of *Penthouse* magazine.
- There's a Corn God in Gatlin, Nebraska. He is known as "He Who Walks Behind the Rows."
- The Corn God requires a blood sacrifice of young people once they turn nineteen. (This is later lowered to eighteen.)
- A young couple driving through the area hits a young boy who runs out of the corn. At first, they think they've killed him, but then they see that his throat is slashed. Thus begins their adventure with the "children of the corn."
- Gatlin is mentioned in *IT*.
- A Dollar Baby short film called *Disciples of the Crow*, written and directed by John Woodward, was released in 1983. The first *Children of the Corn* feature film came out in 1984. I say "first" because, as of 2011, there were nine *Children of the Corn* films, and a new one, *Children of the Corn: Runaway* is reportedly in the development stage. There was also a made-for-TV *Children of the Corn* film in 2009.

The Last Rung on the Ladder

- This story's first publication appearance was in *Night Shift*.
- "Last Rung" is a naturalistic and very sad story about a brother remembering his shared childhood with his troubled sister, Kitty.
- "Last Rung" is heart-wrenching; its final line—"She was the one who always knew the hay would be there"—is one of King's saddest. And "Last Rung"—like *Rita Hayworth and Shawshank Redemption*, *The Body*, and the nonfiction essay "Leaf-Peepers"—is the kind of work that surprises non-Constant Readers who have a preconceived notion of Stephen King only as America's Horrormeister.

- Joseph Reino, Ph.D., writing in *Stephen King: The First Decade*, described "The Last Rung on the Ladder" as "one of the subtlest psychological studies King has ever devised."
- One of the earliest film adaptations of King's work—one of the first Dollar Babies—was *The Last Rung on the Ladder*, which was adapted and directed by my good friend James (Jim) Cole, whose essay "Stephen King Is..." can be found in this volume. The film starred Adam Houhoulis, Melisa Whelden, Nat Wordell, and Adam Howes, and was directed by James Cole from a screenplay by James Cole and Dan Thron.

Essential Stephen King ranking: **65**

The Man Who Loved Flowers
- This story first appeared in the August 1977 issue of *Gallery* magazine.
- "The Man Who Loved Flowers" is a masterful tale, and one more example of just how good Stephen King is as a short story writer.
- The man who loved flowers is in love with Norma. This, we learn, has not been good for Norma...and the circumstances involve a hammer.

Essential Stephen King ranking: **60**

One for the Road
- This story first appeared in the March/April 1977 issue of *Maine* magazine.
- "One for the Road" serves as a sequel to *'Salem's Lot* and takes place two years after the big fire in the novel.

Essential Stephen King ranking: **63**

The Woman in the Room

- This story's first published appearance was in *Night Shift*.
- This story is based on Stephen King's experience caring for his dying mother.
- In *On Writing*, King writes: "When I got into the master bedroom he was sitting beside her on the bed and holding a Kool for her to smoke. She was only semiconscious, her eyes going from Dave [King's brother] to me and then back to Dave again. I sat next to Dave, took the cigarette and held it to her mouth. Her lips stretched out to clamp on the filter." In "The Woman in the Room," King writes: He shakes a Kool out of one of the packages scattered on the table by her bed and lights it. He holds it between the first and second fingers of his right hand, and she puffs it, her lips stretching to grasp the filter. Her inhale is weak. The smoke drifts from her lips."
- In the story, the medication John feeds to his mother is Darvon (containing propoxyphene), which was pulled off the market in 2010 by the FDA, due to the risk of possibly fatal heart rhythm abnormalities.
- Stephen King once described this story in two words: "healing fiction."
- In a June 1983 interview with *Playboy* magazine, King said, "[W]hat really scared me most about the prospect of my mother's death was not being shipped off to some institution, rough as that would have been, but I was afraid it would drive me crazy."
- Renowned director Frank Darabont was a "dollar baby" who acquired the rights from Stephen King for $1 to make a short film of this story. He wrote the script and directed the film. The resulting film, *The Woman in the Room*, was extraordinary and Stephen King loved it. He allowed it to be shown and sold commercially, and Darabont later went on to write and direct: King's *The Shawshank Redemption* in 1994, starring Tim Robbins and Morgan Freeman; King's serial novel, *The Green Mile*,

in 1999, which starred Tom Hanks; and *The Mist*, in 2007, which starred Thomas Jane and Marcia Gay Harden. In *The Mist*, Darabont (who also wrote the screenplay) made the bold decision to change the novella's ending for the film. King reportedly liked the resulting conclusion.

Essential Stephen King ranking: **46**

II. *Skeleton Crew* (1985)
The Mist

- This novella first appeared in the 1980 anthology *Dark Forces*.
- In 2007, Frank Darabont wrote and directed the film adaptation of the novella.
- Darabont changed the ending of the novella for his film.
- In 2017, a new TV series adaptation of *The Mist* aired on Spike TV.
- The story takes place in Bridgton, Maine. After a violent thunderstorm the town is encased in a thick mist, in which all manner of supernatural and possibly prehistoric creatures live and kill whomever wanders in.
- The novella suggests that the mist and the creatures within may have been due to a failed government experiment—The Arrowhead Project— to breach other dimensions.
- In a 2006 interview with *The Paris Review*, King said, "I once wrote a short novel called *The Mist*. It's about this mist that rolls in and covers a town, and the story follows a number of people who are trapped in a supermarket. There's a woman in the checkout line who's got this box of mushrooms. When she walks to the window to see the mist coming in, the manager takes them from her. And she tells him, 'Give me back my mushies.' We're terrified of disruption. We're afraid that somebody's going to steal our mushrooms in the checkout line."

Essential Stephen King ranking: **33**

Here There Be Tygers

- This story first appeared in the Spring 1968 issue of *Ubris.*
- This is one of King's earliest short stories.
- King captures grammar school flawlessly in this tale about an eight-year-old who needs to go to the bathroom, but is afraid to ask because of his mean teacher, who he knows will embarrass him about it. His bathroom visit results in the death of a classmate. Or does it?
- "Here there be tygers" is a phrase used on medieval maps to indicate expected dangers. Other phrases included "here there be dragons," "here are lions," and written on the Borgia Map in the Vatican Library, "Here there are even men who have large four-foot horns, and there are even serpents so large that they could eat an ox whole."
- King reuses the phrase "Here there be tygers" in his 1988 short story "The Reploids."
- As of the end of 2017, as confirmed on StephenKing.com., Dollar Baby film rights are still available to this story.

The Monkey

- This story first appeared in the November 1980 issue of *Gallery* magazine.
- King got the idea for the monkey during a visit to New York. He passed a street merchant who had a battalion of little toy wind-up monkeys lined up on a blanket on a street corner, and the sight so frightened King that he returned to his hotel room and wrote almost the whole story in longhand.
- In the "Notes" to *Skeleton Crew*, King said of "The Monkey": "[The monkeys] looked really scary to me, and I spent the rest of my walk back to the hotel wondering why. I decided it was because they reminded me of the lady with the shear...the one who cuts everyone's thread one day."

- In "The Monkey," the newspaper that ran the story "Mystery of the Dead Fish" was *The Bridgton News*. Bridgton was the Maine town where Dave Drayton and his family lived in *The Mist* and is also the real Maine town where King and his family have a house on Long Lake.
- The original manuscript of "The Monkey" is in the Stephen King Archives in the Special Collections Library at Stephen King's alma mater, the University of Maine in Orono, Maine.
- "The Monkey" was once adapted by horror writer Dennis Etchison for a radio performance on Halloween night, October 31, 1985, to benefit UNICEF.

Essential Stephen King ranking: **88**

Cain Rose Up

- This story first appeared in the Spring 1968 issue of *Ubris*.
- In "Cain Rose Up," a depressed college student named Curt Garrish succumbs to the frustration of college life by randomly shooting people with a rifle from his dorm window. This story, originally published when King was in college, was revised somewhat for its *Skeleton Crew* appearance.
- "Cain Rose Up" fictionalizes the real-life murderous rampage of Charles Whitman, a former Marine and academically overloaded college student who went on a shooting spree from a twenty-seven-story tower on August 1, 1966 at the University of Texas in Austin. Whitman ultimately killed twelve people and wounded thirty-three others. King had long been fascinated by Whitman's story and decided to try his hand at putting himself into the mind of a student pushed just a tad too far. He was, as the story reveals, extremely successful at "understanding" Whitman and those like him.
- The *Skeleton Crew* version is more visceral and effectively communicates Garrish's completely delusional state of mind, a state

of mind that actually rationalizes his brutal murders as a fulfillment of what he perceives as a mandate from God that he believes is hidden in Genesis: "God made the world in His image, and if you don't eat the world, the world eats you." The story concludes with Garrish murmuring to himself, "Good God, let's eat."

- In a June 1983 interview with *Playboy* magazine, King mentioned Charles Whitman: [When asked "Where do you think you'd be today without your writing talent?"] "I might very well have ended up there in the Texas tower with Charlie Whitman, working out my demons with a high-powered telescopic rifle instead of a word processor. I mean, I know that guy Whitman. My writing has kept me out of that tower."

- In a September 24, 1988 interview with *Salon* magazine, King talked about Charles Whitman and the Texas Tower incident: "I think most men are wired up to perform acts of violence, usually defensive, but I think that we're still very primitive creatures, and that we have a real tendency toward violence. Most of us are like...well, most of us are like most airplanes. Remember TWA Flight 800, the one that exploded over Long Island Sound? That was an electrical problem, or at least they feel that it was probably an electrical problem, and a fire started in the wiring. And when you see a guy who suddenly snaps, a guy who goes nuts, a Charles Whitman, who goes to the top of the Texas tower and shoots a whole bunch of people, when a guy goes postal—that's the current slang—that's a guy with a fire in his wires, basically."

- A short film version of "Cain Rose Up" was released in 2013. It starred Harris Matthews as Curt Garrish and was directed by Ranjeet S. Marwa from his own screenplay.

- The novella *Apt Pupil* concludes with a similar sniper scene as in "Cain Rose Up," but the movie version of *Apt Pupil* rewrites King's ending.

Essential Stephen King ranking: **86**

Note: See Rick Hautala's essay "Steve Rose Up" in this volume. Rick's piece is followed by a remembrance by his widow, Holly Newstein Hautala.

Mrs. Todd's Shortcut

- This story first appeared in the May 1984 issue of *Redbook* magazine.
- Homer Buckland, intentionally named for the poet Homer, is the caretaker of the Todds' house in Maine. The ending of the story elevates it to a transcendent level and leaves us with a palpable sense of what it feels like to be left behind.
- Homer's cadence takes a little getting used to, but the payoff is worth it.
- According to Stephen King, his wife Tabitha is the real Mrs. Todd. In the "Notes" section of *Skeleton Crew*, King writes, "My wife is the real Mrs. Todd; the woman really *is* mad for a shortcut, and much of the one in the story actually exists. She found it, too."
- The story mentions Joe Camber from *Cujo* getting killed by his own dog.

Essential Stephen King ranking: **66**

The Jaunt

- This story first appeared in the 1981 issue of *The Twilight Zone Magazine*.
- "The Jaunt" is one of my favorite Stephen King short stories. It is about teleportation as a means of travel, including using it to teleport to other planets.
- In the "Notes" to *Skeleton Crew*, King said of "The Jaunt": "This was originally for *Omni*, which quite rightly rejected it because the science is so wonky. It was Ben Bova's idea to have

the colonists in the story mining for water, and I have incorporated that in this version."

- King has said that the term "jaunting" is an homage to the science fiction novel *The Stars My Destination* by Alfred Bester.
- It's always fascinating when authors postulate what the future will be like and the reality that ensues doesn't even come close to their vision. In the "energy crisis" years of the late 1970s and early 1980s ("The Jaunt" was written around 1980), 1987 seemed like a long way off and King decided to set the discovery of Jaunting during that year.
- "The Jaunt" includes details from a book written about The Jaunt called *The Politics of The Jaunt*. This device gives King the opportunity to go even deeper into the story and give readers a lot of exciting background regarding the discovery of teleportation and the sometimes-tragic events surrounding its early use.

Essential Stephen King ranking: **58**

The Wedding Gig

- This story first appeared in the December 1980 issue of *Ellery Queen's Mystery Magazine*.
- "The Wedding Gig" is a traditional crime story, but with odd characters, including a three-hundred-pound woman who becomes a mob boss.
- There have been no film adaptations of this story, although as of spring 2018, the story was not listed as available for adaptation on StephenKing.com, so rights may have been sold.

Paranoid: A Chant

- "Paranoid: A Chant" was first published in *Skeleton Crew*.
- The original title of this poem was "Paranoid/A Chant."

- "Paranoid: A Chant" is a poem that describes the mental deterioration of a narrator who manifests symptoms of paranoid schizophrenia.

- When I was a Practitioner in Residence at the University of New Haven, I regularly taught this poem in my English Composition and Literature classes. I developed and taught the theory that the narrator of "Paranoid: A Chant" is who J. Alfred Prufrock (of T. S. Eliot's "The Love Song of J. Alfred Prufrock") would devolve into if he did not treat his (or her—the gender of the narrator is non-specific) nascent paranoia, alienation, and depression.

- Director Jay Holben acquired the rights to make a short film of the poem. He titled it "Paranoid" and it starred Tonya Ivey as the narrator. King fans were surprised he used a female narrator since most readers of the poem always believed they were hearing the ravings of a mad*man*.

- *Paranoid* director Jay Holben generously wrote a long letter for me to read to my English composition students, in which he discusses his adaptation of the poem. This is his concluding thought about the movie:

  I wanted to get under people's skin a bit. I wanted them to have a chance to look inside the mind of a woman who isn't particularly healthy and not really enjoy being there…Stephen King's *Paranoid* isn't intended to be an audience pleaser as much as a thought provoker—hopefully very much in the vein of King's original prose.

- *Paranoid* star Tonya Ivey also kindly wrote a letter to my students talking about her work in the poem. Here's an excerpt:

  Paranoid was a first for me in many ways. It was the first time I had a leading role in a film, first time I had discrepancies with a director about being in my underwear (strangely, this gets easier?), first time I had done a voice-over & the first time I got to work on truly great material.

I am a Stephen King fanatic. I used to stay up all night reading his books, terrified of sleep & terrified to get out of bed. Reading his stories during my formative years helped mold my thoughts on narrative & character development...Working on a project that had his name anywhere near it was a humbling experience for me.

Essential Stephen King ranking: **99**

The Raft

- This story first appeared in the November 1982 issue of *Gallery* magazine.
- "The Raft" is a classic horror story that echoes Joseph Payne Brennan's legendary early-1950s short story "Slime," and is one of King's simplest, yet scariest narratives.
- Four college kids get trapped on a raft in the middle of a lake when something under the water begins moving toward them...and attacking.
- King wrote a short story in 1968 called "The Float," which he submitted to the men's magazine *Adam*. The story was accepted and payment—$250—was promised on publication. King eventually received a $250 check from *Adam*, but it is possible that the story was never published. In the "Notes" section of *Skeleton Crew*, King asked anyone who had seen the original version of the story to contact him, but so far, it seems as though "The Float" exists only in the dead zone.
- *The Raft* was one of the segments of the 1987 film, *Creepshow 2*. It starred Paul Satterfield, Jeremy Green, Daniel Beer, and Page Hannah. It was directed by Michael Gornick from a screenplay by George A. Romero.

Essential Stephen King ranking: **70**

Word Processor of the Gods

- This story first appeared in the January 1983 issue of *Playboy* magazine.
- Like in "Obits," "Umney's Last Case," and *Duma Key*, this story features a writer who has the power to create and destroy through his work.
- In this story, Richard Hagstrom is left a word processor by his late nephew Jonathan. Whatever Richard types, happens. [**Spoiler Alert**]: So he kills off his obnoxious son and wife first. And then types "I am a man who lives alone. Except for my wife Belinda, and my son Jonathan."
- "Word Processor of the Gods" was adapted for a Season 1 episode of the TV series *Tales from the Darkside*. It was written by Michael McDowell, directed by Michael Gornick, and broadcast November 25, 1984.

The Man Who Would Not Shake Hands

- This story first appeared in the 1981 anthology *Shadows 4*.
- Why won't he shake hands? Because whomever he touches, dies.
- This story is set at a "club" at 249B East 35th Street in New York City, the same club where the novella *The Breathing Method* is set. This story takes place in 1919, *The Breathing Method* in December 197-. The character Emlyn McCarron from *The Breathing Method* is mentioned in this short story.
- In both this story and *The Breathing Method*, Stephen King's credo—"It is the tale, not he who tells it."—is cited.

Beachworld

- This story first appeared in the Fall 1984 issue of *Weird Tales* magazine.
- This is a classic horror/sci-fi hybrid story: It's about an astronaut trapped on a [**Spoiler Alert**] sentient sand planet.

- An eighteen-minute adaptation of this story was released in 2015. It was written and directed by Chad Boling.

The Reaper's Image

- This story first appeared in the Spring 1969 issue of *Startling Mystery Stories* magazine.
- The Grim Reaper appears in a haunted mirror. Chaos ensues.
- A film adaptation is reportedly in development.

Nona

- This story first appeared in the 1978 anthology *Shadows*.
- A man known only as The Prisoner meets a woman named Nona in Joe's Good Eats one night and goes on a bloody murderous rampage with her. Nona—a gorgeous creature who [**Spoiler Alert**] nonetheless transforms into a giant rat while embracing The Prisoner—may or may not have been real and the whole story of the killing spree is told by The Prisoner from his jail cell—just before he plans on killing himself.
- "Nona" is one of King's "Castle Rock" stories. The Prisoner's mother came from Castle Rock and The Prisoner grew up in Harlow, a town we are told is across the river from Castle Rock.
- "Nona" marked King's first use of his haunting (haunted?) "Do you love?" leitmotif. In the story, Nona the rat thing asks The Prisoner this question in the Castle Rock graveyard. Four years later, in the *Skeleton Crew* story, "The Raft," Randy asks the malevolent, devouring thing in the water the same question.
- An interesting reference in "Nona" is when The Prisoner tells us, "One of my 'brothers,' Curt, ran away." In King's short story "Cain Rose Up" (also in *Skeleton Crew*), the main character is a college student named Curt Garrish, obviously inspired by the Texas Tower sniper Charles Whitman. In "Cain Rose Up," Curt begins killing people from his college dorm window. If this is the "Curt" The Prisoner is referring to, it is interesting

that he uses the phrase "ran away," since "Cain Rose Up" ends with Garrish continuing to shoot people from his college dorm window.

- Two "Dollar Baby" film adaptations of "Nona" have been produced, one in 2014 and one in 2016. See IMDB.com for details.

Essential Stephen King ranking: **48**

In my 1998 book, *The Lost Work of Stephen King*, I discuss King's college *Garbage Truck* columns. In one of these columns, King reviewed the movie *Easy Rider* and discussed the diner scene in the movie in which blue-collar workers taunt and bait the long-haired (for the time) Dennis Hopper and Jack Nicholson, calling them the "purtiest girls" they ever saw. King talks about the "tension and impending violence" in this scene and how this kind of hassle is familiar to any young person with long hair who hazards entering any place where he is clearly the outsider. In "Nona," King gave us this scene:

> The third thing that struck me was The Eye. You know about The Eye once you let your hair get down below the lobes of your ears. Right then people know you don't belong to the Lions, Elks, or the VFW. You know about The Eye, but you never get used to it.
>
> Right now the people giving me The Eye were four truckers in one booth, two more at the counter, a pair of old ladies wearing cheap fur coats and blue rinses, the short-order cook, and a gawky kid with soapsuds on his hands.

In "Nona," it isn't long before one of the truckers makes a crack about Christ coming back, another one plays "A Boy Named Sue" on the jukebox, and, finally, The Prisoner is confronted by a Neanderthal who asks him if he actually is "a fella." The scene in *Easy Rider*, plus King's own experiences as a "longhair" in the sixties, seems to have influenced this gripping scene in "Nona." As I suggested in *Lost Work*, it seems that King was editorially commenting on his own experiences and using the character of The Prisoner to express his own feelings about being an outsider.

For Owen

- This poem's first publication was in *Skeleton Crew*.
- This poem tells the story of King walking his son Owen to school and imagining the other students as fruit. It is written in unrhymed free verse comprising thirty-four lines.
- Since Stephen King is Stephen King, of course, there are certain lines in this phantasmagorical fantasy that add a tone of darkness to an otherwise light-hearted tale:
  - "I could tell you things but better not."
  - "I could tell you that dying's an art and I am learning fast.
- **Personal Story**: I attended Owen's book-signing for *Double Feature* in New London, Connecticut when his book first came out and I brought my personal copy of my own book *The Complete Stephen King Encyclopedia*. I was hoping Owen would sign it on the page on which I had written about this poem. He explained he couldn't because he had decided early on in his career that he would only sign things that he had written. This makes a lot of sense and I completely respect his decision. (Some writers *will* sign stuff in which they're written about. An example would be George Harrison's sister Louise signing my *Beatles Book of Lists* on the page on which I had written about her. In fact, she signed it twice, ten years apart.) Owen likely realized early on that if he did not draw a line, people would be asking him to sign his father's works. Granted, those books would become immediately collectible, but he knew it would create a firestorm of requests and it would not surprise me if, as an artist, he felt it would be a betrayal of his own creative impetus. I have never been the type of fan who expects anything from an artist. You ask. They say yes? Great. They pass? That's fine with me. As it should be with all fans.

Survivor Type

- This story first appeared in the 1982 anthology *Terrors*.
- This story set the bar a tad higher for horror writers. In it, a man starving to death on a deserted island [**Spoiler Alert**] begins hacking off and eating parts of himself to survive.
- In a 1985 interview with Charles Grant in *Monsterland Magazine*, King said of "Survivor Type": "As far as short stories are concerned, I like the grisly ones the best. However, the story 'Survivor Type' goes a little bit too far, even for me."
- Self-cannibalism is called autosarcophagy.
- In the "Notes" to *Skeleton Crew*, King said, "We were living in Bridgton at the time, and I spent an hour or so talking with Ralph Drews, the retired doctor next door. Although he looked doubtful at first (the year before, in pursuit of another story, I had asked him if he thought it was possible for a man to swallow a cat), he finally agreed that a guy could subsist on himself for quite a while—like everything else which is material, he pointed out, the human body is just stored energy. Ah, I asked him, but what about the repeated shock of the amputations? The answer he gave me is, with very few changes, the first paragraph of the story."
- The story is written as a diary of sorts and the entry "Febba" tells us "Nothing left below the groin." One could assume that at this point, Richard Pine has consumed everything from his upper thighs to his feet, on both sides. He kept his naughty bits, obviously for their survival functionality, i.e. the expelling of waste.
- The story ends with the line "lady fingers they taste just like lady fingers."
- A thirty-minute horror short film adaptation of "Survivor Type" was released in 2012. It was written and directed by Billy Hanson.

Essential Stephen King ranking: **44**

Uncle Otto's Truck

Uncle Otto's Truck? ©2017 Valerie Barnes

- This story first appeared in the October 1983 issue of *Yankee* magazine.
- In the "Notes" to *Skeleton Crew*, King said, "The truck is real, and so is the house."
- "Uncle Otto's Truck" was included in the DAW Books anthology, *The Year's Best Horror Stories Series XII,* in 1984.
- In "Uncle Otto's Truck," Quentin Schenck tells us that his Uncle's Cresswell truck "gave up in spectacular fashion. It went like the wonderful one-hoss shay in the Holmes poem." King is referring here to the poem "The Deacon's Masterpiece" by Oliver Wendell Holmes. The 120-line poem's first stanza is:

  > Have you heard of the wonderful one-hoss shay,
  > That was built in such a logical way
  > It ran a hundred years to a day,
  > And then, of a sudden, it—ah, but stay,
  > I'll tell you what happened without delay,
  > Scaring the parson into fits,
  > Frightening people out of their wits,—
  > Have you ever heard of that, I say?

- The moment when Quentin looks up and sees [**Spoiler Alert**] the Cresswell outside the window of his uncle's house can actually make you jump.

Essential Stephen King ranking: **80**

Morning Deliveries (Milkman #1)

- This short story's first publication was in *Skeleton Crew*.
- Spike Milligan is a milkman who leaves deadly "extras" in his customer's daily deliveries, including deadly nightshade, a tarantula, an acid gel, eggnog spiked with belladonna, and an empty milk bottle filled with cyanide gas.
- This story and "Big Wheels: A Tale of The Laundry Game" were adapted from an unfinished novel called *The Milkman*.

- **Big Wheels: A Tale of The Laundry Game (Milkman #2)**
- This story first appeared in the 1980 anthology *New Terrors*.
- Two guys—Rocky and Leo—get drunk and crash into a gas station in an attempt to get an inspection sticker renewed before midnight.
- When they leave the gas station, they are followed by serial killer Spike Milligan (from "Morning Deliveries"), who kills a random driver and convinces Bob to kill his wife and burn down his house.
- A short film adaptation *The Milkman*, based on "Big Wheels," was released in 2017. It was written and directed by Raymond Mamrak and starred Mamrak. Proceeds went to the Make-a-Wish Foundation.

Gramma

- This story first appeared in the Spring 1984 issue of *Weirdbook* magazine.
- "Gramma" is based on Stephen King's years living in Durham, Maine when his mother, Ruth, took care of her aged parents. In an interview for my *Complete Stephen King Encyclopedia*, Chris Chesley, King's childhood friend and collaborator (*People, Places, and Things*), talked about the roots of this tale:

  When I first knew Steve, his mother was taking care of his grandparents. They lived in the house with

Steve and his mother, and Steve's story "Gramma" from *Skeleton Crew* came out of that. In that story, the grandmother has been transformed into a supernatural thing about which a child has to make a decision. Should I give this...what seems to be a monster...should I give this creature the tea? Well, that giving of the tea is based directly upon his life at that time, when he was a boy between ten and twelve. The grandparents lived in the downstairs front room. The grandmother was invalided. She was not able to talk. And for kids that age, someone who is invalided and very old is kind of a horrifying presence. And so Steve had that experience, and it was borne home on him, and you can see the connection between that experience, and how affected he must have been by that situation to be motivated to later turn it into such a powerful story. When I read the story—sitting there by myself in the night—it raised the hackles on my neck, even though I knew from whence the story was derived. And I thought to myself at the time, think of how much he took in. Think of how affected he was by that in order to have the psychological motivation to spit it back out by writing this hair-raising story.

- In a June 1983 interview with *Playboy* magazine, King said, "Then there was my father's mother, Granny Spansky, whom David and I got to know when we were living in the Middle West. She was a big, heavyset woman who alternately fascinated and repelled me. I can still see her cackling like an old witch through toothless gums while she'd fry an entire loaf of bread in bacon drippings on an antique range and then gobble it down, chortling, 'My, that's crisp!'"

- In *Danse Macabre*, King also refers to Granny Spansky, writing "my paternal grandmother enjoyed frying half a loaf of bread in bacon fat for breakfast..."
- "Gramma" is one of King's "Castle Rock" stories. The Castle Rock Strangler's mother, Henrietta Dodd (from *The Dead Zone*), makes a cameo appearance, as does Joe Camber from *Cujo* (his hill is mentioned) and Cora Simard from *The Tommyknockers* (she gossips with Henrietta on eleven-year-old George Bruckner's party line).
- On February 14, 1986, the CBS series *The New Twilight Zone* broadcast the adaptation "Gramma," starring Barret Oliver, Darlanne Fluegel, and Frederick Long. The teleplay was written by Harlan Ellison and the episode was directed by Bradford May.

Essential Stephen King ranking: **69**

The Ballad of the Flexible Bullet

- This story first appeared in the June 1984 issue of *The Magazine of Fantasy & Science Fiction*.
- What is the "flexible bullet"? Insanity. The poet Marianne Moore is credited with the image of the "flexible bullet."
- This story introduced Constant Readers to "Fornits." Fornits are good-luck elves who live inside writers' typewriters and provide good luck and creative insight. They shoot good luck dust known as "fornus" out of handguns.
- The writer Reg Thorpe's personal Fornit is named Rackne.
- "The Ballad of the Flexible Bullet" is the title of the short story submitted to editor Henry Wilson by Reg Thorpe. To humor Thorpe, Wilson tells him that he, too, has a Fornit and that her name is Bellis.
- The story mentions Sylvia Plath, the acclaimed writer and poet who committed suicide.

- In 2015, there was talk of a possible short film "Dollar Baby" adaptation of this story, but nothing has yet come to fruition.

The Reach

- This story first appeared in the November 1981 issue of *Yankee* magazine.
- This story was originally titled "Do the Dead Sing?"
- Stella Flanders, a ninety-five-year-old Maine widow with terminal cancer, has never been off Goat Island. She has never crossed the Reach, a body of water between two bodies of land that is open at both ends, separating Goat Island from the mainland. By way of explanation, Stella tells her grandchildren, "Your blood is in the stones of this island, and I stay here because the mainland is too far to reach."
- One day, Stella begins seeing ghosts, starting with the specter of her late husband Bill. That winter, she sees Bill standing on the frozen Reach like "Jesus-out-of-the-boat" and she begins to walk across the ice.
- "The Reach" is the kind of short story that ends up being dissected in high school and college English literature classes because this poignant story functions equally well at both the literal and the blatantly symbolic level. In addition to being a true Maine slice-of-life story with vivid characters and realistic settings, its images are also easily interpreted as metaphors for the journey towards transcendence and the curse/blessing duality of death.
- King's writing is superb in this story. A favorite example is when he writes of old Richard walking up a path, "his arthritis riding him like an invisible passenger."
- Elizabeth Hand, in a September 1999 review of *Hearts in Atlantis* in the *Village Voice Literary Supplement*, specifically singled out "The Reach" as one of King's works that achieves "genuine power and resonance."

- There is a scene in "The Reach" in which Stella recalls keeping a pot of lobster stew going on the stove at all times. Lobsters were plentiful and cheap back then, and, thus, what we know as an expensive delicacy today, was considered "poor man's soup" in Maine in 1978. Stella remembers hiding the pot when the minister came calling because of her embarrassment. This anecdote is based on King's childhood and he has told this story in interviews, remembering his mother keeping lobster stew on the stove and hiding the pot when company came.

- In May 2012, after the Cannes Film Festival, it was reported that "The Reach" was the latest Stephen King story to get a film adaptation. *The Hollywood Reporter* said that Park Entertainment would be developing the film in the $12–$14 million budget range and that they were currently looking for a director. There have been no updates on this adaptation since then.

- "The Reach" won the 1981 World Fantasy Award for best short fiction.

- "The Reach" is probably my all-time favorite Stephen King short story.

Essential Stephen King ranking: **35**

III. *Nightmares & Dreamscapes* (1993)
Dolan's Cadillac

- This novella originally appeared in five parts in five issues of *Castle Rock: The Stephen King Newsletter* from February through June 1985.

- Stephen King loves relevant epigraphs for his works and, in the original five-part serialization of *Dolan's Cadillac* in the *Castle Rock* newsletter (February-June 1985), he used one "revenge-themed" epigraph for each segment:

  1. "Revenge is a dish best eaten cold" (Spanish proverb).

2. "God says, 'Take what you want, and pay for it'" (Spanish proverb).

3. "Vengeance is mine, saith the Lord" (Old Testament).

4. "Meet revenge is proper and just" (The Koran).

5. "Vengeance and pity do not meet" (Sheridan).

- In the revised version of the story that appeared in *Nightmares & Dreamscapes*, King eliminated all the epigraphs except the first.

- *Dolan's Cadillac* is King's modern update of Poe's 1846 short story "The Cask of Amontillado." In Poe's tale, the aristocrat Montresor exacts exquisite revenge on Fortunato, whose "thousand injuries" he had borne for too long, by entombing him alive in a wine cellar. In *Dolan's Cadillac*, the widower Robinson assesses a similar retribution by entombing the organized crime figure Dolan in his gray Cadillac beneath a Las Vegas desert highway. (In 2000, King published "The Old Dude's Ticker," a modern retelling of Poe's "The Tell-Tale Heart.")

- The film *Dolan's Cadillac* was released in 2009 starring Christian Slater, Emmanuelle Vaugier, and Wes Bentley. It was directed by Jeff Beesly from a screenplay by Richard Dooling. There was talk in 2001 of a film adaptation of the story starring Sylvester Stallone as Dolan and Kevin Bacon as Robinson, which did not come to fruition.

Essential Stephen King ranking: **42**

The End of the Whole Mess

- This science fiction short story first appeared in the October 1986 issue of *Omni* magazine.

- "The End of the Whole Mess" is a Kafkaesque look at one possible future—and how the end of mankind may not come about due to a devastating, apocalyptic war, but from a much more benign catalyst: good intentions. Congresswoman and

Vanity Fair writer Clare Boothe Luce might have said it best: "No good deed goes unpunished."

- This story was made into a short film as one of the episodes of the 2006 TV series *Nightmares & Dreamscapes*. It starred Ron Livingston and Henry Thomas.

- In one of the most entertaining scenes in the story, young Bobby the genius builds a glider with forward-facing wings and Howard launches him (successfully) into the air off his American Flyer red wagon. In the story, King notes that plans for forward-wing fighter planes were on the drawing boards of both the American and Russian air forces. He was right. In 1986, NASA was working on the Grumman X-29, a fighter plane with forward wings. In *Orders of Magnitude: A History of the NACA and NASA, 1915-1990*, Roger E. Bilstein wrote, "The Grumman X-29 [was] a plane whose dramatic configuration matched that of the HiMAT [a plane built with Highly Maneuverable Aircraft Technology]. The X-29 had a single, vertical tail fin and canard surfaces—not unique in the 1980s. What made the X-29 so fascinating was its sharply forward-swept wings."

- In the "Notes" to *Nightmares & Dreamscapes*, King wrote, "Dave King is what we New Englanders call 'a piece of work.' A child prodigy with a tested IQ of over 150 (you will find reflections of Dave in Bow-Wow Fornoy's genius brother in 'The End of the Whole Mess') who went through school as if on a rocket-sled, finishing college at eighteen and going right to work as a high-school math teacher at Brunswick High. Many of his remedial algebra students were older than he was. Dave was the youngest ever to be elected Town Selectman in the state of Maine, and was a Town Manager at the age of twenty-five or so. He is a genuine polymath, a man who knows something about just about everything."

Essential Stephen King ranking: **62**

Suffer the Little Children

- This story first appeared in the February 1972 issue of *Cavalier* magazine.
- Teachers love their students. Most of the time. But what would happen if a teacher—who may or may not be mentally ill—believes that her students are evil doppelgangers who want to kill her? Well, she'd have to kill them *first*, right?
- Throughout his career, King has used teachers as important characters for several tales. These include *Carrie, The Shining, Rage,* "Sometimes They Come Back," *The Dead Zone, Christine,* "Here There Be Tygers," and this tale, "Suffer the Little Children."
- Two "Dollar Baby" adaptations of the story have been made, in 2006 and 2015. Reportedly, a feature film version is in development with Sean Carter writing and directing.

The Night Flier

- This story first appeared in the 1988 anthology *Prime Evil.*
- "The Night Flier" is about a vampire pilot who travels from place to place to do his business.
- Richard Dees, a tabloid reporter, believes the Flier is a lunatic who's actually a vampire wannabe. Does he learn otherwise?
- A film version written and directed by Mark Pavia came out in 1997 starring Miguel Ferrer as Richard Dees.

Popsy

- This story first appeared in the 1987 anthology *Masques II.*
- King has said that Popsy could also be the Night Flier.
- A child trafficker snatches the wrong kid.
- Three short film versions of this story have been made. They were released in 2009, 2014, and 2016.

It Grows on You

- This story first appeared in the Fall 1973 issue of *Marshroots*, then in a revised version in August 1982 in *Whispers*, and then in a yet-again revised version in *Nightmares & Dreamscapes*.
- In the notes to *Nightmares & Dreamscapes*, Stephen King said that this story can serve as an epilogue of sorts to his novel *Needful Things*.
- "It Grows On You" is about a house that adds wings to itself.
- The *Whispers* version of "It Grows on You" was nominated for the 1983 Locus Award for Best Short Story.
- There are no film versions of this story, but it is not listed on King's website as being available for adaptation, so rights may have been sold.

Chattery Teeth

- This story first appeared in the Fall 1992 issue of *Cemetery Dance* magazine.
- A salesman is given a pair of oversized chattering teeth and told they don't work any more. It turns out the teeth are possessed by a protection demon who kills a hitchhiker the salesman picks up and later threatens an aggressive dog.
- "Chattery Teeth" was produced as a segment of the 1997 movie *Quicksilver Highway*, written and directed by Mick Garris.

Dedication

- This story first appeared in the anthology *Night Visions 5* in 1988.
- Many find this to be one of King's more disgusting stories. Perhaps not as disgusting as "A Very Tight Place," but still pretty gross.
- A maid eats semen from the bed sheets of a famous writer, possibly as part of a spell.

The Moving Finger

- This story first appeared in the December 1990 issue of *The Magazine of Fantasy & Science Fiction.*
- Questions elicited by "The Moving Finger": First, what would you do if a living finger poked itself up out of your bathroom sink drain? And second, if the finger turns out to be incredibly long, how big is the creature attached to it? And third, if you burned and ultimately amputated the finger, how pissed off do you think the owner of said finger would get?
- A film version of the story was the series finale of the TV series *Monsters* in 1991.

Sneakers

- This story first appeared in the anthology *Night Visions 5* in 1988.
- "Sneakers" is about a haunted toilet stall. King has said that he figured since he had written about haunted houses, it was now time to write about "a haunted shithouse."
- John Tell sees a pair of dirty white sneakers when he glances under the door of the first stall in the third-floor bathroom in the building where he is working as a recording mixer on the new Dead Beats' album. No one else can see the sneakers and, ultimately, John learns they belong to the ghost of a murdered cocaine deliveryman, who ultimately reveals to John who killed him, allowing the ghost to move on to his next plane of existence, whatever it might be.
- King made an interesting revision when he reprinted "Sneakers" in *Nightmares & Dreamscapes*. In the original appearance of the story (in the limited edition *Night Visions 5* edited by Douglas E. Winter), King has Paul Jannings describe The Dead Beats by saying, "These guys make The Dead Kennedys sound like the Beatles." In the *Nightmares & Dreamscapes* version, King changes "Dead Kennedys" to "Butthole Surfers."

- The three main characters of the story are John, Paul, and George.
- In his essay "The Neighborhood of the Beast" in *Mid-Life Confidential*, King tells us, "I played briefly in a band during my senior year—organ, not guitar—but I didn't last much past the original rehearsals. My rock-and-roll aspirations (such as they were) foundered, as almost all my other extra-curricular activities did, on the fact that I lived seven miles from town, and had no car even after I had managed to get my driver's license."
- There really is a "Dead Beats" band, but they spell their name "Deadbeats."

Essential Stephen King ranking: **90**

You Know They Got a Hell of a Band

- This story first appeared in the 1992 anthology *Shock Rock*.
- This story is the ultimate rock 'n' roll fantasy: dead rock stars form a band in "Heaven."
- In the "Notes" of *Nightmares & Dreamscapes*, King says, "What I felt here—the impetus for the story—was how authentically creepy it is that so many rockers have died young, or under nasty circumstances; it's an actuarial expert's nightmare."
- The title of this story comes from an old Righteous Brothers song called "Rock and Roll Heaven."
- In a 2006 interview with *The Paris Review*, King talked about the role of music in his writing at that point in his life: "Now I'll only listen to music at the end of a day's work, when I roll back to the beginning of what I did that day and go over it on the screen. A lot of times the music will drive my wife crazy because it will be the same thing over and over and over again. I used to have a dance mix of that song 'Mambo No. 5' by Lou Bega. It's a cheerful, calypso kind of thing, and my wife came upstairs one day and said, 'Steve, one more time...you die!'"

(Shortly after the movie *IT* came out in 2017, fans started putting pop songs under the scene of Pennywise dancing. One of these homemade videos was Pennywise dancing to "Mambo No. 5," apparently at Stephen King's request.)

- A short film of this story was released on August 2, 2006 as Episode 8 of Season 1 of the Stephen King TV series *Nightmares & Dreamscapes: From the Stories of Stephen King*. It starred Kim Delaney and Steven Weber and was directed by Mike Robe from his own screenplay adaptation of the story.

Essential Stephen King ranking: **83**

Home Delivery

- This story first appeared in the 1989 anthology *Book of the Dead*.
- This is a Stephen King science fiction zombie story. (Pre-*The Walking Dead*, by the way.)
- The main character is widow Maddie Pace, who lives on Jenny Island (actually Gennesault) off the coast of Maine and who lost her husband in a fishing boat accident.
- [**Spoiler Alert**]: An alien satellite dubbed Star Wormwood is in stationary orbit above the earth and its obvious mission is to reanimate the earth's dead. Star Wormwood is one of King's greatest horrors: it is literally a giant ball of ravenous alien worms. A joint U.S./Chinese visit to the satellite to investigate goes horrifically wrong and one of the last transmissions is: "Oh my Christ they're in my head, *they're eating my fuckin br*—", followed by static.
- The residents of Jenny have to deal with the island's dead rising out of the cemeteries and attacking the living. And even though Maddie's husband Jack was lost at sea, he might be able to find his way home…right?

- Renowned artist Glenn Chadbourne adapted "Home Delivery" for the book *The Secretary of Dreams*, a collection of King comics published by Cemetery Dance in 2006.

Rainy Season

- This story first appeared in the Spring 1989 issue of *Midnight Graffiti* magazine.
- King simply submitted it unsolicited to the magazine. They built an entire issue around it. King's cover letter read:

  "Enclosed is a short story, 'Rainy Season,' which I thought might be right for *Graffiti*. It's pretty gross."
- Bizarre rains have been part of the literature of the bizarre for decades. This story nods to that tradition with the events that take place, adding in the tried and true narrative element of an ancient curse.
- **[Spoiler Alert]**: Every seven years in Willow, Maine, it rains toads. And not just your ordinary, garden variety toads. *Killer* toads. *Carnivorous* toads. It's all part of the "ritual," a recurring event that locals expect, accept, and prepare for, but do not understand. All they know is that every seven years, when visitors come to town on June 17th, a resident always warns them about the rain of predacious toads expected that evening. The visitors always scoff, the toads always come, the visitors are always eaten, the toads always melt away in the morning sun, and the town then enjoys another seven years of peace and prosperity.
- "Rainy Season" is a terrific horror story, but also a sly commentary on tourism and how natives feel about those seasonal visitors—"summer people"—who pack up and leave when they have exhausted their interest in a place, and need to get back to something more important.
- "Rainy Season" is a great deal of fun, mainly because King plays it straight. There are no *Creepshow*-style histrionics, nor comic

book conventions—we believe that toads fall from the sky and that the way John and Elise react is the way *normal* people would react. Unbelieving at first, but then desperate to survive when the truth is made clear.

- *Rainy Season*, a twenty-one-minute film adaptation of "Rainy Season," was released in March 2017. It was directed by Vanessa Ionta Wright from her own screenplay adaptation of the story. It starred Brian Ashton Smith and Anne-Marie Kennedy. It won the "Best Stephen King Dollar Baby of 2017" award.

My Pretty Pony

- This story first appeared as a 250-copy limited artist edition in 1989 published by the Whitney Museum of Modern Art. It was an oversized, illustrated book with stainless steel cover, digital clock, nine lithographs, and eight screenprints.
- The short story "My Pretty Pony" is a chapter from an aborted Richard Bachman novel called *My Pretty Pony*. The novel died; the story survived.
- "My Pretty Pony" is a tender story of the relationship between a grandfather and his grandson, and how one day shortly before his death, the grandfather gives "instruction" (never advice) to his rapt grandson. Stanley Wiater, author of *The Stephen King Universe*, once told me that this story suggested to him what would result if "Ernest Hemingway and Ray Bradbury collaborated on a story."
- In the "Notes" to *Nightmares & Dreamscapes*, King wrote, "*My Pretty Pony* I junked...except for a brief flashback in which Banning, while waiting to begin his assault on the wedding party, remembers how his grandfather instructed him on the plastic nature of time. Finding that flashback—marvelously complete, almost a short story as it stood—was like finding a rose growing in a junkheap. I plucked it, and I did so with great gratitude."

- **[Spoiler Alert]**: Since the moment I first read "My Pretty Pony" back in 1988, I have never forgotten the passage where King evocatively and poignantly describes the grandfather's death: "...Grandpa's pony had kicked down Grandpa's fences and gone over all the hills of the world. Wicked heart, wicked heart. Pretty, but with a wicked heart."

Essential Stephen King ranking: **40**

Sorry, Right Number

- *Sorry, Right Number* is a teleplay written as an episode of the horror anthology series *Tales from the Darkside*. The episode aired on November 22, 1987.
- *Sorry, Right Number*'s first text publication—as a screenplay—was in *Nightmares & Dreamscapes*.
- The main character, Bill Weiderman, is a novelist. His novel *Ghost's Kiss* was made into a TV movie. He was played by Darrin Stevens. His wife Katie was played by Barbara Weetman.
- The premise is powerful: Can you call yourself in the past to warn yourself about something terrible that's about to happen?
- The title *Sorry, Right Number* is a reference to the 1948 film *Sorry, Wrong Number*, starring Burt Lancaster and Barbara Stanwyck.

The Ten O'Clock People

- This story's first publication was in *Nightmares & Dreamscapes*.
- Is there any building in America where smoking is allowed inside anymore? This story is about people who work in a building where smoking is completely *verboten* and they have to go outside (often at ten o'clock) to smoke. (And a quick Google search reveals that, yes, there are still states where smoking is allowed in workplaces, restaurants, and bars.)

- The truly strange premise for this terrific story is that horrible bat-like creatures (batmen) with oozing tumors on their face and a taste for humans (especially eyeballs, it seems) have infiltrated the highest levels of American business and culture (the Vice President is one). Their determined plan is to take over the world, ultimately using the human race as their own personal All-You-Can-Eat buffet. A few "lucky" humans—including the main character of this tale, Brandon Pearson—are the only ones can see these bat creeps in their true form.

- In the "Notes" to *Nightmares & Dreamscapes*, King wrote of this story, "The expensive buildings are now all no-smoking zones as the American people go calmly about one of the most amazing turnabouts of the twentieth century; we are purging ourselves of our bad old habit, we are doing it with hardly any fanfare, and the result has been some very odd pockets of sociological behavior. Those who refuse to give up their old habit—the Ten O'Clock People of the title—constitute one of those.... I hope it says something interesting about a wave of change which has, temporarily, at least, re-created some aspects of the separate-but-equal facilities of the forties and fifties."

- "The Ten O'Clock People" has a black hero. Duke Rhinemann is described as a "good-looking young black man." When we consider King's comment about the move away from smoking creating a throwback to archaic social mores, the race of the hero can perhaps be interpreted metaphorically, as well as on a purely narrative level.

- The batmen of "The Ten O'Clock People" resemble the Can-toi creatures mentioned in *Low Men in Yellow Coats* and the *Dark Tower* series.

Essential Stephen King ranking: **93**

Crouch End

- This story's first publication was in the 1980 anthology *New Tales of the Cthulhu Mythos*.
- This story was inspired by a trip the Kings made to London to visit Peter Straub, and it references the work of H. P. Lovecraft.
- Lonnie Freeman goes missing in Crouch End and his hysterical wife reports seeing monsters. She believes her husband is trapped in one. She couldn't be right, could she?
- A short film of this story was released on July 12, 2006 as Episode 2 of Season 1 of the Stephen King TV series *Nightmares & Dreamscapes: From the Stories of Stephen King*. It was directed by Mark Haber from a screenplay adaptation of the story by Kim LeMasters.

The House on Maple Street

- This story's first publication was in *Nightmares & Dreamscapes*.
- Tabitha King read the audio version of this story.
- This science fiction short story was inspired by an illustration in Chris Van Allsburg's children's book *The Mysteries of Harris Burdick*. King was sent the book by his producer friend Richard Rubenstein with a note that said, "You'll like this."
- The name of the main characters, the four Bradbury children, is a tribute to science fiction and fantasy writer Ray Bradbury.
- The story has an evil stepfather and a house, like the house in "It Grows On You," that grows and changes on its own—ultimately in order to rescue the kids from their evil stepfather.
- •In the "Notes," King tells us that his wife, Tabitha, and his son, Owen, each wrote a story based on illustrations from the Van Allsburg book. He writes, "I wish I could offer my wife's and son's stories as well."

The Fifth Quarter

- This story first appeared in the April 1972 issue of *Cavalier* magazine.
- This is the only short story King wrote using the pseudonym "John Swithen."
- "The Fifth Quarter" is about a heist, a secret map, and murderous revenge.
- This story was filmed as part of the *Nightmares & Dreamscapes: From the Stories of Stephen King* TV miniseries.

The Doctor's Case

- This story first appeared in the 1987 anthology *The New Adventures of Sherlock Holmes*.
- Who killed the sadistic Lord Hull? And will Doctor Watson solve the mystery and bring the perpetrator to justice?
- A short film adaptation is scheduled for September 2018 release. A longer adaptation was released in January 2018. (The longer version starred Denise Crosby, who also appeared in the first *Pet Sematary* film.)

Umney's Last Case

- This story's first publication was in *Nightmares & Dreamscapes*.
- This is Stephen King's personal favorite story in *Nightmares & Dreamscapes*.
- This story is part Raymond Chandler pastiche, part time travel tale, and part contemplation on the nature of writing and the creation of characters and other places and times. "Umney's Last Case" flows effortlessly towards its inevitable conclusion, and neatly takes a final U-turn into a chilling cliffhanger.
- In the "Notes" to *Nightmares & Dreamscapes*, King spoke about "Umney's Last Case": "For a long time I steered clear of that Chandlerian voice, because I had nothing to use it for...noth-

ing to say in the tones of Philip Marlowe that was mine....Then one day I did."

- Samuel Landry's New York agent in the modern world is named Verrill, a certain tribute to Stephen King's longtime editor and friend, Chuck Verrill.
- "Umney's Last Case" is an important story in the Stephen King canon and the one that Penguin Books chose to celebrate in 1995 with a special single-volume edition (a "Penguin Single") commemorating the publishing company's sixtieth anniversary. These eighty-eight-page mini-books are now collector's items.
- A short film of this story was released on July 19, 2006 as Episode 3 of Season 1 of the Stephen King TV series *Nightmares & Dreamscapes: From the Stories of Stephen King*. It starred William H. Macy, Jacqueline McKenzie, and Tory Mussett. It was directed by Rob Bowman from a teleplay adaptation of the story by April Smith.

Head Down

- This nonfiction essay first appeared in the April 16, 1990 issue of *The New Yorker*.
- "Head Down" is about Owen King's Little League team.
- The original title of "Head Down" was "The Boys of Summer."
- In the "Notes" to *Nightmares & Dreamscapes*, King spoke about the genesis of this essay: "My method of working when I feel out of my depth is brutally simple: I lower my own head and run as fast as I can, as long as I can. That was what I did here, gathering documentation like a mad packrat and simply trying to keep up with the team....Hard or not, 'Head Down' was the opportunity of a lifetime, and before I was done, Chip McGrath of *The New Yorker* had coaxed the best nonfiction writing of my life out of me."

- "Head Down" later appeared in the 1991 anthology *The Best American Sports Writing* and the 2002 collection *Baseball: A Literary Anthology.*

Brooklyn August

- This poem first appeared in the 1971 issue of *Io: A Journal of New American Poetry (#10).*
- It is about baseball and connects thematically to "Head Down."
- The poem's first line is "In Ebbets Field the crabgrass grows."

The Beggar and the Diamond

- This story's first publication was in Nightmares & Dreamscapes.
- King introduces the story with the following "Author's Note":
  This little story—a Hindu parable in its original form—was first told to me by Mr. Surendra Patel, of Scarsdale, New York. I have adapted it freely and apologize to those who know it in its true form, where Lord Shiva and his wife, Parvati, are the major characters.
- In the parable, God places a diamond in the path of Ramu, a complaining man who has decided to pretend he is blind to prove to himself that his life could be much worse. He doesn't see the diamond, which God then replaces with a branch which, God says, will serve him as a walking stick for the rest of his days.
- At the conclusion of the story, the Archangel Uriel, who has been observing the events of Ramu's story, asks God, "Have You given me a lesson, Lord?" God responds, "I don't know, have I?"

IV. *Everything's Eventual* (March 2002)

Autopsy Room Four

- This story first appeared in King's 1997 Philtrum Press collection *Six Stories*.
- There is a "complication" during surgery called "anesthesia awareness." It means what it sounds like: a patient wakes up paralyzed during surgery and is aware of everything that's going on. In some cases of anesthesia awareness, physical sensation also returns, either fully or partly.
- Stephen King took this premise and used it to describe the situation the story's protagonist, Howard Cottrell, finds himself in when he awakens and discovers he's paralyzed and lying, not on a surgical table, but on an autopsy table.
- "Autopsy Room Four" is inspired by the 1947 short story "Breakdown" by Louis Pollock, in which the protagonist awakens after a car accident fully paralyzed and needs to find a way to communicate with the people tending to him and prove that he's alive.

The Man in the Black Suit

- This story first appeared in the October 31, 1994 issue of *The New Yorker* magazine.
- King won the 1994 O. Henry Award for Best Short Story for this story.
- The narrator—diarist, actually—of this story is an old man in his eighties named Gary, writing from his final residence—a room in a nursing home. When he was nine, Gary met the Devil—"live" and in person—on the banks of the Castle Stream in Maine. The Dark Man told Gary that his mother was dead and that he was now going to eat Gary alive. Gary managed to flee the riverbank and make it home, but throughout his life, he was traumatized by one stark reality: he escaped the Devil through sheer luck, and not by the "intercession of the

God I have worshipped and sung hymns to all my life." This cold, dark fact now terrorizes the old man because if God was not there for him that day, will he be waiting for him when he crosses over into the realm where He and "the man in the black suit" both hold offices?

"The Man in the Black Suit" foreshadowed one specific narrative element of Stephen King's 1996's serial novel *The Green Mile*. In *The Green Mile* (as in "The Man in the Black Suit"), the story is told to the reader by an old man (Paul Edgecombe) writing in his diary while living in a nursing home. King has used the diary/epistolary format in other works, most notably in "The End of the Whole Mess," "Survivor Type," and *The Plant*.

In King's introduction to *Six Stories*, he wrote, "['The Man in the Black Suit' comes from] a long New England tradition of stories which dealt with meeting the devil in the woods...he always comes out of the woods—the uncharted regions—to test the human soul."

A short film adaptation of this story was made in 2004. It was written and directed by Nicholas Mariani and starred Geoff Hansen and John Viener.

"The Man in the Black Suit" was adapted into a groundbreaking opera in 2001 by American Opera Projects. Music was by Eve Beglarian and the libretto was co-written by Beglarian and Grethe Barrett Holby. It was directed by Holby. The following is the Project Summary written by the performing arts group, Ardea Arts:

The Man in the Black Suit, an opera by Eve Beglarian and Grethe Barrett Holby based on the award-winning story by Stephen King, addresses issues of faith, evil and the world beyond us. The story takes place in rural Maine in the early twentieth century, told by a man in his nineties recounting a pivotal childhood experience—an encounter with evil that changes his life, and the life of his family, forever. The opera mines fundamental questions he faces as he awaits the end of his life.

Director Grethe Barrett Holby is working to etch the emotional topography of this intensely philosophical story into the libretto and the physical production simultaneously—using light, water, reflections, sounds generated directly by movement and dramatic action—a unique way of working, particularly in the world of opera. Collaborating with the composer on the opera and the libretto from the outset has ensured that the production and directorial ideas both inform and are informed by the musical ideas from the very inception of the project, allowing all elements—libretto, music and production—to grow together organically as a conceptual whole.

Composer Eve Beglarian is working to merge aspects of traditional opera with new technology in order to mirror the hallucinatory hyper-reality of the story in music and sound. The story is shot through with the sounds of nature. In addition to the more conventional forces of voices, strings, and guitars, the score will include live sound effects (known as foley) using techniques borrowed from film. Further innovation includes a mix performer performing as an instrumentalist in the pit, playing the electronics and processing live under the direction of the conductor, allowing the electronic materials to be performed with the same immediacy and responsiveness as the acoustic instruments.

This is not an opera that explicitly examines the conventions of opera on one hand or the avant-garde on the other. It is not a piece that cares about the distinction between opera and music-theater. It is a piece that utilizes electronics without making electronics the issue. It is at core hugely dramatic without ever being self-consciously theatrical. It's not made to speak to the field—of music, of opera, whatever. It's made to speak to human beings. It's made to speak to you.

All That You Love Will Be Carried Away

- This story first appeared in the January 29, 2001 issue of *The New Yorker*.
- This is a naturalistic story in which all the horrors are psychological: depression, alienation, and suicide are among the topics King deals with in this story of a frozen food salesman on what might be his last day.
- I used this King story in my University of New Haven Composition and Literature course. We read the original story and then watched the James Renner short film adaptation of the story, which starred Joe Bob Briggs and Harvey Pekar. My topic question focused on what students thought happened at the end of the story.

The Death of Jack Hamilton

- This story first appeared in the December 24 & 31, 2001 issue of *The New Yorker*
- Homer Van Meter, a member of John Dillinger's gang, tells the story of the gunshot and gangrene death of fellow gang member Jack Hamilton.
- In the afternote to this story, King writes "As a kid, I was fascinated by tales of the Depression-era outlaws, an interest that probably peaked with Arthur Penn's remarkable *Bonnie*

and Clyde....Jack Hamilton's lingering death is a documented fact; my story of what happened at Doc Barker's hideout is, of course, pure imagination...or myth, if you like that word better; I do."

In the Deathroom

- This story first appeared in the 1999 *Blood and Smoke* audiobook. Its first print appearance was in *Secret Windows*.
- A *New York Times* reporter is abducted and imprisoned in an interrogation room in South America.
- One of the torture devices is an electric shock device that looks like a stainless steel dildo with a rubber grip.
- A short film of this story directed by Luke Cheney was released in 2009.

Everything's Eventual

- This story first appeared in the October/November 1997 issue of *The Magazine of Fantasy & Science Fiction*.
- "Everything's Eventual" is science fiction with a touch of the fantastic. Once again, King looks at "wild talents," those human beings gifted (some would say cursed) with wondrous abilities that can be used for good or evil. (*Carrie, Firestarter, The Shining, The Dead Zone*, and "The End of the Whole Mess" are other examples of King writing about such "gifted" individuals.)
- It was reported to me by an unimpeachable source that Stephen King told Peter Straub that the character of Dinky is a "Breaker," like Ted in the novella *Low Men in Yellow Coats* (in *Hearts in Atlantis*), thereby connecting this tale to the world of *The Dark Tower, The Stand*, and other King *Dark Tower* works.
- In *Low Men in Yellow Coats*, it is explained that the Dark Tower "holds everything together." There are Beams protecting the Tower, while "Breakers," working for the Crimson King, en-

deavor to destroy the Beams. The Breakers, it is made clear, do not do this work voluntarily. If Dinky is, indeed, a Breaker, then it is quite possible that Mr. Sharpton and his Trans Corporation may figure into future events in the story of Roland the Last Gunslinger and his quest to find the Dark Tower.

- "Everything's Eventual" is one of those occasional King works in which the author references himself. In Part 17 of the novella, Dinky tells us, "There was this show me and Pug used to watch one summer back when we were little kids. *Golden Years*, it was called. You probably don't remember it."

- A full-length feature film adaptation of this story, *Everything's Eventual*, was released in 2009. It starred Michael Flores and Joe Jones. It was directed by J. P. Scott from a screenplay by Chad Callaghan.

- The short film *Everything's Eventual* was released in 2011. It starred Billy Schnase and Bill Dablow. It was directed by Maxwell Heesch from his own screenplay adaptation of the story.

L. T.'s Theory of Pets

- This story was originally published in the 1997 Philtrum Press collection *Six Stories*.

- This story was released as an audiobook in 2001. It was a recording of Stephen King himself reading the story live at Royal Festival Hall in London.

- A married couple buy each other pets. The pets get along, but each animal hates the opposite spouse. And there may or may not be a serial killer loose in Nevada.

- This story is listed on Stephen King's website as available for adaptation.

- In his Note for this story, King says it was inspired by a "Dear Abby" column about giving pets as a gift and that it is his favorite in the collection.

The Road Virus Heads North

- This story was originally published in the 1999 anthology *999*.
- Richard Kinnell buys a painting that can depict the future. The painter was a crazy genius who burned all his paintings (except the one Richard buys) before committing suicide. After seeing the painting change, Richard throws it away, but then finds it at his home when he arrives. Will the painting foretell Richard's fate?
- A short film of this story was released on July 26, 2006 as Episode 5 of Season 1 of the Stephen King TV series *Nightmares & Dreamscapes: From the Stories of Stephen King*. It starred Tom Berenger and Marsha Mason and was directed by Sergio Mimica-Gezzan from a screenplay by Peter Filardi.

Lunch at the Gotham Café

- This story was originally published in the 1995 anthology *Dark Love*.
- This story was later published in the 1997 Philtrum Press limited edition collection *Six Stories*, and as an audio story (read by Stephen King) in the 1999 *Blood and Smoke* audiobook.
- This is an odd story in which an estranged couple are attacked by a maniacal chef screaming "Eeeeee" in the Gotham Café. Even after Steve saves his soon-to-be-ex-wife's life, she still despises him and leaves him at the restaurant where he muses about the chef's insanity…and starts saying "Eeeeee." King said in his Note accompanying this story that he thought the couple were crazier than the chef. And he would know, right?
- A short film adaptation of this story was released in 2005. It was written by Peter Schink, Julie Sands, and Bev Vincent, and directed by Jack Edward Sawyers. Cameos in the film were made by Stephen King, Mick Garris, and Steve Wozniak.

That Feeling, You Can Only Say What It Is in French

- This story was originally published in the June 22 & 29, 1998 issue of *The New Yorker*.

- That "feeling" King is describing in the story's title is *déjà vu*. Merriam-Webster defines *déjà vu* as "the illusion of remembering scenes and events when experienced for the first time," and "a feeling that one has seen or heard something before."

- "That Feeling, You Can Only Say What It Is In French" mostly takes place in the mind of Carol Shelton, on her way to a second honeymoon vacation with her husband Bill to celebrate their twenty-fifth anniversary. As they are driving to their hotel, Carol begins getting "those feelings"...flashes of vivid recall known as *déjà vu*, a weird biological short circuit in the brain that makes the experiencer interpret new events as memory.

- This is one of King's stories set outside of Maine. "That Feeling, You Can Only Say What It Is In French" takes place in Florida, where, not so coincidentally, Stephen and Tabitha King now have a home where they spend most winters, and where Stephen went to recuperate following his 1999 accident. (During King's recovery, his wife Tabitha took some photos of him on a Florida beach that were to be used as publicity materials and by the media.)

Riding the Bullet

- This story first appeared as a 2000 e-book, the world's first mass market work of fiction.

- *Riding the Bullet* was nominated for the 2000 Bram Stoker Award for Best Long Form fiction.

- Alan Parker hitchhikes to see his mother at a hospital where she was brought after suffering a stroke. He's picked up by a guy who may or may not be dead and given the power to decide who lives: him or his mother?

- A film version of the story written and directed by Mick Garris was released in 2004.

Luckey Quarter

- This story's first publication was in the June 30/July 2, 1995 edition of *USA Today* magazine. This story also appeared in King's collection *Six Stories*.
- Who among us has not imagined what we'd do if we won a fortune? (I've written imaginary checks to people.) Darlene Pullman gets a "luckey" quarter tip at her job as a hotel chambermaid and starts winning big with it. Or does she?

V. *Just After Sunset* (2008)
Willa

- This story first appeared in the December 2006 issue of *Playboy* magazine.
- "Willa" is a superb ghost story that would have almost certainly been a *Twilight Zone* episode had King been writing during that show's heyday (and if, y'know, he wrote for the series, and, y'know, if Rod Serling liked it.)
- You find yourself in a rundown train station. Your fiancée is missing. You decide to walk through a desolate landscape to look for her. But to find her, you'll have to pay a visit to…the Twilight Zone.

The Gingerbread Girl

- This story first appeared in the July 2007 issue of *Esquire* magazine.
- A young mother is in almost unbearable grief over the crib death of her newborn daughter Amy. She takes to running, splits with her husband, and holes up at her father's house on the Gulf on Florida. One day she sees a dead blonde in the

trunk of her "not very nice" neighbor and ends up in the ultimate fight for her life.

- Some readers have said "The Gingerbread Girl" feels like a Richard Bachman story. They're right.

Harvey's Dream

- This story first appeared in the June 30, 2003 issue of *The New Yorker*.

- In the *Just After Sunset* "Notes" section, King tells us that this entire story came to him in a dream and that he wrote it in one sitting, acting as a transcriptionist. Similarly, Mozart used to talk about being a transcriptionist for the music he heard in his head. He believed the music was already written and that all he did was write it down.

- The main character, Harvey, has a dream that may or may not be precognitive. And may or may not involve the death of a loved one.

Rest Stop

- This story first appeared in the December 2003 issue of *Esquire* magazine.

- In a story that nods to both Stephen King's "Richard Bachman" pseudonym and his novel *The Dark Half*, a writer who uses an alias summons that persona to rescue a woman from what seems like horrific abuse.

- "Rest Stop" won the National Magazine Award for Fiction in 2004.

Stationary Bike

- This story first appeared in the 2003 anthology *Borderlands 5*.

- Richard's in trouble: his cholesterol and unhealthy eating have raised his risk of an early death. So he decides to exercise on a stationary bicycle in his basement. But before long, the bike becomes a vehicle that serves as a portal to another world, a world where he meets the "workmen" whose job it is to clear the crap out of his arteries. They're not pleased with Richard's new healthy lifestyle and, considering it's a Stephen King story, that cannot bode well for Richard, right?

- "Stationary Bike" has a *Rose Madder* sensibility to it, and even a twinge of the painting-themed *Duma Key*.
- A 2012 short film adaptation of this story called *Bike* was written and directed by David Toms and starred Steve Hope Wynn as Richard.

The Things They Left Behind

- This story first appeared in the 2005 anthology *Transgressions: Volume Two*.
- This story asks the question, "Is there any closure for 9/11?" Any further comments about this tale would veer into spoiler territory.

Graduation Afternoon

- This story first appeared in the March 2007 issue of *Postscripts*.
- King wonders if this story was the result of him quitting the anti-depressant Doxepin, which he took not because he was depressed, but because it was supposed to help with the chronic pain he was experiencing following his near-fatal accident in 1999.
- This story, like "Harvey's Dream," was "transcribed" from his subconscious.
- A beautiful townie and a rich kid are in a relationship, and it's graduation afternoon. Then something horrible happens. That's a terrible synopsis of a terrifying story, but any more would spoil the big reveal that changes everything.
- "And you thought 9/11 was bad for New York City..." could easily be a tagline for this story.

N.

- This story was first published in its entirety as prose in *Just After Sunset*.
- In a self-interview on stephenking.com, King said of this story:

    [*N.*] is a riff on Arthur Machen's "The Great God Pan," which is one of the best horror stories ever written. Maybe the best in the English language. Mine isn't anywhere near that good, but I loved the chance to put neurotic behavior—obsessive/compulsive disorder—together with the idea of a monster-filled macroverse. That was a good combination. As for Machen vs. Lovecraft: sure, Lovecraft was ultimately better, because he did more with those concepts, but "The Great God Pan" is more reader-friendly. And Machen was there first. He wrote "Pan" in 1895, when HPL was five years old.

- *N.* was adapted as *Stephen King's N.*, a twenty-five-part graphic video series totaling thirty minutes, as part of the marketing campaign for *Just After Sunset*. The episodes were drawn by artist Alex Maleev and colored by comic-book colorist José Villarrubia.
- In September 2017, Gaumont Television announced that they were developing an adaptation of *N.*, which would be retitled *8*.

The Cat from Hell

- This story first appeared in the June 1977 issue of *Cavalier* magazine.
- I'm a huge fan of cats, so the basic premise of this story—an old man hires someone to put a hit on a cat—was disconcerting to me. Yes, I know it's only a story, but my *agita* comes from the same impulse that makes me skip over any videos on YouTube or Facebook that show an animal in distress. One I did see (mainly because I wanted to write about it) was of a

bull committing suicide after his horns were set on fire during a bullfight, and it messed me up for days.

- A scene at the end will feel familiar to anyone who has seen *Alien*.

The New York Times at Special Bargain Rates

- This story first appeared in the October/November 2008 issue of *The Magazine of Fantasy & Science Fiction*.
- This story harkens back to King's screenplay *Sorry, Right Number*, in which a wife gets a phone call from her dead husband. Or does she?
- A TV series of this story called *Grand Central* is in development at ABC.

Mute

- This story first appeared in the December 2007 issue of *Playboy* magazine.
- A book salesman named Monette (he wears a pin that says "Ask Me About The Best Fall List Ever!") picks up a deaf and mute hitchhiker, and proceeds to tell him—the guy's deaf, right?—about his wife's adultery and embezzlement.
- However, Monette begins to worry when the hitchhiker disappears at a stop and something terrible later happens to his wife.
- Monette goes to confession. Does he have a reason to be absolved of a sin?

Ayana

- This story first appeared in the Fall 2007 issue of *The Paris Review*.
- A young black girl kisses a dying man…and the man doesn't die. Is it a miracle?
- This story has one of King's best lines: "The medical diagnosis of 'miracle' is 'misdiagnosis.'"

A Very Tight Place

- This novella first appeared in the May 2008 issue of *McSweeney's* magazine.
- This might be one of the grossest stories King has ever written. Seriously.
- The main character, Curtis Johnson, has been living an ongoing feud with his irascible neighbor Tim Grunwald over property rights in Florida. His dog even died as a result of the skirmish. To say they hate each other is an understatement. Grunwald lures Johnson to an abandoned construction site and traps him in a Port-O-San. With no possible chance of being rescued, Johnson needs to seriously get his shit together. (Sorry.)
- If you've ever wanted to know what it's like to be trapped in a tipped-over Port-O-San, this story will satisfy that curiosity.

VI. *The Bazaar of Bad Dreams* (2015)
Mile 81

- This story was first published as an e-book in 2011.
- The version of "Mile 81" that appears in *The Bazaar of Bad Dreams* is revised, with several more deaths.
- Could an alien being disguise itself as a station wagon and then eat people? Anything's possible in Stephen King World!

Premium Harmony

- This story first appeared in the November 9, 2009 issue of *The New Yorker*.
- This is a naturalistic story set in Castle Rock about a marriage, two deaths, and smoking. It's also about a dog, obesity, and the logistics of a French kiss.
- "Premium Harmony" asks the reader to consider the unasked questions, "Is it wrong to be relieved when someone dies?" And, "If not, why not?"

- In the introductory note to "Premium Harmony," King talks about other writers' influence on one's own writing and says that if "Premium Harmony" reads like a Raymond Carver story, it is because he wrote it after reading two dozen of Carver's short stories. King admits that he had missed Carver in his reading and, only after being asked to review his collected stories for the *New York Times Book Review*, did he realize Carver's phenomenal talent.

- In the introduction, King talks about loving the losers Carver wrote about, but that he didn't think Carver had much of a sense of humor. King admits he himself sees humor in everything and that some of that came through in "Premium Harmony."

Batman and Robin Have an Altercation

- This story first appeared in the September 2012 issue of *Harper's* magazine.

- Another of King's "Alzheimer's" stories. Several characters in his later works either have a form of dementia, or are caregivers for someone suffering from cognitive impairment.

- A son takes his elderly father to lunch every Sunday. One week, he gets into an accident in which his dementia-muddled father saves the day.

The Dune

- This story first appeared in the Fall 2011 issue of *Granta* magazine.

- A retired judge sees the names of people who soon die written in the sand on property his family owns in Florida.

- The end of this story is great, and unexpected.

- As with other King tales in which the protagonist is provided terrible information, possibly via supernatural means, we are left wondering if the judge is really seeing the names—or is there something else going on?

- In the Note in *The Bazaar of Bad Dreams* introducing "The Dune," King wrote, "I was in Florida, walking our dog on the beach. Because it was January, and cold, I was the only one out there. Up ahead I saw what looked like writing in the sand. When I got closer, I saw it was just a trick of sunlight and shadow, but writers' minds are junkheaps of odd information, and it made me think of an old quote from somewhere (it turned out to be Omar Khayyam): 'The Moving Finger writes, and having writ, moves on.' That in turn made me think of some magical place where an invisible Moving Finger would write terrible things in the sand, and I had this story. It has one of my very favorite endings."

Bad Little Kid

- This story was previously unpublished in English.
- This story was originally published in German and French as an e-book.
- George Hallas is in prison for killing a "bad little kid," a kid who showed up throughout his life and left death and destruction in his wake. The day before his execution, he warns his attorney, Leonard Bradley, to watch out for the kid because he's still out there. Bradley finds something in his car shortly thereafter that suggests that Hallas was right.

A Death

- This story first appeared in the September 2015 issue of *The New Yorker*.
- King dedicates this story to the writer Elmore Leonard and, in the Intro, says that when he had the idea for the story, he wanted the language to be "dry and laconic." (It is.) he also said

he had no idea where the story would go, but knew that the language would take him there. (It did.)

- "A Death" is about a murder, and truth, and faith, and gullibility…and a shitty silver dollar.
- The story is set in Dakota Territory before it became part of the United States. Reading it, we can justifiably speculate that King might be a fan of the HBO series *Deadwood.*

The Bone Church

- This long narrative poem first appeared in the November 2009 issue of *Playboy* magazine.
- The actual Bone Church is described by King as "a million years of bone and tusk, / a whited sepulchre of eternity, a thrashpit of prongs / such as you'd see if hell burned dry to the slag of its cauldron."
- The poem consists of a man sitting at a bar and telling his bizarre story for drinks. The story is of an expedition to the Bone Church during which everyone except the narrator died.
- In the Intro, King talks about a friend, Jimmy Smith, reading King's long-lost original version of the poem at the University of Maine Poetry Hour in 1969 or 1970. It was well-received. King decided to try rewriting it, and this version is the result.

Morality

- This novella first appeared in the July 2009 issue of *Esquire* magazine.
- This tale asks the question, "What would you do to get out of trouble, especially financial trouble?"
- King has said that this story was inspired by his own financial troubles when in college and when first married.
- *Morality* won the Shirley Jackson Award for Best Novelette for 2009.
- *Morality* was included as a bonus story in *Blockade Billy.*

Afterlife

- This short story first appeared in the June 2013 issue of *Tin House* magazine.
- This is a great story about reincarnation. If you could choose between starting your original life over from birth, or stopping the cycle once and for all, what would you do?

Ur

- This novella first appeared as an e-book for the Amazon Kindle platform in 2009. An audiobook edition was released in 2010 by Simon & Schuster. The 2015 version in *The Bazaar of Bad Dreams* is heavily revised.
- A pink Kindle can access alternate historical timelines and English professor Wesley Smith has to decide how to use this new power and knowledge.
- The "low men in yellow coats" from the novella of the same name make an appearance and make the decision for Wesley as to what to do with what he has learned from the Kindle much easier.

Herman Wouk Is Still Alive

- This short story first appeared in the May 2011 issue of *The Atlantic* magazine.
- This story won the 2011 Best Short Fiction Bram Stoker Award.
- "Herman Wouk Is Still Alive" is dedicated to Owen King and Herman Wouk.
- This is not a supernatural horror story, but it is, indeed, a horror story. Any piece of fiction that includes the dismemberment of children and a huge number of deaths is undoubtedly horrific.
- A poor, single mother living on welfare wins some money on a lottery scratch ticket and convinces her childhood friend to go on a road trip...with their multiple kids, in a rented van, paid

for with some of her winnings. After drinking while driving, she decides to see how fast the van will go. [**Spoiler Alert**]: It's pretty goddamn fast.

- The other characters in this story are two aging poets who are on their way to the University of Maine to read from their works. They are unwitting participants in a multifaceted tragedy.
- As of this writing, Herman Wouk is, indeed, still alive and is 102 years old. What he said was his final book, *Sailor and Fiddler: Reflections of a 100-Year-Old Author,* was published in January 2016.
- Herman Wouk read King's story and sent him a complimentary note. He also invited King to visit.

Under the Weather

- This short story first appeared in the 2011 paperback edition of the novella collection, *Full Dark, No Stars.*
- There's a foul odor coming from Brad Franklin's apartment. The superintendent thinks it might be rats. And, by the way, no one's seen your wife for quite some time, Mr. Franklin.
- Can imagination overpower death? And is someone dead just because they're apparently sleeping late? And is it true that beloved pets will eat their master's body if they're dead?

Blockade Billy

- This novella was first published as a Scribner hardcover in May 2010.
- Not everyone is who they say they are, and a catcher who seems too good to be true, and who brings good luck to a baseball team, could actually be hiding a dark, evil secret.
- The first edition of *Blockade Billy* was published by *Cemetery Dance* and included a "Blockade Billy" baseball card.

Mister Yummy

- This short story was first published in *Bazaar of Bad Dreams.*
- Ollie Franklin and Dave Calhoun are two old men living out their final days in the Lakeview Assisted Living Center.
- Ollie recalls his younger days living as a gay man in America in the 1980s and talks about seeing a beautiful young man that everyone called Mister Yummy.
- Even though he never saw him again, suddenly Ollie is visited by Mister Yummy at the nursing home. Why is he there? Or is Ollie just seeing his pending death?

Tommy

- This narrative poem was first published in the March 2010 issue of *Playboy* magazine.
- "Tommy" begins:

    Tommy died in 1969.

    He was a hippie with leukemia.

    Bummer, man.

- "Tommy" is a flashback to the peace-and-love sixties and it tells the story of Tommy's death, funeral, and aftermath. Tommy was gay and wore a button that said, "I'm Here and I'm Queer." He wanted to be buried wearing it, but his mother hid it under his vest.
- "Tommy" may or may not be about someone from King's past. He dedicates it to "D. F."
- King has a vivid recall of the sights, sounds, and sensibilities of the sixties and, in "Tommy," his ability to describe that era is on full display.

The Little Green God of Agony

- This short story was first published in the 2011 anthology *A Book of Horrors.*

- "The Little Green God of Agony" is a classic horror story that is one of King's best. It can be said that it sprung from a terrible source: the 1999 accident that almost killed him. The story is about pain, but not really. It's more about where pain comes from, and as we discover, it's not always just from injury to the body, or delusions of the mind.

- When the sixth wealthiest man in the world is injured in an airplane crash landing (a plane he was flying), he suffers through years of surgeries and therapy that ultimately result in him being bedridden and refusing physical therapy.

- As a last resort, Andrew Newsome calls on a preacher, Reverend Rideout, who has a reputation for being able to heal people and who Andrew believes can help him. Andrew's five-thousand-dollar-a-week nurse Kat McDonald thinks Rideout is a fraud and tells her boss so. He summarily fires her, but the Reverend insists that if he fires her, he'll leave, too.

- Could it be that when we're injured or sick, we become "infested" with little demonic gods of agony that torture us until they're expelled or they kill us?

- Andrew Newsome ends up going through a gruesome "exorcism" of sorts that results in the death of one person in the sickroom, and the possible "infesting" of another. Plus, we learn that the little green god of agony likes to eat eyes.

- King's short stories are unvaryingly superb. This one is no exception.

- As of this writing, there have been no film adaptations of "The Little Green God of Agony."

That Bus Is Another World

- This short story was first published in the August 2014 issue of *Esquire* magazine.

- A man stuck in traffic and late for an important appointment witnesses what looks like a murder on the bus next to him.

Should he call the police? Someone on the bus had to have seen it, right? If he calls, he'll miss his appointment. And can he be sure he saw what he thought he saw?

Obits

- This short story was first published in *Bazaar of Bad Dreams*.
- "Obits" won the 2016 Edgar Award for Best Short Story.
- If you could kill someone simply by writing their obituary, would you? No? What if it was someone you absolutely despised? Or someone who had injured you in an abominable way? "Obits" tells the story of Michael Anderson, a writer who one day writes an obit for his boss, Jeroma, because she had refused him a raise. Next thing he knows, she's dead. And with that, we're off to the races.
- Does Anderson go rogue and start killing off people left and right? How does he react when he learns that his power has grown so that people with the *same name* as the subject of the deadly obit also die? King puts us right in the middle of Anderson's mind and soul as he grapples with what to do next.
- As of this writing, there are no film adaptations of "Obits."

Drunken Fireworks

- This short story was first published in 2015 as an audiobook.
- "Drunken Fireworks" is funny: two old-time Downeasters, mother and son, with a ton of insurance and lottery money, square off against an Italian "connected" family on the opposite side of the lake in a fireworks "arms race."
- James Franco is reportedly developing the film version of this story.

Summer Thunder

- This short story was first published in the 2013 anthology *Turn Down the Lights*.

- In the Intro to this story in *The Bazaar of Bad Dreams*, King writes, "What better place to end a collection than with a story about the end of the world?"
- What would you do if you were one of only a few people who survived the nuclear apocalypse that took almost everyone? You're going to die of radiation poisoning or…something else.
- Peter Robinson's dog Gandalf is his only companion after his wife and daughter are killed in Boston in the nuclear blast. Gandalf's fate bothers me more than Robinson's ultimate final decision.

Cookie Jar

- This novella (novelette?) of close to 8,300 words was first published in the *Bazaar of Bad Dreams* paperback.
- Rhett Alderson's thirteen-year-old great-grandson, Dale, visits him at the Good Life Retirement Home to interview him for a school project.
- *Cookie Jar* harkens to *The Green Mile* in how it has a retired senior citizen recounting an epic story from his past, and also *Blockade Billy* which uses a similar framing device.
- Rhett's mother had a cookie jar that was always full, no matter how many cookies were removed. Rhett deliberately emptied it one day and discovered his mother's secret: it was a portal to another world. Rhett wills the cookie jar to Dale and one of Rhett's last thoughts after knowing Dale would empty it as soon as got his hands on it, was "After that, you're on your own."

III.
THE NOVELLAS

King's novellas are extraordinary. Here is a look at his collected novellas.

I. *Different Seasons* (1978)
Rita Hayworth and Shawshank Redemption

- This novella's subtitle is "Hope Springs Eternal."
- This novella was adapted as the movie *The Shawshank Redemption*, written and directed by Frank Darabont. It has consistently been the highest rated and most popular movie on the Internet Movie Database's Top Rated Movies list.
- *Shawshank*'s character Brooks Hatlen was named in honor of King's former University of Maine English professor Burton Hatlen. Hatlen has written many papers and articles about King's work and King has acknowledged Hatlen's encouragement of his writing when he was attending UMO. One of Hatlen's articles about Stephen King's work is "Why Stephen King is a Maine Writer," published in the online journal *Joshua Maine*.
- During a September 20, 2000 live AOL chat, King said, "I like a lot of the Castle Rock films, like *Stand By Me, The Shawshank Redemption*, and *The Green Mile*, because they see past the horror to the human beings. I'm a lot more interested in the people than the monsters."

- King fans have always loved this novella. Only *The Mist* and *The Body* topped it in a survey of hundreds of King fans conducted for my 2001 book, *The Essential Stephen King*. It is one of the four exemplary works in *Different Seasons*, perhaps King's finest novella collection. But as is often the case, Frank Darabont's *The Shawshank Redemption*, the 1994 movie version of the novella, brought a much larger audience to the source story and surprised a great many critics and readers who had fit Stephen King neatly into a "Horror Only" box. This happened on a smaller scale with Rob Reiner's *Stand By Me*, but the film garnered nowhere near the response that greeted *The Shawshank Redemption* after the movie came out in 1994.

- King wrote *Rita Hayworth and Shawshank Redemption* immediately after completing *The Dead Zone*. The intimate first-person narrative form, the well-defined characters, and the implicit tension and terror of the prison setting, all combine to make this one of King's most engaging and beloved.

- In 1994, the film adaptation of *Rita Hayworth and Shawshank Redemption* was released as *The Shawshank Redemption*. It starred Tim Robbins, Morgan Freeman, Bob Gunton, William Sadler, James Whitmore, David Proval, Jude Ciccolella, and Paul McCrane. It was directed by Frank Darabont from his screenplay.

Essential Stephen King ranking: **29**

Apt Pupil

- This novella's subtitle is "Summer of Corruption."
- *Apt Pupil* asks the question, how could the Nazis have done what they did? How could thousands of men—Nazi "soldiers"—report for duty every day and methodically and cold-bloodedly exterminate human beings—including women and young children—as though they were nothing more than cattle slated for slaughtering that particular "workday"?

- Todd Bowden, a thirteen-year-old "all-American kid" obsessed with the Holocaust, discovers a horrible truth about one of his neighbors, an old man named Arthur Denker. Denker is really Kurt Dussander, a Nazi death camp commandant now known around the world as the "Blood-Fiend of Patin."
- In a June 1983 interview with *Playboy* magazine, Stephen King was asked if he had an obsession with mass murderer Charles Starkweather and the nature of evil: "Obsession is too strong a word. It was more like trying to figure out a puzzle, because I wanted to know why somebody could do the things Stark-weather did. I suppose I wanted to decipher the unspeakable, just as people try to make sense out of Auschwitz or Jonestown. I certainly didn't find evil seductive in any sick way—that would be pathological—but I did find it compelling. And I think most people do, or the bookstores wouldn't still be filled with biographies of Adolf Hitler more than thirty-five years after World War Two. The fascination of the abomination, as Conrad called it."
- Stephen King wrote *Apt Pupil* in two weeks after finishing writing *The Shining*. These two incredibly intense works so wiped out King that he did not write another word for three whole months. "I was pooped," he has admitted.
- In 1998, the film *Apt Pupil* was released starring Brad Renfro, Ian McKellen, and David Schwimmer. It was directed by Bryan Singer from a screenplay by Brandon Boyce.

Essential Stephen King ranking: **30**

The Body

- This novella's subtitle is "Fall from Innocence."
- *The Body* is another of Stephen King's works that shuts people up when they attempt to dismiss him as "just a horror writer." (*Rita Hayworth and Shawshank Redemption* and "The Last Rung

on the Ladder" do the same thing, in equally as effective a manner.) But as is often the case when a movie adaptation of a King work becomes an enormous hit, sometimes the original work is overshadowed. In the case of the novella *The Body*, Rob Reiner's enormously popular 1986 movie version *Stand By Me* has effectively usurped the text version in the annals of popular culture and is the work that has the higher-profile presence. In fact, I have heard people refer to the novella itself as *Stand By Me*.

- *The Body* is set in Castle Rock, Maine. Maine landmarks and characters abound, including Cujo, Constable Bannerman, Harrison State Park, The Mellow Tiger, *The Castle Rock Call* (the newspaper in which Gary from "The Man in the Black Suit" published a weekly column for years), Lewiston, Motton, Pownal, and more.

- In *Danse Macabre*, King talks about the genesis of *The Body*: "According to Mom, I had gone off to play at a neighbor's house—a house that was near a railroad line. About an hour after I left I came back (she said), as white as a ghost. I would not speak for the rest of that day; I would not tell her why I'd not waited to be picked up or phoned that I wanted to come home; I would not tell her why my chum's mom hadn't walked me back but had allowed me to come alone. It turned out that the kid I had been playing with had been run over by a freight train while playing on or crossing the tracks...My mom never knew if I had been near him when it happened..."

- There are two brothers mentioned in *The Body* with the last name of Darabont: Stevie and Royce. *The Body* was published in 1982. Stephen King had known *Shawshank Redemption* director Frank Darabont since 1980 when he sold Frank the rights (for $1.00) to make a short film of King's *Night Shift* story "The Woman in the Room." As a result, it seems likely that these two characters' moniker is a nod to the esteemed director.

- In 1986, the film adaptation of *The Body* was released as the movie *Stand By Me*. It starred Wil Wheaton, Richard Dreyfuss, River Phoenix, Corey Feldman, Jerry O'Connell, Kiefer Sutherland, and Casey Sziemasko. It was directed by Rob Reiner from a screenplay by Raynold Gideon and Bruce A. Evans.
- The movie *Stand By Me* is ranked at #193 on IMDB.com's list of top Rated Movies.

Essential Stephen King ranking: **27**

The Breathing Method

- This novella's subtitle is "A Winter's Tale."
- In an interview in the June 1983 issue of *Playboy* magazine, King talked about this novella: "In my novella *The Breathing Method* in *Different Seasons*, I've created a mysterious private club in an old brownstone on East 35th Street in Manhattan, in which an oddly matched group of men gathers periodically to trade tales of the uncanny....That men's club really is a metaphor for the entire storytelling process. There are as many stories in me as there are rooms in that house, and I can easily lose myself in them."
- One of the most interesting bits of (true) cultural trivia King inserts into this story is his recounting of the accepted practice in 1935 of encouraging overweight expectant mothers to, incredibly, *take up smoking*. A popular advertising slogan of the time was "Reach for a Lucky instead of a sweet."
- *The Breathing Method* is dedicated to Peter and Susan Straub and may have been directly inspired by Straub's "Chowder Society" men's club in *Ghost Story*. Regardless of its genesis, though, for all its horror and its gruesome conclusion, this is one of King's literary works, told in a leisurely tone, yet not lacking punch or pleasure.

- In addition to being a compelling and horrifying Christmas tale having nothing to do with Christmas (except that a birth takes place on Christmas Eve), *The Breathing Method* is notable for being the first time King used his totemic phrase: "It Is The Tale, Not He Who Tells It."

- In *The Stephen King Universe,* authors Stanley Wiater, Christopher Golden, and Hank Wagner wrote in 2001, "It is telling to note that thus far [*The Breathing Method*] is the one piece in this collection that has not been filmed. Nor is it likely to be, given the hideousness of the conclusion...." I'd like to add that when one considers the anthology in which this novella appears, the continued reluctance of filmmakers to adapt *The Breathing Method* for the silver screen is a powerful statement about its genuinely horrific ending. After all, *Different Seasons* has already provided filmmakers with source material for three exceptional films: Rob Reiner's *Stand By Me* (*The Body*); Frank Darabont's *The Shawshank Redemption* (*Rita Hayworth and Shawshank Redemption*); and Bryan Singer's *Apt Pupil* (*Apt Pupil*). 2018 Update: IMDb.com has a film called *The Breathing Method* listed as "in development" with no further details.

Essential Stephen King ranking: **75**

II. *Four Past Midnight* (1990)
The Langoliers

- This novella's first publication was in *Four Past Midnight*.
- Ten passengers on a plane awaken to find everyone else has disappeared, including the pilot and co-pilot. They land in an alternate Bangor, Maine, and learn that there are creatures called Langoliers whose job it is to eat the past.
- In *The Langoliers*, it is said that Albert Kaussner plays a Gretch violin. I think this might have been a misspelling of Gretsch, a renowned maker of stringed instruments.

- In a September 7, 2017 interview with *The New York Times*, Stephen King said this about flying versus driving: "I travel by plane when I have to—I travel by car when I possibly can. The difference is if your car breaks down, you pull over into the breakdown lane. If you're at 40,000 feet and your plane has trouble, you die. I feel more in control when I'm driving than when I'm flying. You hope that the pilot won't have a brain embolism and die at the controls."
- In an April 3, 1998 interview with Dennis Miller on HBO, King talked about the genesis of *The Langoliers*: "I kept thinking that it would be great if you could knock yourself out while you were flying. That would be the ideal...So I was flying with some guys who had a small jet and I said, 'This would be really great if only you didn't have to be aware through the whole thing. If you could just get on and there'd be a black place in your mind.' And the guy says to me, 'Well, we can lower the oxygen back there and you'd go right out.' And I said, 'Do it.' And they wouldn't do it, but...but I got a story out of it."
- The TV miniseries *Stephen King's The Langoliers* aired on ABC in 1995. It starred Patricia Wettig, Bronson Pinchot, Dean Stockwell, Kate Maberly, David Morse, Mark Lindsay Chapman, Chris Collet, Kimber Riddle, and Frankie Faison. It was directed by Tom Holland from Holland's own screenplay.

Secret Window, Secret Garden
- This novella's first publication was in *Four Past Midnight*.
- *Secret Window, Secret Garden* is a powerful and scary story that, like the equally effective *The Dark Half*, *Misery*, and *Bag of Bones*, takes us inside the mind of a bestselling author and makes us realize that, sometimes, that's a pretty spooky place. King is very good when writing about writers and the writing process. *Secret Window, Secret Garden* is no exception to that rule.

- King's 1989 novel *The Dark Half* and this 1990 novella are both about writers and the power that fiction can have over both the writer and the reader. Written around the same time, they are evocative and probing looks into the psyche of the writer/artist, but they also share something else in common. They are both works in which King mentions assassinated Beatle John Lennon by name. In *The Dark Half*, Liz Beaumont hopes that the people now paying attention to her newly-famous husband are not like the "mad crocodile-hunter who...killed John Lennon." In *Secret Window, Secret Garden*, Mort Rainey describes John Shooter as wearing "round wire-framed 'John Lennon' glasses." In 1980, a few days after Lennon was killed, King published a eulogy for the slain Beatle called "Remembering John."
- This is one of King's most psychologically astute tales, and the final revelation [**Spoiler Alert**] of who John Shooter actually was and how he was connected to Mort Rainey is, in my mind, one of the most satisfying (and terrifying) denouements in a King story. (And who was John Kintner, and how did he figure into all this?)
- *Secret Window, Secret Garden* was released as the film *Secret Window* in 2004. It starred Johnny Depp, John Turturro, Maria Bello, and Timothy Hutton. It was directed by David Koepp from his own screenplay adaptation of the novella.

Essential Stephen King ranking: **38**

The Library Policeman
- This novella's first publication was in *Four Past Midnight*.
- King's inspiration for this tale came from his then ten-year-old son Owen who told his father he was afraid to return overdue books to the library because of the Library Police.
- In "Three Past Midnight," King's forenote to *The Library Policeman*, he writes, "About thirty pages in, the humor began to go

out of the situation. And about fifty pages in, the whole story took a screaming left turn into the dark places I have traveled so often and which I still know so little about. Eventually I found the guy I was looking for, and managed to raise my head enough to look into his merciless silver eyes. I have tried to bring back a sketch of him for you, Constant Reader, but it may not be very good. My hands were trembling quite badly when I made it, you see."

- In 2001, The Book of the Month Club published a hard-cover Reader's Calendar that contained all kinds of information about writers and books. The BOMC reprinted part of the "How King Kills" section from my *Complete Stephen King Encyclopedia*, and they made sure to include my entry for *The Library Policeman*, which read, "Killed by a funnel-snouted, eye-sucking, shape-changing alien librarian."

- *The Library Policeman* is one of those occasional works of King in which he refers to himself in the third person. (Others include *Thinner*, "The Blue Air Compressor," and "The Night Flier.") In the story, Junction City librarian Ardelia Lortz makes it quite plain to Sam Peebles that she is no fan of King's books: "[I] have no desire...to read a novel by Robert McCammon, Stephen King, or V. C. Andrews." (Ardelia also tells Sam that Robert McCammon's novel *Swan Song* is the favorite novel of her children patrons. She even had a copy put in Vinabind.)

- Currently, there are no film adaptations of this novella.

Essential Stephen King ranking: **34**

The Sun Dog

- This novella's first publication was in *Four Past Midnight*.
- In the forenote to *The Sun Dog*, King said, "This story came almost all at once one night in the summer of 1987, but the thinking which made it possible went on for almost a year."

- Kevin Delevan, a teenage Castle Rock, Maine resident, receives a self-developing Polaroid Sun camera for his fifteenth birthday. He is thrilled with his gift, except that after he snaps his first picture, he realizes that his Sun camera is no ordinary Sun camera. No matter what Kevin looks at through the viewfinder, what develops is a photo of a black dog in front of a white fence. What is most perplexing to both Kevin and his dad, though, is that with each snapshot Kevin takes, the Sun dog appears to be getting closer and closer to the viewer.

- Stephen King's longtime editor, Chuck Verrill, has been honored several times in King's works by King naming characters after him. The most prominent mention would be the *Creepshow* segment "The Lonesome Death of Jordy Verrill." There is also a character named "Verrill" (a literary agent) in "Umney's Last Case," and the Verrill name pops up again, here, in *The Sun Dog*. In this *Four Past Midnight* novella, Eleusippus Deere's sister Meleusippus was once married to a gentleman named Verrill. Mr. Verrill was killed in the Battle of Leyte Gulf in 1944.

Essential Stephen King ranking: **37**

III. *Hearts in Atlantis* (1999)

- In his "Author's Note" in *Hearts in Atlantis*, King said, "Although it is difficult to believe, the 60s are not fictional; they actually happened. ... I have tried to remain true to the spirit of the age. Is that really possible? I don't know, but I have tried."

- In 2001, the film *Hearts in Atlantis* was released starring Anthony Hopkins and Anton Yelchin. It was written by William Goldman and directed by Scott Hicks. Although the film used the title of the book, the movie was based on the novella *Low Men in Yellow Coats* and parts of "Heavenly Shades of Night Are Falling" from the collection.

Low Men in Yellow Coats

- This novella is a *Dark Tower* story.
- When Bobby Garfield is eleven years old, a man named Ted Brautigan moves into the boarding house where Bobby lives with his widowed mother. Bobby and Ted soon establish a friendship and a bond and Bobby eventually learns that Ted is on the lam. Not from the cops, however, but from the low men in yellow coats, minions of the Crimson King, whom we already know from the *Dark Tower* series and *Insomnia*. Why do the low men want Ted? Because he is a "breaker," a being who can break the Beams that lead to the Dark Tower, and the Crimson King wants to use him (against his will) to destroy the Beams and, thus, make the Dark Tower fall and destroy all of space and time. Ted is captured, however, due, in part, to Bobby's rejection ("chickening out") of him. Bobby's guilt sets him on the wrong path for many years of his life, until he receives an envelope from Ted (who has apparently escaped the Crimson King), filled with rose petals, a resonant and recognizable image to readers familiar with the *Dark Tower* narrative.

Hearts in Atlantis

- A story about University of Maine freshman Pete Riley, who gets caught up in a dangerous obsession with the card game Hearts. (And this obsession was literally dangerous—the hellhole of Vietnam awaited flunked-out college students.) Pete also gets romantically involved with none other than Carol Gerber, now an antiwar activist who was once rescued by Bobby (from "Low Men in Yellow Coats") when they were young and who will tragically die (or will she?) in a fire.
- King talks about playing endless card games when he was a student at the University of Maine in his *Hearts in Suspension* essay, "Five to One, One in Five." (See that section in this volume.)

Blind Willie

- "Blind Willie" connects the first two stories in the anthology through the character of Willie Shearman, one of the kids who violently assaulted Carol Gerber in *Low Men in Yellow Coats* and who has never been able to emotionally atone for his sins.
- This story was originally published in *Antaeus: The Final Issue* in October 1994, and later appeared with minor revisions in 1997 in King's Philtrum Press anthology *Six Stories*.
- The version in *Hearts in Atlantis* is heavily revised from its first two publications.

Why We're In Vietnam

- This story is about John "Sully-John" Sullivan, a friend of Bobby's from *Low Men in Yellow Coats*, and a Vietnam vet whose life was saved by the previous story's Willie Shearman. This tale boasts one of the most powerful scenes in the book, a terrifying sequence in which things fall from the sky onto the highway where Sully-John sits in traffic. This scene is really a depiction of Sullivan's death that ends on an exquisitely poignant and undeniably supernatural moment involving, of all things, a baseball glove—and another message from Ted Brautigan.
- A section of this short story was originally published by King's Philtrum Press as a chapbook called "The New Lieutenant's Rap," which was given to party guests at an April 6, 1999 celebration in New York City marking King's twenty-fifth year in publishing. This segment was heavily revised for its eventual appearance in *Hearts in Atlantis*.

Heavenly Shades of Night Are Falling

- *Hearts in Atlantis* concludes with the brief story "Heavenly Shades of Night Are Falling," which was added to the book after the manuscript had been turned in to the publisher. In this story, Bobby learns a truth about Carol Gerber, and Ted Brautigan, and ultimately himself. This story makes yet another *Dark Tower* connection when we learn that Raymond Fiegler, the leader of the group that did the bombing in which Carol was killed, taught Carol a trick. He taught her how to become dim (an *Eyes of the Dragon* reference), which means that Fiegler, another "RF" character, is probably yet another manifestation of our old friend Randall Flagg.

Essential Stephen King ranking: **14**

IV. *Full Dark No Stars* (2010)
1922

- Wilfred's wife wants to sell land she owns and, if she does, it will render Wilfred's adjacent land unfarmable. Because it's a Stephen King story, murder, a well, a dead cow, murderous robberies, and rats—lots of rats—become integral parts of Wilfred's story.
- A film version of *1922* aired on Netflix in October 2017. It was written and directed by Zak Hilditch and starred Thomas Jane and Molly Parker. (Jane also starred in *The Mist* and *Dreamcatcher*.)
- *1922* takes place in Hemingford Home, Nebraska, where Mother Abagail lives.

Big Driver

- Tess, a mystery writer on her way home from a signing appearance, is given "advice" to avoid I-84 and take a lesser-known road home. But she is actually being steered to a place where she'll be stranded…and experience a nightmare beyond anything she's ever written.
- Is murder as revenge ever justified? *Big Driver* explores this question, and Tess Thorne makes life-changing decisions after her tragic experience.

- The Lifetime film *Big Driver* was released in 2014. It starred Maria Bello, Ann Dowd, Olympia Dukakis, and Joan Jett, was written by Richard Christian Matheson, and was directed by Mikael Salomon.

Fair Extension

- What if the devil offered you a deal? Dave Streeter is told that his cancer will be cured, he will live at least another fifteen years, and he will prosper. But he has to pay 15 percent of his salary for these fifteen years, and he has to choose someone upon whom will be levied terrible misfortune. Would you do it? (**Spoiler Alert**: Dave takes the deal.)
- *Fair Extension* is set in Derry, Maine. (A Mrs. Denbrough is mentioned.) We all know what goes on in Derry. But now, we learn that not only is Derry the home turf of Pennywise, but apparently Satan as well.
- Does Dave ultimately pay for surrendering to the dark side? Or is he left at the end of the novella wanting "more"?

A Good Marriage

- The marriage in *A Good Marriage* is anything but, but for years it manifested the trappings of one.
- What would you do if you discovered your husband was a serial killer? That is the premise of this novella.
- King said that the bad guy in *A Good Marriage* is based on the true story of Dennis Rader, the ordinary father and husband and all-around good citizen who had a secret life as the "Bind Torture Kill" (BTK) Killer who murdered ten people between 1974 and 1991 in and around Wichita, Kansas. Rader is currently serving ten consecutive life sentences in Kansas.
- In 2014, upon the release of the movie adaptation of *A Good Marriage*, written by Stephen King, Dennis Rader's daughter, Kerri Rawson, publicly denounced King and the movie and

accused King of exploiting her father's ten victims and their families. King responded that Bob Anderson, the killer in his story, is a banal little man and that the novella is actually about a strong woman, his wife Darcy. He also said that the drive to understand is the basis for art and that is what he strove for in the novella and movie. *A Good Marriage* stars Joan Allen, Anthony LaPaglia, Kristen Connolly, and Stephen Lang.

V. *Gwendy's Button Box* (with Richard Chizmar)

"There are three ways up to Castle View from the town of Castle Rock: Route 117, Pleasant Road, and the Suicide Stairs…"

- Richard Chizmar is a writer and the founder of the magazine and publishing house *Cemetery Dance*.
- In an interview with King and Chizmar on the *Cemetery Dance* website, King says:

    I had the idea for the story last July, and thought it was a little like Richard Matheson's "Button, Button," but could be its own special thing. I liked it because it basically postulates putting the fate of the world in the hands of a child (like Trump). I didn't know how to finish it. So it just sat there until this January. I didn't seek out a collaborator; one kind of fell into my lap. I've corresponded via email with Rich Chizmar for years. I sent him "Gwendy," and basically said, "Do what you want, or it will stay unfinished."…Working with Rich was very easy. For one thing, he knows my stuff, backward and forward—probably better than I do. I didn't give him any direction (that I remember), just let him run with the ball. He did a terrific job of bringing it home. My confidence in him came from reading his short fiction. And he's good with suburban family life. Terrific, actually; very loving, which gives the scary stuff extra bite. He wrote the middle and the end. I did some work on the end, expanding it, and there it was. Tout finis.

- Gwendy's Button Box was a *New York Times* bestseller.

VI. *Elevation*

- Although Scott Carey doesn't look any different, he's been steadily losing weight. There are a couple of other odd things, too. He weighs the same in his clothes and out of them, no matter how heavy they are…
- This novella was announced by King in a December 22, 2017 interview with *Entertainment Weekly* magazine.
- King said, "[*Elevation*] is also a Castle Rock story and, in some ways, it's almost like a sequel to *Gwendy*. Sometimes you seed the ground, and you get a little fertilizer, and things turn out."

Bev Vincent on *Elevation*

Special thanks to Bev for his review of King's latest novella.

Although Castle Rock was supposedly destroyed at the end of *Needful Things*, the small Western Maine town is still doing fairly well, especially during tourist season (King's version is faring considerably better than its counterpart on the recent Hulu series of the same name). Characters have visited Castle Rock in subsequent books, and King returned to it in earnest in *Gwendy's Button Box*, co-written with Richard Chizmar. Inexplicable things are still happening there, though.

King's new novella *Elevation* tells the story of Scott Carey (named after the lead in Matheson's *The Shrinking Man*), a divorced web designer who discovers he's rapidly losing weight. The weird aspect is that he weighs the same naked as when fully dressed with pockets full of coins. He also still looks mildly overweight. Gravity simply appears to be losing its grip on him. His doctor friend wants him to see a specialist, but Scott doesn't want to spend the rest of his life being poked and prodded. He embraces the impossibility of his situation. He feels oddly elevated.

Castle Rock stories are not known for being optimistic and inspirational, but *Elevation* has the same positive feel as *Rita Hayworth and Shawshank Redemption*. The novella blends elements of *Christine* (with its odometer counting down toward zero), *Thinner* (although that was a Bachman novel, and those never end well), and Pixar's animated movie *Up*, yet it's vastly different from all of these.

The supernatural element aside, the story is about Scott "becoming woke." His new neighbors are Deirdre McComb and Missy Donaldson, a married couple who own a vegetarian Mexican restaurant called Holy Frijole. They're having a rough time because Castle Rock is ultra-conservative and many of its residents resent the couple's insistence on emphasizing the "married" part. The restaurant seems doomed. Scott's conflict with them has nothing to do with their sexuality. He just wants them to keep their dogs from crapping in his yard. His determination to win them over and become at least good neighbors pushes him to confront his town's prejudices head on.

The centerpiece of the novella is the Castle Rock Turkey Trot, an annual 12K fundraiser. Scott decides to use his affliction to his advantage to try to break down the social barriers in his long-time home town and mend fences with his neighbors. *Elevation* is uplifting (pun only partly intended), touching, charming, and melancholy. Easily the most optimistic tale King has ever written.

IV.
14 NOTABLE NONFICTION STEPHEN KING WORKS

There is no way to adequately cover all of King's nonfiction in a forum such as this book. King's nonfiction comprises a body of work that deserves its own thoughtful book-length coverage.

However, there are some works that we can look at here, particularly a few books and essays that are King at his most iconic, creative, and entertaining.

- *King's Garbage Truck* (February 1969–May 1970)
- *Danse Macabre* (1981)
- *Nightmares in the Sky* (1988)
- *Mid-Life Confidential: The Rock Bottom Remainders Tour America With Three Chords and an Attitude* (1994)
- "My Little Serrated Security Blanket" *Outside* (December 1995)
- *Secret Windows* (2000)
- *On Writing* (2000)
- *Faithful* (2004)
- *Stephen King's Letter to His Younger Self* (2010)
- "What Ails the Short Story" *The New York Times* (September 30, 2007)
- "Raymond Carver's Life and Stories" *The New York Times* (November 19, 2009)

- *Guns* (2013)
- "Just a Little Talent" *Hard Listening: The Greatest Rock Band Ever (of Authors) Tells All* (2013)
- *Hearts in Suspension* (2016)

King's Garbage Truck (1969–1970)

- *King's Garbage Truck* is a collection of forty-seven columns of commentary, reviews, and critique totaling approximately 35,000 words, which King wrote for the University of Maine student newspaper, *The Maine Campus.*
- Detailed synopses of all forty-seven columns appear in my book *The Lost Work of Stephen King.* A new edition of the original *Lost Work* will be published by the Overlook Connection Press, the publisher of the limited edition of *Stephen King, American Master.* I am currently working on Volume 2 of *The Lost Work of Stephen King.*
- To give a sense of what King wrote about, here are the first lines and word count of all forty-seven columns:

  1. **February 20, 1969 (642 words)** "The Goddard College Dancers, seven students from a small liberal arts school in Vermont, put on a program called *Why We Dance* last Sunday night in Hauck Auditorium."

  2. **February 27, 1969 (515 words)** "You have to feel sorry for William Shakespeare."

  3. **March 6, 1969 (515 words)** "If you watch TV at all lately, you've probably noticed a new trend in entertainment—the cheapie game show."

  4. **March 13, 1969 (690 words)** "There's a Plot afoot."

  5. **March 20, 1969 (670 words)** "I am soliciting."

  6. **March 27, 1969 (600 words)** "This was a pretty good week."

7. **April 10, 1969 (580 words)** "You say it's been a bad week?"

8. **April 17, 1969 (740 words)** "I was in Fun City this weekend for the first time in four years, and it's a strange scene for a country boy who grew up in a small Maine town where there are more graveyards than people."

9. **April 24, 1969 (690 words)** "As President Emeritus of this [several words obscured and illegible] Nitty Gritty Up Tight Society for a Campus with More Cools (which we lovingly refer to as the N. G. U. T. S. C. M. C.—pronounced Nuhgutsmick, for all you linguists out there), I have the happy duty of announcing that we have decided to call a general student strike next week."

10. **May 1, 1969 (600 words)** "SS-1 was the course number of the first special seminar taught here at Maine, during the '68 Fall semester."

11. **May 8, 1969 (914 words)** "Want me to tell you a bad thing?"

12. **May 15, 1969 (715 words)** "Ugly."

13. **May 22, 1969 (780 words)** "I've always been fond of clichés, and one of my favorites is, 'If you can't say something nice, don't say anything at all.'"

14. **June 12, 1969 (518 words)** "Boom! and all at once it's summer."

15. **June 20, 1969 (528 words)** "People have been telling me for years that I've got a sympathetic face."

16. **June 27, 1969 (878 words)** "It's summer, and you're hot."

17. **July 4, 1969 (790 words)** "I was thumbing through a stack of old records last week at the home of a girl who has graduated from Bobby Rydell and chewing gum to Jethro Tull and Tareytons."

18. **July 11, 1969 (1000 words)** "The man's name is Neil Armstrong."

19. **July 18, 1969 (880 words)** "The time has come, folks, the day you've all been waiting for—today is the day we give out the coveted Gritty Awards."

20. **July 25, 1969 (950 words)** "The university's annual Freshman Orientation program, that amiable orgy of tourism, lectures, scheduling, and general all-around rubber-necking has been in full swing now for the last six weeks or so, and the casual observer hardly knows whether to be amused, skeptical, or envious."

21. **August 1, 1969 (790 words)** "I think that of all the people on earth that I would most not want to be, the one who would cop the prize would be Pope Paul."

22. **August 8, 1969 (930 words)** "Last week-end I spent about an hour leafing through some back issues of the *CAMPUS*, glancing at some of the stuff I'd written for the *Garbage Truck* over the last five or six months."

23. **September 18, 1969 (780 words)** "And here we all are again, in our places, with bright shiny faces."

24. **September 25, 1969** [Reprint of Column #21]

25. **October 3, 1969 (550 words)** "A funny thing happened to me on my way to class a couple of days ago."

26. **October 9, 1969 (750 words)** "By now, you've probably read at least a dozen reviews of *Easy Rider*, the new Peter Fonda movie."

27. **October 16, 1969 (680 words)** "It has been suggested to me by a lot of people, from Chancellor McNeil, from faculty members, from student senators, and from the general run of the student body, that this is a pretty apathetic campus."

28. **October 23, 1969 (684 words)** "Well, a part of me went into hibernation last week."

29. **October 30, 1969 (990 words)** "Friends and neighbors, we here at the Nitty Gritty Up-Tight Society for a Campus with More Cools (NGUTSCMC—you all remember us—right?) are starting to get a little worried."

30. **November 6, 1969 (782 words)** "In the short course of this year I've already managed to alienate the Maine freshmen and the organized flabs on campus (Owls, Eagles, etc.); now I'm going to see if I can alienate the rest of you by picking what I consider were the best singles and albums of the year—and the worst."

31. **November 13, 1969 (818 words)** "The subject this week is cops."

32. **December 4, 1969 (770 words)** "It's a little bit frightening to wake up in the middle of the night and realize that you may be the only one on earth that realizes why the world is in so much trouble."

33. **December 11, 1969 (590 words)** "Okay, folks, because absolutely nobody asked for it, here it is."

34. **December 18, 1969 (884 words)** "There are strange things in the world."

35. **January 8, 1970 (794 words)** "So there are your 60's."

36. **January 15, 1970 (805 words)** "I, Stephen Edwin King, being of sound mind and body, 22 years of age, and thus past the age of my majority, having no debts outstanding, never having been convicted of felony or misdemeanor, a resident of Durham, Maine, and freeholder in that Town, registered voter, male and of the Caucasian race, do hereby make this my last Will and Testament, revoking all other wills and Codicils."

37. **February 5, 1970 (762 words)** "The subject this week, my friends, is the Boob Tube."

38. **February 12, 1970 (676 words)** "If you're a conservative and a *Bangor Daily News* reader, or even if you're not, gather 'round."

39. **February 19, 1970 (649 words)** "Flowers this week for MUAB, the Memorial Union Activities Board."

40. **February 26, 1970 (532 words)** "Two years ago an excellent actor by the name of George Kennedy won an Academy Award for Best Supporting Actor in a Paul Newman movie called *Cool Hand Luke* ('What we have here is a failure to communicate.')."

41. **March 19, 1970 (687 words)** "The other day I came across a letter I wrote last February 26th, which was the day of The Big Snowstorm of '69."

42. **March 26, 1970 (889 words)** "I've been student teaching for the last eight weeks, and I've been out of touch."

43. **April 9, 1970 (515 words)** "Have you ever thought how exciting some of those boring TV shows would be with a few campus personalities to liven them up?"

44. **April 16, 1970 (787 words)** "Last year, in May, Dick Mieland and I were handing out flyers in the Memorial Union just prior to the Rally for Free Speech (that rally, you may remember, followed the March to End the War, when eggs and other objects were thrown)."

45. **April 30, 1970 (717 words)** "Well, folks, it looks like that season again."

46. **May 7, 1970 (957 words)** "Well, this is almost it—the garbage truck is almost out of gas."

47. **May 21, 1970 (486 words)** "A BLESSED (?) EVENT ANNOUNCED TO THE UNIVERSITY OF MAINE AT ORONO"

- The last line of Stephen King's final *Maine Campus* "Garbage Truck" column was "Take care of yourselves, friends."

Danse Macabre (1981)

- *Danse Macabre* was King's 1981 masterful nonfiction overview of the horror genre. The book was suggested to him by his editor Bill Thompson, who thought that it would prevent King having to answer repeated questions about his thoughts on horror.
- In the forenote to *Danse Macabre*, King wrote, "If you want to know what I think about horror, there's this book I wrote on the subject. Read that. It's my Final Statement on the clockwork of the horror tale."
- *Danse Macabre* is the book in which King first stated his theory about there being three levels of horror: he would first try to terrify the reader; he would then try to horrify the reader; and then he would go for the gross-out.
- In a June 1983 interview in *Playboy* magazine, King expounded on his "triumvirate of horror" aesthetic: "The genre exists on three basic levels, separate but interdependent and each one a little bit cruder than the one before. There's terror on top, the finest emotion any writer can induce; then horror, and, on the very lowest level of all, the gag instinct of revulsion. Naturally, I'll try to terrify you first, and if that doesn't work, I'll try to horrify you, and if I can't make it there, I'll try to gross you out. I'm not proud; I'll give you a sandwich squirming with bugs or shove your hand into the maggot-churning innards of a long-dead woodchuck."
- The woodchuck King is referring to appears in 1979's *The Dead Zone* in the scene where Johnny Smith touches Dr. Brown's hand:

He found himself remembering a picnic in the country when he had been seven or eight, sitting down and putting his hand in something warm and slippery. He had looked around and seen that he had put his hands into the maggoty remains of a woodchuck that had lain under the laurel bush all that hot August. He had screamed then, and he felt a little bit like screaming now.

- It has been close to forty years since King wrote *Danse Macabre*. An update would be welcome, and King did write an essay as the forenote for the 2010 edition called "What's Scary," in which he looked at horror cinema from 1999 through 2009, but as is often the case with long passages of time and books that end at a particular year in coverage, the work to research and write about a topic as broad and deep as the horror genre is overwhelming and clearly not something King wishes to tackle.

Nightmares in the Sky (1988)

- *Nightmares in the Sky* is a coffee-table book of photographs by f-stop Fitzgerald of architectural gargoyles, those stone monster-demons that peer down on us from apartments, office buildings, churches, libraries, museums, courthouses, and other stone structures. King wrote an introductory essay.
- In his essay, he wrote, "Coffee-table book or not, I would suggest a coffee-table might be the worst place for this particular tome; coffee-tables, after all, are low pieces of furniture, accessible to children, and I am as serious as I can be when I say that this is no more a book for children than George Romero's *The Night of the Living Dead* is a movie for them."
- In his essay, King leads us to the question, Why have these faces been deliberately added to the facades and roofs of buildings for so many centuries? Their function is to act as a drain for rainwater, but if form does dictate function, then all that would be necessary would be a pipe. Instead, we have grotesque

faces serving this purpose. Granted, some gargoyles are cherubic angles; but most seem to be these leering, silently shrieking, often insane faces growing out of buildings like, as King aptly describes, "a tumor." And that leads King into a discussion of the symbolic meaning of architectural gargoyles over the ages, thereby achieving what the best art can do—provide a context that opens up the subject and, hopefully, enlightens.

- In section eight of his essay, King writes, "How is this particular effect, which changes in its specifics, but seems to maintain a constant emotional keychord of fear, even horror, achieved?" In the January 1971 issue of *Onan*, a University of Maine student literary magazine, 24-year-old Stephen King published an untitled poem that had as its first line, "In the key-chords of dawn...."

- F-stop Fitzgerald's website tells us: "His book collaboration with horror writer Stephen King, *Nightmares in the Sky*, sold over 180,000 copies and was a national bestseller."

Mid-Life Confidential: The Rock Bottom Remainders Tour America With Three Chords and an Attitude (1994)

- This book chronicles the travels of the Rock Bottom Remainders, Stephen King's band. At the time the book was released, the band consisted of Dave Barry, Tad Bartimus, Roy Blount Jr., Michael Dorris, Robert Fulghum, Kathi Kamen Goldmark, Matt Groening, Josh Kelley, Barbara Kingsolver, Al Kooper, Greil Marcus, Dave Marsh, Ridley Pearson, Jerry Peterson, Joel Selvin, Amy Tan, and Jimmy Vivino.

- King's contribution to the text was the essay "The Neighborhood of the Beast."

- Tabitha King's contribution (she was the tour photographer) was an essay called "I Didn't Get Paid Enough," in which she wrote, "No doubt there are morons out there demanding to know if I don't have enough money. Well, would you work for diddly-shit? No. You wouldn't. Just what I thought. Probably if you had enough money, you wouldn't work at all. So who's got the work ethic here? I have enough money. There's a difference between having enough money and getting paid enough to compensate for the work. I knew you'd understand."

- In "The Neighborhood of the Beast," King "notices" the graffiti on the toilet stall walls wherein he sits and also recounts pithy Graffiti of the Past he couldn't help but remember, such as "Dogs Fuck the Pope (No Fault of Mine)" and "Save Russian Jews, Collect Valuable Prizes." King would revisit bathroom graffiti in the story "All That You Love Will Be Carried Away."

- Speaking of graffiti, the title of King's essay, "The Neighborhood of the Beast" refers to something King saw written on the back of the bathroom door precisely at his eye level: "664/668: THE NEIGHBORHOOD OF THE BEAST." What number sits precisely between "664" and "668"? The ominous number 666, of course, the Biblical sign of The Beast, aka Satan. What that says about being on a tour bus with a bunch of middle-aged rockers is left to the reader's interpretation.

- Rock Bottom Remainders Musical Director Al Kooper considered the Rock Bottom Remainders tour "the nadir of western civilization."

My Little Serrated Security Blanket, *Outside* (1995)

- "My Little Serrated Security Blanket" was written for *Outside* magazine and appeared in their December 1995 issue. The introductory tag line to the article read, "The blacksmith of horror rejoices in the potentialities of an ice ax."

- This brief nonfiction essay (around 500 words) is Stephen King having a great deal of fun in a very well-written piece. He is imagining the kind of damage an ice ax could do to the human body, even though he admits that he "tries not" to think of murder when he looks at the DMM Predator.

- King tells us that the holes the business end of the ax could make in a human body would be "lozenge-shaped."
- King pinpoints the specific areas he would "apply" the ax to: the gut, throat, forehead, nape of the neck, and orbit of the eyeball. And he even knows how far he would put it in: to the "11th serration."
- In a hilarious instance of bizarre synchronicity, the same issue of *Outside* that published King's grisly ode to ice-climbing mayhem also included quite the perky tribute to top-of-the-line first aid kits by none other than our national Doyenne of the Glue Gun, Martha Stewart.

Secret Windows: Essays and Fiction on the Craft of Writing (2000)
Introduction by Peter Straub
- This essay was published for the first time in *Secret Windows*.
- Peter Straub is a longtime friend of Stephen King, as well as his co-author on *The Talisman* and *Black House*. There is also talk of a third co-authored volume.
- Straub opens this Introduction with what King calls in this same volume, a "great hooker":

> Let us deal with a potential embarrassment, or what may seem at least a conflict of interest, right away. In this companion book to *On Writing*, my name pops up often enough to suggest that Stephen King may have adopted the remuneration system perfected by the late Pee Wee Marquette, a diminutive, klaxon-voiced gentleman long ago employed by a jazz club called Birdland to announce the names of the musicians onstage, and who gleefully performed this function as long as the musicians in question slipped him a couple of bucks.

Dave's Rag (1959–1960)

- *Dave's Rag* was a weekly newspaper written, published, and sold by Stephen King and David King.

- **Jumper**
  - ○ "Jumper" was written in 1959, when King was twelve, and Part 1 was published in the December 29, 1959 issue of *Dave's Rag*. The publication dates of Parts 2 and 3 are not known, although it is a safe bet they appeared sometime in 1960.
  - ○ "Jumper" is the story of Jeff Davis, a "police counselor" who, throughout his career, has had to repeatedly convince Robert Steppes not to commit suicide by jumping off high buildings. The story involves some close calls and a giant metal hook.

- **Rush Call**
  - ○ "Rush Call" was written in 1959, when King was twelve, and Part 1 was published in a 1960 issue of *Dave's Rag*.
  - ○ "Rush Call" is a Christmas story about a Scrooge-like character named Dr. Thorpe. One Christmas Eve, he gets a "rush call" to an emergency: a car crash in which a boy with acute appendicitis is trapped. Dr. Thorpe is asked to operate on the boy in the car to remove his appendix, which he does successfully. This was an apparent transcendent experience for him and walking home later that Christmas Day, he discovers he understands the true meaning of Christmas. The story ends with "The Beginning" instead of "The End."

The Horror Market Writer and the Ten Bears: A True Story

- This first appeared in the November 11, 1973 issue of *Writer's Digest* magazine.
- This is a terrific essay in which King lists his Top Ten fears:

1. Fear of the dark
2. Fear of squishy things
3. Fear of deformity
4. Fear of snakes
5. Fear of rats
6. Fear of closed-in places
7. Fear of insects (especially spiders, flies, beetles)
8. Fear of death
9. Fear of others (paranoia)
10. Fear *for* someone else

(This list holds up, wouldn't you agree?)

Foreword to *Night Shift*

- This Foreword, written in February 1977, first appeared in the 1978 *Night Shift* short story collection.
- This is the essay in which King uses the metaphor "the shape of a body under a sheet," a variant of which I borrowed to use as the title of the limited edition of my *Complete Stephen King Encyclopedia*, which was originally called *The Shape Under the Sheet*.
- This is a fine tutorial on writing, as well as an insightful deep-dive look at fear, which, King tells us, "makes us blind."
- As in many forewords, the concluding section of this is an acknowledgments section. King thanks his wife Tabitha, his kids, his early editors, including Bill Thompson, and the editors who bought many of the stories in the collection.

On Becoming a Brand Name

- This first appeared in the February 1980 issue of *Adelina* magazine.
- This long essay was Stephen King's musing on the fact that he was now a "brand." He discussed the fact that "Stephen King" was now a brand name for horror.

- "On Becoming a Brand Name" is very autobiographical, and in it King recounts his efforts to become a successful writer, beginning with his earliest short stories, sold to magazines like *Cavalier*, and moving through his early successes with *Carrie*, *'Salem's Lot*, and *The Shining*, his first bestseller.

Horror Fiction

- This was an excerpt from King's 1981 nonfiction history of the horror genre, *Danse Macabre*.

An Evening at the Billerica Library

- This is a transcript of a very interesting and engaging lecture King gave at the Billerica Library in Massachusetts on Friday, April 22, 1983.
- His requested fee was a "place to bunk and a six-pack."
- King talks about the nature of fame, and says it always surprises him when people ask him, "How does it feel to be famous?" because, he states, "I'm not."
- He recounts the story of his wife Tabitha asking their six-year-old son Owen, "Owen, do you know where Daddy's going?" Owen's reply? "Yes, he's going off to be Stephen King."
- King tells the story of a fry cook asking him if he was Francis Ford Coppola. King said he was and signed an autograph for the guy as Francis Ford Coppola. "That was bad," he said. "God always gets you for that."
- King has long been attributed as the author of the statement, "I have the heart of a small boy. I keep it in a jar on my desk." In this speech, he correctly attributes the quote to Robert Bloch, who was the one who actually said it first.
- In this lecture, King says that the genesis of his story "Here There Be Tygers" was his son, Owen, admitting to him that he got embarrassed when he had to go to the bathroom in school

because they had to raise their hand to ask to go and everyone knew he had to go pee-pee.

- This lecture included a lengthy question-and-answer period. The questions and King's answers are reprinted in the book.

The Ballad of the Flexible Bullet

- This is a reprint of a short story that first appeared in the June 1984 issue of *The Magazine of Fantasy & Science Fiction* and then reprinted in *Skeleton Crew*.

How *IT* Happened

- This is an essay discussing the genesis of King's epic novel *IT*. It first appeared in the October 1986 edition of *Book-Of-The-Month Club News*.
- This is a very engaging essay about the genesis of *IT*, but also about the creative process. King talks about the moment the idea came to him: "The idea was so good it was horrible. It was also irresistible." He said he decided in the summer of 1981 that *IT* had to be written.
- King cites the fairy tale "The Three Billy-Goats Gruff" and *The Hobbit* as inspirations and influences on the overall notion of the novel.
- In this essay, King talks about the Stratford (Connecticut) Public Library, and the corridor connecting the adult and children's sections, reimagining the hallway as a bridge, and how suddenly the book came into being in his imagination and writer's consciousness. I know the Stratford Library well and have spoken there, and can easily see how that corridor can serve as an imaginary bridge to the past, which is exactly the metaphor King employed while writing *IT*.
- King is incredibly self-effacing in this essay, saying that he was disconcerted when he realized that *IT* was a major novel that

could suggest metaphors and a theme. Regarding the idea of the bridge, he wrote:

In this second idea I sensed something worse than a symbol; I sensed a theme, and this made me nervous. I'm not a bright novelist, no Graham Greene or Paul Bowles. If I wrote a book with a conscious theme I would end with a bunch of sound and fury. I'm a storyteller; my virtues are honesty, good intent, and the ability to entertain people of my own level of intellect.

Banned Books and Other Concerns: The Virginia Beach Lecture

- This talk took place at the Virginia Beach Public Library on September 22, 1986, the day after King's thirty-ninth birthday.
- The lecture was recorded and transcribed by George Beahm, author of *The Stephen King Companion*.
- King again revisited his "truth inside the lie" theme:

I think that the real truth of fiction is that fiction is the truth; moral fiction is the truth inside the lie. And if you lie in your fiction, you are immoral and have no business writing at all.

- King talks about when Studs Terkel's book *Working* was temporarily banned from the Pittsburgh school system due to complaints by a few parents about the language. The punchline to King's story is that when the kid whose mother started complaining originally took the book out, he was the first student to check it out in three years. When the school board banned the book, there were sixty-three stamps in the book.
- In this talk, King addresses the fact that some of his books have been banned in schools, specifically mentioning *Cujo*, *'Salem's Lot*, and *The Shining*. This was when he gave some of his most well-known and repeated advice to students:

I would just say to you as students who are supposed to be learning, that as soon as the book is gone from the library, do not walk—run to your nearest public library or bookseller and find out what your elders don't want you to know. Because that's what you need to know! Don't let them bullshit you and don't let them guide your mind, because once it starts, it never stops. Some of our more famous leaders have been book-banners, like Hitler, Stalin, Idi Amin.

Turning the Thumbscrew on the Reader

- This essay was first published in the June 1987 issue of *Book-of-the-Month-Club News*.
- In this essay, King talks about writing *Misery*, and then veers off into writing about writing.
- King uses the opportunity of this essay to tell one of the greatest stories ever told about James Joyce. Joyce was agonizing over the fact that he had written seven words that day, but didn't know in what order they should appear.
- King also makes a statement with which many of us would disagree: "I don't have the ability to write the dazzling prose line." Horse hockey. What about these I've previously mentioned? "Sooner or later, life takes in its breath, pauses, and then tilts towards winter." ("Leaf-Peepers.") Or this passage from *The Regulators*? "...and surrounding everything like an auditory edging of lace, the soothing, silky hiss of lawn sprinklers."

"Ever Et Raw Meat?" and Other Weird Questions

- This essay was first published in the December 6, 1987 edition of *The New York Times Book Review*.
- King talks about the questions fans ask him. He organizes them by category:
  - **The One-of-a-Kind Questions**: These include: "I see you have a beard. Are you morbid of razors?"; "Will you soon write of pimples or some other facial blemish?"; "Why do

you keep up this disgusting mother worship when anyone with any sense knows a MAN has no use to his mother once he is weened?"; and "Ever et raw meat?"

○ **The Old Standards**: These include: "Where do you get your ideas?" (King says he gets his in Utica.) "How do you get an agent?" (King's answer is "sell your soul to the Devil.") "Do you have to know somebody to get published?" (King responds, "Yes; in fact, it helps to grovel, toady and be willing to perform twisted acts of sexual depravity at a moment's notice, and in public if necessary.") "How do you start a novel?" (King explains, "I usually start by writing the number 1 in the upper right-hand corner of a clean sheet of paper.")

○ **The Real Weirdies:** These include: "You writing any good books lately?"; "Don't you wish you had a rubber stamp?"; and "How come you're not reading one of your own books?" (His answer to this one is, "I know how they all come out.")

A New Introduction to John Fowles's *The Collector*

- This Introduction was first published as a twelve-page booklet distributed with the 1989 Book-of-the-Month club edition of *The Collector* by John Fowles.

What Stephen King Does for Love

- This essay was first published in the April 1990 issue of *Seventeen* magazine.
- What does Stephen King do for love? He reads.
- This is one of the more important nonfiction essays Stephen King has ever written. In this revealing essay, King discusses at length the influences on his writing, his resistance to reading what was assigned him in school, and the differences between reading for love and reading because you're told to, which is a

paradigm King describes as consisting of two continents called "Wanna Read" and "Gotta Read."

- This essay was out of print until Stephen King himself reprinted it in his 2000 collection *Secret Windows*, which contained essays and short stories having to do with writing. *Secret Windows* was published by the Book of the Month Club as a companion volume to King's *On Writing*.

- In this excerpt, King talks about Charles Dickens:

  I remember putting down *A Tale of Two Cities* and asking myself if this could really be the same man who had written *The Pickwick Papers*. It hardly seemed possible; *Pickwick* had been awful, *Cities* was wonderful. So, I discovered, was *Oliver Twist*...and if *Hamlet* is the greatest play ever written, then *Great Expectations* may be the greatest novel. And if you think I'm kidding, try it. I defy you not to finish it after reading the first fifty pages. That sucker kicks.

- These are the writers King mentions in the essay: Herman Melville, Danielle Steele, Dean Koontz, William Shakespeare, George Eliot, Emily Dickinson, John D. MacDonald, Ed McBain, Shirley Jackson, J. R. R. Tolkien, Reginald Rose, Tad Mosel, Rod Serling, Charles Dickens, Wilkie Collins, Ken Kesey, Tom Wolfe, Robert Howard, Andre Norton, Jack London, Margaret Mitchell, Agatha Christie, Margaret Millar, Joseph Heller, Thomas Hardy, Theodore Dreiser, Frank Norris, Edgar Allan Poe, Robert Frost, Ernest Hemingway, John Updike, James Fenimore Cooper, John Steinbeck, and himself.

- "What Stephen King Does For Love" is Stephen King at his most engaging; it is Stephen King as Teacher. Reading this essay brought to mind something that Clive Barker, King's contemporary and fellow horror writer, once said about reading: "I forbid my mind nothing," making the same point that King has often made about censorship and forbidding kids to read certain works. King has often advised kids to go to the public library or bookstore and read what their parents and teachers most definitely do not want them to read (including some of his own books).

Two Past Midnight: A Note on *Secret Window, Secret Garden*

- This essay first appeared in *Four Past Midnight* in 1990.

Introduction to Jack Ketchum's *The Girl Next Door*

- This essay was written for, and first appeared in the 1995 Overlook Connection Press edition of *The Girl Next Door* by Jack Ketchum.
- King is a big fan of Jack Ketchum (which is the widely known pseudonym of the late Dallas Mayr) and, in this essay, he puts Ketchum's work, particularly *The Girl Next Door*, in context as one of the great suspense novels of all time. He'll make you want to read it, if you haven't already.

Great Hookers I Have Known

- This essay, written when Joe Hill was thirteen and Owen King was ten, is about opening lines—"hookers"— in fiction.
- King opines that, of his kids, he thinks Joe would probably be the one to make a living at writing. Of course, we now know that both Joe and Owen are full-time professional writers.
- King mentions a great "hooker" Joe came up with for a story: "God owes me a hundred bucks."
- At the time he wrote this essay, King said his favorite hooker from his own work was the opening line of *'Salem's Lot:* "Everybody thought the man and the boy were father and son."
- This essay is worth tracking down if only for the list of great opening lines King provides. (He says he ruled out Elmore Leonard from consideration or else he would have taken up the entire list.)

A Night at the Royal Festival Hall: Muriel Gray interviews Stephen King, 1998

- This is an interesting interview done with King at his most forthcoming when *Bag of Bones* was released. At one point, he uses his *IT* dedication, fiction is "the truth inside the lie" in an answer.

- King discusses his macular degeneration in this interview and essentially says he's okay and hopes for the best. The audience was brought down a notch when he was asked about it, but he broke the tension by saying, "I bought a dog!" That's a classic Kingism: "What if you go blind?" "I'll have a seeing-eye dog!"

- King mentions Peter Straub's comment that "Stevie hasn't discovered sex" when asked about the explicit sex in *Bag of Bones* and explains that he has discovered it, but never really had anything to say about it until that book.

- King admits that he would write for free, but encourages the audience to buy his book because he has a kid in college, other kids who need things, and that his wife has a bunch of relatives. King usually isn't so blunt about money in interviews.

- In this interview, King states unequivocally that he believes in an afterlife. He uses the analogy of a paper cup and an expensive crystal wine goblet. He believes human beings are akin to the goblet, and that we wouldn't throw away an expensive glass after one use. "We're not Dixie cups," he says.

An Evening with Stephen King, 1999

- This is a transcript of a talk King did at the University of Vermont. He was invited by Dr. Tony Magistrale.

- In this talk, King muses about a short story he never wrote (or at least never published—he may have written it) called, "Beauty Becomes You." It's about a hairdresser who does the hair of the dead.

- This talk includes one of my all-time favorite King quotes: "I did make some notes and I'm going to say a few things. But before I do that, I just want to remind you we're all having a fairly good time now for people who will die someday."

TONY MAGISTRALE REMEMBERS STEPHEN KING'S VISIT TO THE UNIVERSITY OF VERMONT

- Stephen and I played a game of tennis together after his talk and I asked him if he wanted to take a sauna before being driven back to his hotel. He looked at me and said, "Where I come from, there are no saunas."

- Another time, Stephen and I were walking back from dinner at a downtown Burlington, Vermont restaurant. They had been kind enough to close their doors for the night to accommodate my twenty students enrolled in the King seminar. Strangely enough, the wait staff all wanted to work that particular night. After dinner, around midnight, King and I were walking back to my car. It was a dark and spooky March night as I recall, and we came upon a deserted building that had large pieces of plywood around its perimeters. One piece had a hole in it about the size of a head at shoulder height. King said to me, "Tony, I dare ya to put your hand in there." I responded with, "Let's review. There is no one on the streets and it's midnight. No moon, full dark. And I'm walking alone with Stephen King. No, *you* put YOUR hand in there." King's reply was, "Not on your life."

- King admits to having a touch of obsessive-compulsive disorder and admits that sometimes he checks the stove "seventeen, eighteen times before going to bed."
- In this talk, King talks about having just written the short story "1408." He recounts that Room 1402 of the Park Lane Hotel in New York City inspired the story after he stayed there and learned from the bellboy that the room he was in was where the actor Gig Young had committed suicide in the closet. The truth is that the bellboy (who King described as "the world's oldest") was mistaken. Three weeks after Gig Young's wedding in 1978, Gig Young shot his new wife Kim Schmidt and then killed himself in their condo apartment in the Osborne Apartments on West 57th Street in New York.
- At one point, King says, "Do I believe the Red Sox will ever win the World Series? Not in my lifetime! That's not gonna happen." Five years later, in 2004, the Red Sox won the World Series, and that year, King published a book about the team's winning season, co-written with Stewart O'Nan, called *Faithful.*

In the Deathroom
- This is the first text appearance of a story that first appeared in the 1999 *Blood and Smoke* audiobook.

On Writing: A Memoir of the Craft **(October 2000)**
- *On Writing* is part writing tutorial and part autobiography.
- It is widely considered one of the best writing books ever published.
- One of my English Department colleagues at the University of New Haven assigns *On Writing* to his Composition students every semester.
- *On Writing* is in several parts:
  - First Foreword
  - Second Foreword

- ○ Third Foreword
- ○ C. V.
- ○ What Writing Is
- ○ Toolbox
- ○ On Writing
- ○ On Living: A Postscript

Faithful (2004)

- This book was co-written with Stewart O'Nan and is about the Boston Red Sox's 2004 season in which they won the World Series.
- On May 4, 2007, the *Boston Herald* announced that HBO would be developing a six-part miniseries based on the book for airing in 2008. King was quoted as saying, "The script is just goddamn hilarious." As of this writing, this miniseries has not aired.

What Ails the Short Story, *The New York Times* (2007)

- This essay first appeared in the *New York Times* on September 30, 2007 and begins, "The American short story is alive and well." But he continues, "Do you like the sound of that? Me too. I only wish it were actually true."
- In this essay, King talks about his experience editing *The Best American Short Stories 2007*.
- King concludes with "So—American short story alive? Check. American short story well? Sorry, no, can't say so. Current condition stable, but apt to deteriorate in the years ahead."

Raymond Carver's Life and Stories, *The New York Times* (2009)

- This is King's review of the biography *Raymond Carver: A Writer's Life* by Carol Sklenicka and the Library of America edition of *Raymond Carver: Collected Stories*, edited by William L. Stull and Maureen P. Carroll. (I have the Library of America edition

King reviews and it is a great collection of brilliant writing by a legendary American icon. King is a Carver fan.)

Stephen King's Letter to His Younger Self (2010)

This one is self-explanatory.

stephen king

Bangor, ME 04401

June, 2010

Dear Me,

I'm writing to you from the year 2010, when I have reached the totally ridiculous age of sixty-two, in order to give you a piece of advice. It's simple, really, just five words: *stay away from recreational drugs*. You've got a lot of talent, and you're going to make lots of people happy with your stories, but—unfortunate but true—you are also a junkie waiting to happen. If you don't heed this letter and change the future, at least ten good years of your life—from age 30 to 40—are going to be a kind of dark eclipse where you disappoint a lot of people and fail to enjoy your own success. You will also come close to dying on several occasions. Do yourself a favor and enjoy a brighter, more productive world. Remember that, like love, resistance to temptation makes the heart grow stronger.

Stay clean.

Best regards,

[signature: Stephen King]

Guns (2013)

- This long, important essay was written by King after the Sandy Hook Elementary School shooting on December 14, 2012 in Newtown, Connecticut.
- *Guns* has seven parts:

  1. **The Shake**: A twenty-one-part deconstruction of how America responds to a mass shooting

  2. *Rage:* The story of his Richard Bachman novel and why he decided to pull it from publication

  3. **Drunks in a Barroom**: A contemplation on the state of political discourse in America

  4. **Culture of Violence**: King's contention that there is no "culture of violence" in America and that it is a fiction created by the right-wing gun advocates, politicians, and the NRA

  5. **From My Cold Dead Hands**: Musings on guns and the people who own them

  6. **No Solutions; Reasonable Measures**: King's three-part solution

  7. **Epilogue**: King tells of the most recent (at the time) mass shooting

- King on the state of political discourse in America: "Political discourse as it once existed in America has given way to useless screaming.... We're like drunks in a barroom. No one's listening because everyone is too busy thinking about what they're going to say next, and absolutely *prove* that the current speaker is so full of shit he squeaks."

- King offers a "trio of reasonable measures to curb gun violence." He lists them in order of likelihood.

  1. Comprehensive and universal background checks

2. Ban the sale of clips and magazines containing more then ten rounds

3. Ban the sale of assault weapons such as the Bushmaster and the AR-15

Just a Little Talent

- This is an essay that appeared in the collection *Hard Listening: The Greatest Rock Band Ever (of Authors) Tells All*, which was published exclusively as an ebook in 2013.
- The title comes from a quote from King's mother: "Almost everybody has one thing they're really good at. If you've got just a little talent for something else, be grateful."
- In this essay, King talks about music, opening with the day his friend Chris Chesley called him to come over and listen to the new Dave Van Ronk album he had gotten for his birthday.
- They learned the song "Bed Bug Blues" from the record and that was sort of the beginning of King's second career as a rock musician.
- He also talks about his early guitars, playing with the Remainders, and Dave Barry teaching him how to play barre chords.

Hearts in Suspension (2016)

- *Hearts in Suspension* is a collection of essays published by the University of Maine Press to celebrate the fiftieth anniversary of Stephen King's admission to the University of Maine.
- The book includes a new nonfiction essay by King called "Five to One, One in Five" in which, according to the dust jacket, "King sheds his fictional persona and takes on the challenge of a nonfiction return to his undergraduate experience."
- *Hearts in Suspension* also includes an introduction by Jim Bishop, King's English professor at UMO, and essays by twelve "fellow students and friends" from King's college days, including works by Harold Crosby, David Bright, Diane McPherson,

Jim H. Smith, Philip Thompson, Keith Carreiro, Sherry Dee, Bruce Holsapple, Larry Moscowitz, Frank Kadi, Michael Alpert, and Jim Bishop (in addition to his Introduction).

- The book also includes a reprint of King's novella *Hearts in Atlantis* (with a new 2016 Introduction), four reprints of original *King's Garbage Truck* columns, specifically, May 15, 1969; July 11, 1969; May 7, 1970; and May 21, 1970. (See the section on *King's Garbage Truck* in this volume for word counts and first lines of these four columns.)

Five to One, One in Five

For me, remembering college is like taking a bite of cotton candy: it fills the mouth but melts almost at once, leaving just a lingering taste of sweetness behind.
Stephen King

- King wrote this essay especially for *Hearts in Suspension*. It runs from page twenty-three through page seventy-six in the book, totaling fifty-three pages.
- One of the reasons I'm a big fan of Stephen King's nonfiction is exemplified by this essay. It reads like fiction and King is able to elicit true engagement with the work through his recognizable, accessible, and entertaining writer's voice.
- This is an important essay, which I will attempt to thematically deconstruct (no, I won't use the current trendy abomination "unpack"), and it includes a reprint of the complete text of King's seminal poem "The Dark Man." (See the essay on "The Dark Man" by Dr. Michael Collings in this volume.)
- In the Introduction to this essay, King cites his "fiction is the truth inside the lie" mantra to explain how "most of the stories that follow are mostly true."

- In the first section of this essay, King posits an idea about near-death experiences, triggered by a memory from college in which he just missed getting killed in a 1969 car crash. He asks, if sometimes we see our past life flash before our eyes just before death, as some say, isn't it possible that some people might see their future life in the same way moments before they get their face ripped off in a car slamming into a tree at a very high speed? Interesting idea. King, of course, muses that he would have seen his life as a husband, father, teacher, writer, and so forth if he had been in the car that he had only moments before exited.

- King then talks about taking a tour of the University of Maine, and explains in detail just how poor his mother and he and his brother, David, were during his high school years. How poor? At one point, they had an outhouse. That's how poor.

- King relates showing up for his draft-mandated military physical egregiously hungover and tripping on Purple Microdot acid. He was rejected for bad eyes and high blood pressure, which he admits did not surprise him considering the condition he was in at the time.

- The next section of this essay is about rage. No, not the novel (although that does make an appearance, albeit brief), but King's personal sense of rage during his college years. He writes that looking back now at his college-era writings, he can see the anger, the furious disenchantment that he now considers revelatory: "It took me years to look back on those early stories and poems and realize how angry I was, how fucking *furious*, through most of the time I spent at the University of Maine.... In today's society, one of my stories, 'Cain Rose Up,' would have put me under scrutiny as a possible school shooter." King admits that he may have been overreacting considering his actual empirical circumstances: "[I] wasn't going hungry; I was no Oliver Twist asking for a second helping....I had friends, I had a sex life of sorts…[y]et the rage was there, a steady stream of magma that came out only in the fiction I was writing…"

- King concludes his discussion of his college rage with this assessment of his poem "The Dark Man" and a self-aware conclusion:

    It's only now, looking at this poem after many years, that I can see past the juvenile romanticism and the influences (Walt Whitman, Gerard Manley Hopkins, Ray Bradbury, LSD, the Doors, even the film *Hush, Hush Sweet Charlotte*) to what may have been the well-spring of that rage: I felt like an outsider. I felt alone. And that was okay, because the anger was fuel. Besides, I liked the darkness.

    I felt at home there.

- King then talks about his college roommate Harold Crosby, a young man who was as straight-laced and serious as King was not. Harold wanted to become a dentist, and today he is a dentist. He also has an essay in *Hearts in Suspension* in which he remembers King's typewriter going all the time and muses that one of his biggest regrets is not asking King to sign and give to him one of the typed stories he'd ask him to read.

- King then also discusses his at-the-time Republicanism and says he is now a liberal Democrat who most assuredly rejects the Republican operating principle of "Good luck, buddy, you're on your own."

- King talks about voting for Richard Nixon in 1968, about reading *In Dubious Battle* and *The Grapes of Wrath*, and about spending four hours picketing a grocery store in Bangor on behalf of the United Farm Workers who went on strike against grape growers in California to fight for a minimum wage. Interestingly, King makes mention of his cognitive dissonance regarding his picketing: "I did not see the dichotomy between my support of the UFW and my Republican beliefs, which included the freedom to pay your workers whatever you could get away with." He concludes this section with the statement, "Fiction has the power to change lives."

- In the next section, King talks about Vietnam, napalm, and moving into a cabin in University Cabins, a group of cabins that housed four students each and which were arranged in a circle "like a wagon train preparing to withstand an Indian attack."
- King reveals he had reached a point where he believed that killing the Vietnamese ostensibly for peace was insane. He remembers a poster that appeared in the UMO Memorial

Union—KILLING FOR PEACE IS LIKE FUCKING FOR CHASTITY—that was quickly taken down.

- King moves on to talk about protests on campus and the taking of his iconic "STUDY, DAMMIT!" photo. (He was hungover.) He states that he believes he looks totally insane in the picture and that he's got a "Charlie Manson" vibe going on. He says the picture captures "the angry, unquiet spirit of a man who would eventually go on to create Annie Wilkes and Pennywise the Clown." Yup.

- King also talks about being a member of the Students for a Democratic Society (SDS) and relates the story of a protest in which he was involved, known as the Chicken Crisis. The protest consisted of bringing three live chickens—named Humphrey, Nixon, and Wallace—into the UMO Union and just letting them hang out. The protestors and the chickens were eventually evicted and cooked and eaten (the chickens, that is. C'mon. Who doesn't like a little dangling modifier joke now and then?).

 Stephen King ✔ @Step... · 22h ∨
Satan to Manson: "Yo, Charlie! What took you so long, broheim? Have a seat by the fire, and let me stick this red-hot poker up your butt!"

💬 919 🔁 11.2K ♡ 57.9K ✉

- In the next section, King talks about tragic events that took place between 1968 and 1970, a time that gave us the assassinations of Robert Kennedy, Martin Luther King, and student protesters at Kent State. King talks about taking a teaching job at Hampden Academy and the personal psychological battle he waged wondering if, by complying with his new job's "no long hair" requirement, he'd be surrendering to the Man. He decided a paying job was more important than a ponytail. It reads like a short story.

- The next section is about King's early years as a teacher, an occupation he accepted rather than sought out. He was married and had a kid, after all, so he taught high school and considered teaching elementary school. He felt he could teach Frost to fifth graders and many of them might "get it." However, the big problem for writers with teaching is that it drains the energy out of you. (I can attest to this firsthand.) King uses the metaphor of the teacher connecting jumper cables from his or her head to the students' heads and draining out all of the creative juice. So, he took a job at a laundry—the New Franklin Laundry, a decision which resulted in a few really good short stories. This freed up his mind to write. "No papers to grade, no lesson plans to fill out."

- King then talks about the five English teachers who influenced him, naming specifically Merton Ricker, Jim Bishop, Burton Hatlen, Ted Holmes, and Graham Adams. (All writers have a list like this. Mine are John Schread (Notre Dame High School), Dick Allen (University of Bridgeport), and Jay Halpern (University of New Haven. My literary agent, John White, also a writer, also had a big influence on me, but I never had him as a teacher.).

- In the next section, King recounts working in a textile mill on the three-to-eleven-o'clock shift after high school classes in the spring and summer before college. He was offered the opportunity to work over the Fourth of July holiday cleaning out the basement, but took the week off without pay due to exhaustion, and slept most of that week. Later, a co-worker told him there had been rats the size of cats down there, and thus, King's story "Graveyard Shift" was born. He sold it to *Cavalier* for two hundred dollars.

- King then spends time discussing alcohol abuse, specifically his own. "An alcoholic can no more choose not to drink than a man with diarrhea can choose not to shit," he proclaims, and tells the story of the two times he got arrested for being drunk. One he got off, claiming he was only "drunk walking," but the second time he was convicted of petty larceny and fined five hundred dollars because, while drunk, he drove around Orono and stole forty or more traffic cones. He felt they were a hazard.

- He moves on to his early experiences with cocaine and his first few acid and mescaline trips. He also talks about not liking the high of pot, calling it "dope for dopes."

- In the next section, King reminisces about the fall semester of his junior year. What's interesting to students and followers of King's work is what he has to say about specific titles. At the time he was writing *Sword in the Darkness*, a novel he felt was as good as Ross Lockridge's *Raintree County*, and which he realized wasn't, and is now grateful it was never published. He admits that he has written some "novels that aren't very good." A footnote connected to this claim reads, "*The Tommyknockers* comes to mind." He then talks about being persuaded by Dino De Laurentiis to direct *Maximum Overdrive*, his film version of his short story "Trucks." In another footnote, he writes that "[*Maximum Overdrive*] was filmed with a crew that spoke only Italian. I will *never* live that down."

- King concludes the essay with remembrances of his graduation and his final thoughts about entering the "real world." He admits sneering with his friend Flip at what that real world might involve for them: "checked golf pants, potbellies, ranch-style homes in the suburbs with attached two-car garages, 2.5 kiddies, and barbecues on Saturday afternoon." He then acknowledges being shamed by a friend named Karen who, with "a troubled smile," admitted to them that her parents had had barbecues on Saturday afternoons when she was growing up, telling them, "We had fun. I don't hate my parents for having those Saturday afternoon barbecues. I love them for it."

- King's last thought is that Karen's rebuke may have been "a reminder that even when Atlantis sinks, it's possible to swim away."

V.
POEMS

And poets, in my view, and I think the view of most people, do speak God's language—it's better, it's finer, it's language on a higher plane than ordinary people speak in their daily lives.
Stephen King

Stephen King is a poet. Many creative artists work in all formats of their art. Stephen King is an example of a wide-ranging artist with a strong creative impetus to express himself in whatever form is required for the end result for which he strives. His creative library includes novels, short stories, novellas, nonfiction essays, screenplays, plays, and poems. This is a list of the handful of poems King has published over the years. It is followed by an insightful essay by King authority, Dr. Michael Collings, about what might be King's most important poem, "The Dark Man."

Poem Title	Published In	First Published
Harrison State Park '68	*Ubris*	Fall, 1968
The Dark Man	*Ubris*	Fall, 1969
Donovan's Brain	*Moth*	1970
Silence	*Moth*	1970
Brooklyn August	*Io*	1971
In the Key-Chords of Dawn	*Onan*	1971
Untitled	*Onan*	Spring, 1971

Untitled	*Contraband*	October 31, 1971
Woman with Child	*Contraband*	October 31, 1971
The Hardcase Speaks	*Contraband*	December 1, 1971
For Owen	*Skeleton Crew*	June, 1985
Paranoid: A Chant	*Skeleton Crew*	June, 1985
Dino	*The Salt Hill Journal*	August 1994
Mostly Old Men	*Tin House*	August 2009
The Bone Church	*Playboy*	November, 2009
Tommy	*Playboy*	March, 2010

The Dark Man

This is an excerpt from an original essay Dr. Collings wrote for my book *The Complete Stephen King Encyclopedia* titled "The Radiating Pencils of His Bones: The Poetry of Stephen King."

In this essay, "The Dark Man," Dr. Collings discusses what might be Stephen King's most important poem, seeing as how it provided both a seminal character and seminal themes for much of his later work.

I offer grateful appreciation to my friend for allowing me to reprint this exemplary analytical piece.

The Dark Man
By Dr. Michael Collings

More successful as an independent poem and more indicative of the directions King's imagination will follow, however, is "The Dark Man," published in the Spring 1969 issue of *Ubris* and the 1970 issue of *Moth* (also a publication of UMO [the University of Maine at Orono]), with Burton Hatlen as his advisor. The differences between "Harrison State Park '68" and "The Dark Man" are striking. The earlier poem is verbally and visually diffuse, lacks a clear focus in its elliptical and imagistic approach to violence, and echoes content through its explicit visual arrangement of seemingly unrelated stanzas. The later poem, on the other hand, is from first glance more tightly focused, with its lines and stanzas shaped into conventional format that is clearly a poem. It begins with a strong, almost stridently abrupt image:

> i have stridden the fuming way
> Of sun-hammered tracks and
> Smashed cinders…

Subsequent stanzas repeat the initial syntactical structure, "i have… i have…i have," using that repetition to create an undercurrent of rhythm and power. King's images are implicitly and explicitly violent, rough, often verging on the horrific "desperate houses with counterfeit chimneys"; "glaring swamps/where musk-reek rose/to mix with the sex smell of rotting cypress stumps…"; and:

> i forced a girl in a field of wheat
> and left her sprawled with the virgin bread
> a savage sacrifice…

The poem concludes with a simple, understated assertion of the speaker's ultimate identity: "i am a dark man."

To King's later readers, of course, that phrase will resonate with meaning that far exceeds the confines of a single poem. The "dark man" is nearly as consistent a motif in King's fictions as the "monstrous woman." One dark man, Roland, is the key figure in the Dark Tower cycle, while another, Randall Flagg, forms the evil center of *The Stand* and *Eyes of the Dragon*. More specifically—and more interestingly in terms of "The Dark Man" as suggestive of King's later works—his initial description of Flagg in *The Stand* echoes the atmosphere and feeling, and at times even the specific rhythms and vocabulary of the poem. In the five pages of Chapter 17, King's paragraphs incessantly repeat similar syntactical openings: "Randall Flagg, the dark man, strode south…"; He walked rapidly…"; He walked south…"; "He moved on…"; "He hammered along…"; "He rocked along…"; "The dark man walked and smiled," "He strode on..."; and "He stopped." Only in the final three paragraphs does King shift to another structural form—and the shift is significant because Flagg suddenly becomes aware that "His time of transfiguration was at hand. He was going to be born for the second time..." He becomes, as does the speaker of the final line of the poem, the archetypal Dark Man.

In addition, the images in *The Stand* echo those sketched in the poem. In a sequence that builds on the rape imagery of the final stanza of the poem, King writes of Flagg that:

> The women he took to bed with him, even if they had reduced intercourse to something as casual as getting a snack from the refrigerator, accepted him with a stiffening of the body, a turning way of the countenance. Sometimes they accepted him with tears. They took him the way they might take a ram with golden eyes of a black dog—and when it was done they were *cold*, so *cold*. It seemed impossible they could ever be warm again. (Ch. 17)

And, as with the speaker of the poem, Randall Flagg's world is replete with violence and terror:

> He hammered along, arms swinging by his sides. He was known, well known, along the highways in hiding that are traveled by the poor and the mad, by the professional revolutionaries and by those who have been taught to hate so well that their hate shows on their faces like harelips and they are unwelcome except by others like them who welcome them to cheap rooms with slogans and posters on the walls, to basements where lengths of sawed-off pipe are held in padded vises while they are stuffed with high explosives, to

back rooms where lunatic plans are laid: to kill a cabinet member, to kidnap the child of a visiting dignitary, or to break into a boardroom meeting of Standard Oil with grenades and machine guns and murder in the name of the people. (Ch. 17)

Even in the rhythms, alliterations, and periods of that final extended sentence, one can hear echoes of similar lines in "The Dark Man," down to and including portions that virtually scan as iambic/dactylic units. The poem is 42 lines long, divided into five stanzas of increasingly dark imagery that ultimately have required portions of five novels for King to explore more fully.

VI.
RARITIES

38 NOTABLE UNCOLLECTED & UNPUBLISHED SHORT STORIES & OTHER WORKS

Many typical (i.e., non-fanatical—no offense) Stephen King fans and Constant Readers think that whatever King has in the stores and on the bestseller lists is the sum total of his output. The truth is that King is, and always has been, very prolific, and there are uncollected and unpublished works out there that sometimes show up in a collection, or as a bootleg online.

This feature is a look at a few of these rarities. Special thanks to my friend, the late Rocky Wood, for his exemplary work in tracking down many of these obscure works. Also, when deciding which rarities to discuss in this book, I went with stories about which there is some known information, such as title, plot, and/or theme. When all we know is that there was a story written by King decades ago, and it isn't available anywhere, I skipped it.

(See my book *The Lost Work of Stephen King* for more on Stephen King rarities. Volume 1 is available from the Overlook Connection Press; Volume 2 is in the works.)

People, Places and Things, Vol. 1

- This early collection of typed stories has on its cover page "First Printing, 1960" and "Second Printing, 1963." It was discovered by Stephen King or a member of his staff in a box of papers, and the nineteen-page collection includes short stories by King and his then-friend Chis Chesley. The story "Never Look Behind You" was a collaboration between King and Chesley. Here's a look at the stories by Stephen King in the collection.

The contents page of *People, Places, and Things*, Vol. 1.
The black shape is a hole in the paper.

The Hotel at the End of the Road

- Two hoods on the run end up paralyzed in a museum of the living dead. The clerk tells them, "You'll be well-preserved. And you won't die." This marked King's first use of zombies, and the hotel seems to foretell King's later masterful use of haunted places, especially the Overlook Hotel (from *The Shining*) and the Marsten House (from *'Salem's Lot*).

I've Got To Get Away!

- A robot becomes suddenly conscious and tries to flee the assembly line at the "atomic factory" where he works. This story is an early example of King's frequent motif of out-of-control technology. (See: *Christine*, "Trucks," "The Mangler," "Word Processor of the Gods," *The Tommyknockers*, "Obits," for example.) (See "The Killer" in this volume.)

The Dimension Warp

- This story is listed on the Contents page of *People, Places and Things*, but does not appear in the collection. No known copies of it exist. From the title, though, it's pretty clear it's a science fiction story.

The Thing at the Bottom of the Well

- This is a very important early Stephen King story. A sadistic little creep named Oglethorpe ends up at the bottom of a well. His body is found with his arms and legs pulled off, just the way he used to pull the wings off of flies, inflict other tortures on animals, and deliberately try to hurt people. (He ties a rope across the stairs so the maid will trip and fall into the cellar.) It is one of the earliest, if not *the* earliest use of King's archetypal "thing in the sewer" monster that later became Pennywise in *IT*. The monster under the bed, the boogeyman in the closet— this thing at the bottom of the well appears to be the ancestral grandfather of all these fiendish King bad guys.
- Stephen King has never allowed "The Thing at the Bottom of the Well" to be republished, although, interestingly, he did allow his one-page story "The Hotel at the End of the Road" (also from the People, Places and Things collection) to be published in the 4th (1993) and 5th (1996) editions of *The Market Guide for Young Writers*, published by Writers Digest Books.

The Stranger

- Kelso Black, one of the bad guys from "The Hotel at the End of the Road," kills a guard during a robbery and is then visited by a stranger who seems to be Lucifer himself. The stranger tells Black that he created a contract with him when he murdered the guard and he's there to cart him off to Hell. This seems to be King's first use of the Dark Man—a personification of evil—who would later become Randall Flagg (and other "R. F." manifestations) in *The Stand*, the *Dark Tower* series, and *The Eyes of the Dragon*.

I'm Falling

- This story is listed on the Contents page of *People, Places and Things*, but does not appear in the collection. No known copies of it exist. In the "Forward," [sic] however, we're told to "let Steve King's I'M FALLING transport you into a world of dreams."

The Cursed Expedition

- Two astronauts are eaten by Venus, which, to their horror, they discover is alive. This story is one of King's first uses of the idea of being consumed by a living planet—a fate that later also proves to be the fate of Rand in *Skeleton Crew*'s "Beachworld." Also, he uses Venus as the villain, which he will do later in "I Am the Doorway."

The Other Side of the Fog

- A sudden, unexplained fog becomes a time machine and poor Pete Jacobs keeps "running through the whiteness" trying to get back home. Just as "Night Surf" was an early forerunner of *The Stand*, "The Other Side of the Fog" is an early precursor to *The Mist*.

Never Look Behind You

- A man who had been picking "the people's pockets clean of money" for years is visited by a woman in rags who kills him with a flash of fire to his throat. Two men later discover the dead George and one says, "I'm glad he's gone." The story ends with the line, "That one was lucky. He didn't look behind him."

The Village Vomit

- King talks about this satirical spin-off of the high school newspaper *The Drum* in his essay "Everything You Need To Know About Writing…in Ten Minutes":

    When I was a sophomore in high school, I did a sophomoric thing which got me in a pot of fairly hot water, as sophomoric didoes often do. I wrote and published a small satiric newspaper called *The Village Vomit*. In this little paper I lampooned a number of teachers at Lisbon (Maine) High School, where I was under instruction. These were not very gentle lampoons; they ranged from the scatological to the downright cruel.

    Eventually, a copy of this little newspaper found its way into the hands of a faculty member, and since I had been unwise enough to put my name on it (a fault, some critics argue, of which I have still not been entirely cured), I was brought into the office. The sophisticated satirist had by that time reverted to what he really was: a fourteen-year-old kid who was shaking in his boots and wondering if he was going to get a suspension…what we called "a three-day vacation" in those dim days of 1964.

    [T]he guidance counselor arranged what he no doubt thought of as a more constructive channel for my talents. This was a job—contingent upon the editor's approval—writing sports for the *Lisbon Enterprise*, a twelve-page weekly of the sort with which any small-town resident will be familiar.

- King credits the paper's editor effusively:

    This editor was the man who taught me everything I know about writing in ten minutes. His name was John Gould—not the famed New England humorist or the novelist who wrote *The Greenleaf Fires* but a relative of both, I believe.

- Speaking of "Everything You Need To Know About Writing… in Ten Minutes," here are ten tips King offers to aspiring writers:
    - Be talented
    - Be neat
    - Be self-critical
    - Remove every extraneous word
    - Never look at a reference book while doing a first draft
    - Know the markets
    - Write to entertain
    - Ask yourself frequently, "Am I having fun?"
    - [Learn] how to evaluate criticism
    - If it's bad, kill it

The Pit and the Pendulum

- According to Rocky Wood, "King wrote 'The Pit and the Pendulum,' which he and Chris Chesley sold copies of at Durham's elementary school. It 'novelized' the 1961 movie of the same name. All trace of the story has been lost."
- King talked about this story in Douglas Winter's *Stephen King: The Art of Darkness*:

    One day I went to Brunswick to see the American International Film of *The Pit and the Pendulum* with Vincent Price, and I was very impressed by it—very, very scared. And when I went home, I got a bunch of stencils, and I wrote a novelization of the movie, with chapters and everything—although it was only twelve pages long. I bought a ream of typewriter paper, and I bought a stapler and some staples, and I printed, on Dave's machine, about two hundred and fifty copies of this book. I slugged in a price of a dime on them, and when I took them to school, I was just flabbergasted. In three days, I sold something like seventy of these things. And all of a sudden, I was in the black—it was like a license to steal. That was my first experience with bestsellerdom. But they shut me down. They took me to the principal's office and told me to stop, although there didn't seem to be any real reason. My aunt taught in that school, and it was just not seemly; it wasn't right. So I had to quit.

Also see "Trigger-Finger" and "The Undead" in this section.

Trigger-Finger and The Undead

- In *Stephen King: Uncollected and Unpublished*, Rocky Wood discusses these two "lost" stories:

    A possibly unique piece of King Ephemera appeared on eBay in late 2012. The seller offered a one page flyer Stephen King had created to advertise stories from his cottage publishing venture, Triad Publishing Co. This was also the name King used to publish *People, Places and Things* (1960 and 1963) and "The Star Invaders" (June 1964). The flyer was posted to a fellow fan in New York and is postmarked 5 pm, 6 September 1963 at the Pownal, Maine Post Office. It advertises three stories for sale—King's print adaptation of the American-International Film, *The Pit and the Pendulum*..."Trigger-Finger" and "The Undead."

- Rocky also reproduced the full text of the flyer (all punctuation and formatting is as original):

"Dear Monster-Fan,

The crypt has just opened, and we here at Triad are letting out three of the most MONSTROUS tales to come your way in a blue moon. Here they are:

THE UNDEAD – a chilling excursion into the twilight world of Vampires, Terror, and…THE UN-DEAD! Here's a sample: "'Madly tumbling over each other, the kids piled back into the rod. One didn't make it. His head was split open like a ripe melon. The rod peeled out, spot-lighting one of the horrors in the glare of its headlights. It skidded…' 20 pages of TERROR! A Triad classic, only 35¢.

TRIGGER-FINGER – what happens when a trigger-happy intelligence agent invades Castro's Cuba in search of a beautiful U.S. space-scientist? PLENTY! Only 20¢.

THE PIT AND THE PENDULUM – this is NOT Poe's classic. It's adapted from the A-I shocker, starring Vincent Price. What's it about? Torture…premature burial…and the shambling horror that walked the darkened corridors of the storm-ravaged castle! Also, only 20¢.

These horrors are brought to you by TRIAD, INC. They are guaranteed to shock, or your money back! So get on the hearse, and read these terrors on the way to the crypt!

YES!! I wanto [sic] be scared outta ten year's growth! Send me the Triad Horrors I've checked. / THE UN-DEAD 35¢ / THE PIT & THE PENDULUM 20¢ / TRIGGER-FINGER 20¢ / SEND TO: TRIAD

PUBLISHING CO., C/O STEVE KING, R.F.D. #1, POWNAL, MAINE / (Enclose payment with money-order, please!)

- Wood continues:

    When queried about "Trigger-Finger" and "The Undead," King said, "I don't remember either one, which isn't surprising. Around the time I discovered *Famous Monsters, Spacemen, Creepy* and *Eerie,* those stories just poured out!"

The Star Invaders

- "The Star Invaders" is a seventeen-page short story in typescript that King wrote when he was in his teens and which he self-published as a "Gaslight Book" when he was seventeen. The text is spaced at 1½ lines and the sheets measure 8 ½" x 5 ½" and is one of King's earliest short stories still extant.
- Dr. Michael Collings said of "The Star Invaders": "The great strength of the story is its nascent characterization, coupled with an occasional image that would resonate through much of King's fiction."
- The story includes a scene that foreshadows the "closet" scenes in *Carrie,* as well as the "tiger" scene in "Here There Be Tygers":

    Lord, they had locked him in a small room! It seemed even smaller than before. Jerry felt a cold sweat break out on his brow. He remembered back thirty years. He had been a kid then, a really small kid. His father had been a bear on discipline, and every time he'd done something wrong, he was locked in the closet to meditate...

    He had gotten to hate that closet. It was small and stuffed with clothes. The arid smell of moth-balls made him cough, and to his terrified four-year-old mind, it always seemed that a tiger crouched in the corner.

- Another important image from "The Star Invaders" is the green light associated with the alien's invading ships. King would later use green fire as an image for evil in both *The Eyes of the Dragon* and *The Tommyknockers*.

Codename: Mousetrap

- This short story was originally published in *The Drum*, the Lisbon High School newspaper, on October 27, 1965 under the byline "Steve King." It has not been reprinted. King was eighteen when it was published.

- In *Stephen King: Uncollected, Unpublished* by my dear friend the late Rocky Wood, we are treated to a detailed synopsis of this story:

  In this America Under Siege story a man breaks into a supermarket with a recently installed burglar alarm. The burglar, Kelly, becomes somewhat wary after reading "B. J. Burgular Alarms" [sic] had installed a new burglar (also misspelled "burgular") alarm. The bottom of the note read: "Code Name: MOUSETRAP." It was a very large store, "Twenty cash-registers, full of Friday night receipts, faced him blankly." Suddenly, a buzzer sounded and the lights came up, causing Kelly to run for it.

  With that, "…the soup display began to move. It clattered toward him, spilling individual cans, and revealing the glitter of stainless steel beneath."[…]"Now he could clearly see the shape of the Mousetrap. Three limber-jointed steel tentacles snaked out at him. An insectivorous row of TV eyes stared at him. In the silence of the store, he could actually hear the clitter of the relays in its electronic brain."

As he ran from the creature, he "…could not believe what he saw—and when he did, he let out a small moan"—dozens of beefsteaks were rolling over the meat counter and coming after him along with a "…rump roast with two glittering antenna…that…crashed into his leg and clutched him with bright steel claws. 98 cents a pound, he though widly [sic], my rump roast certainly isn't as cheap as it use [sic] to be." Dodging a "V formation of sirloins" and a shopping cart, "waving tentacles like a wild Medusa on wheels" Kelly crashed through a plate-glass window and onto the pavement.

"His arms dripped blood, and he picked jagged shards of glass out of them numbly. But I made it, he thought, getting up. I made it! And then the parking-meter grabbed him."

- As Wood acknowledges, this story utilizes a favorite theme of King: technology coming alive and manifesting a murderous instinct. Other examples of King's use of this theme include *Christine*, "Trucks," "The Mangler," and *The Tommyknockers*.

I Was a Teenage Grave Robber

- This was Stephen King's first published story. King was eighteen when this thriller first appeared in a 1965 issue of *Comics Review*. It was published the following year, 1966, in *Stories of Suspense* as "In a Half-World of Terror."
- "I Was a Teenage Grave Robber"—with its fabulous, classic fifties B-movie title—is the story (in nine typed, single-spaced chapters) of young Danny Gerad, a destitute orphan who is recruited by Rankin, emissary and assistant to mad scientist Steffen Weinbaum, to work as a grave robber.
- There are some interesting elements in this story that foreshadow later King images and works. In an early harbinger of King's

magnum opus, *IT*, King has Danny Gerad musing about the nightmares of childhood as he enters the "Stygian blackness" of Weinbaum's garage: "All my childish fears of the dark returned. Once again I entered the realm of terror that only a child can know."

- One memorable passage from the story:

    A huge, white maggot twisted on the garage floor, holding Weinbaum with long suckers, raising him towards its dripping, pink mouth from which horrid mewing sounds came. Veins, red and pulsing, showed under its slimy flesh and millions of squirming tiny maggots in the blood vessels, in the skin, even forming a huge eye that stared out at me. A huge maggot, made up of hundreds of millions of maggots, the feasters on the dead flesh that Weinbaum had used so freely.

- In a 1973 essay, "The Horror Writer and the Ten Bears," King revealed his "Top Ten" list of personal fears. His number one "bear" was: "Fear of the dark."

- This story also contained one of King's earliest uses of the image of a rat, specifically in the line, "I was cut off by a sound that has haunted me through nightmares ever since, a hideous mewing sound, like that of some gigantic rat in pain." (It was actually the sound of a giant maggot.)

- In this tale, King also uses the adroit and appropriately "King-ish" image of "the velvet darkness of the night."

The Invasion of the Star-Creatures

- King talks about this early story in *On Writing*.

- King states that he wrote and self-published forty-eight copies of this short story in the summer following eighth grade. He sold around forty-three or forty-four copies of the story during summer vacation.

Happy Stamps

- King talks about writing this story in *On Writing*. The idea came to him after his mother stuck her tongue out at him and he saw that it was green from licking S&H stamps. It was written circa 1959–1960.

I thought how nice it would be if you could make those damned stamps in your basement, and in that instant a story called "Happy Stamps" was born. The concept of counterfeiting Green Stamps and the sight of my mother's green tongue created it in an instant.

The hero of my story was your classic Poor Schmuck, a guy named Roger who had done jail time twice for counterfeiting money—one more bust would make him a three-time loser. Instead of money, he began to counterfeit Happy Stamps...except, he discovered, the design of Happy Stamps was so moronically simple that he wasn't really counterfeiting at all; he was creating reams of the actual article. In a funny scene— probably the first really competent scene I ever wrote— Roger sits in the living room with his old mom, the two of them mooning over the Happy Stamps catalogue while the printing press runs downstairs, ejecting bale after bale of those same trading stamps.

"Great Scott!" Mom says. "According to the fine print, you can get anything with Happy Stamps, Roger—you tell them what you want, and they figure out how many books you need to get it. Why, for six or seven million books, we could probably get a Happy Stamps house in the suburbs!"

Roger discovers, however, that although the stamps are perfect, the glue is defective. If you lap the stamps and stick them in the book they're fine, but if you send them through a mechanical licker, the pink Happy

Stamps turn blue. At the end of the story, Roger is in the basement, standing in front of a mirror. Behind him, on the table, are roughly ninety books of Happy Stamps, each book filled with individually licked sheets of stamps. Our hero's lips are pink. He runs out his tongue; that's even pinker. Even his teeth are turning pink. Mom calls cheerily down the stairs, saying she has just gotten off the phone with the Happy Stamps National Redemption Center in Terre Haute, and the lady said they could probably get a nice Tudor home in Weston for only eleven million, six hundred thousand books of Happy Stamps.

"That's nice, Mom," Roger says. He looks at himself a moment longer in the mirror, lips pink and eyes bleak, then slowly returns to the table. Behind him, billions of Happy Stamps are stuffed into basement storage bins. Slowly, our hero opens a fresh stamp-book, then begins to lick sheets and stick them in. Only eleven million, five hundred and ninety thousand books to go, he thinks as the story ends, and Mom can have her Tudor.

- King submitted "Happy Stamps" to *Alfred Hitchcock's Mystery Magazine*. It was rejected with a note wishing him luck with the story. It has never been published.

The 43rd Dream

- This (rhyming) short story, discovered by one of Stephen King's high school teachers, first appeared in the Lisbon High School newspaper *The Drum* on January 29, 1966. The byline was "Steve King."
- Lisbon High teacher Prudence Grant discovered the story in her files as she was preparing to retire and ultimately sold the only known copy of the newspaper on eBay for 416 dollars.

- In an interview on NPR, Grant spoke of King being taunted and pranked when he was in grade school and noted that several characters in *Carrie* seemed to have been modeled on Lisbon High faculty and staff members.
- The story itself is beyond strange: it completely fits the title, although "dream" could justifiably have been replaced with "drug trip" and it would have worked to describe the events of the story.
- A description of the story that appeared in Justin Brooks' *Stephen King: A Primary Bibliography of the World's Most Popular Author* reads: "A high school student tells about being abused by a cross-eyed police officer of looking like John Wilkes Booth, being beaten by a crowd with Hula Hoops, and getting served at a bar by bartender Jack the Ripper."

A Possible Fairy Tale

- "A Possible Fairy Tale" is an anti-Vietnam War essay that King wrote in 1970 when he was a student at the University of Maine.
- This essay appeared in the May 8, 1970 issue of the University of Maine's student newspaper *The Maine Campus*'s special publication, *The Paper*.
- *The Paper* was an attempt by some UMO students to call attention to the war in Vietnam and to the Nixon administration's refusal to acknowledge the strong resistance of many Americans to our involvement. The front page of the paper had a peace sign as part of its masthead, and the entire front page was taken up by photos of an antiwar rally.
- These were the eleven elements of King's "fairy tale" (paraphrased):

1. **Friday, May 8, 1970**: The University of Maine joins the nationwide campus strikes against the war in Vietnam.

2. **Saturday, May 9**: One million people participate in an antiwar sit-in at the White House.

3. **Sunday, May 10**: The White House sit-in swells to an astonishing 1.2 million people.

4. **Monday, May 11**: The campus strikes continue; all the members of the Teamsters union decide to strike until President Nixon withdraws our troops from Cambodia.

5. **Tuesday, May 12**: National Guard troops refuse to enter the Berkeley campus; twelve platoons of Army troops and Marines refuse to go to Cambodia.

6. **Wednesday, May 13**: The members of the United Auto Workers union join the nationwide strikes; there are calls for Vice-President Spiro Agnew's impeachment.

7. **Thursday, May 14**: President Nixon addresses the nation and pleads for support. Railworkers join the strikes, while the sit-in around the White House grows to two million people. Democratic Senator Eugene McCarthy, who had been strongly opposing the Vietnam War since 1968, describes the activities so far as "a groove."

8. **Friday, May 15**: A bill is expected to pass the House today forbidding President Nixon to spend any more money in southeast Asia.

9. **Saturday, May 16**: Postal workers, dock workers, and some federal government employees join the nationwide strikes. There is talk that articles of impeachment against Spiro Agnew will be drawn up by Thursday, May 21.

10. **Sunday, May 17**: President Nixon tells the nation that he is withdrawing five hundred thousand troops from Vietnam and that the Cambodia invasion is over.

11. **Monday, May 18**: Soviet premier Aleksei Kosygin "calls Nixon...[and] congratulates him on 'an act of sanity and humanity.'" The two leaders decide on a summit "to discuss complete disarmament."

- A ceasefire in Vietnam on January 28, 1973 ended our direct involvement in southeast Asia. The last U.S. troops left Vietnam on March 29 of that year, but we continued to bomb Cambodia while retrieving American prisoners of war.

Queen of Spades

- This (presumably lost) short story was written by King as an assignment in Ted Holmes's writing class when King was in college. In "Five to One, One in Five," King said it was hugely influenced stylistically by William Faulkner, and that it was the only short story for which he received an A+ while in college.

Slade

- *Slade* is an eight-installment, 6,500-word comedic novella (a parody of the traditional Western) by "Steve" King that King wrote while attending the University of Maine and which was published in *The Maine Campus* during his final semester and in the summer following his graduation.
- The original copies of *The Maine Campus* in which *Slade* appeared were stolen from the University's library sometime in 1988 or 1989.
- *Slade* is "Comedy by Stephen King." It is about Jack Slade, a gunslinger with a grim face and "two sinister 45s." (Slade's guns are always described as "sinister.") As our story begins, Slade is in mourning for his lost love, Miss Polly Peachtree of Paduka [sic], Illinois, who has been killed in an untimely accident: A flaming Montgolfier balloon crashed into her barn as she was milking her cows.

The King Family and the Wicked Witch

- "The King Family and the Wicked Witch" is a short story King wrote for his children in 1977 and which he later gave to a college friend who was then-editor of a Kansas newspaper, *The Flint*. The story was published in the August 25, 1977 edition of the paper.
- The original title of this story was "The King Family and the Farting Cookie."
- The story begins, "On the Secret Road in the town of Bridgton, there lived a wicked witch. Her name was Witch Hazel."
- "The King Family and the Wicked Witch" is very funny and contains some real-life King family details. King mentions the family's red Cadillac and blue truck; and he writes that the mommy was writing poems and cooking.
- There are a couple of Stephen King-esque images in this brief children's tale. King writes that the witch would see the mommy reading Joe a story and "her bony fingers would itch to cast a spell." In *Thinner*, the gypsy man's bony fingers do cast a terrible spell on Billy Halleck. Also, the character of Dom Cardozi in this story could be seen as yet another *Thinner* foreshadowing, this time in the character of Italian mobster, Richard Ginelli.

Before the Play and After the Play

- "Before the Play" is the initially unpublished prologue to *The Shining*. It recounted the early years of the Overlook Hotel.
- This prologue was published in two versions: the version in the August 1982 issue of *Whispers* magazine, and the version in the April 26–May 2, 1997 issue of *TV Guide* magazine. The *TV Guide* version is an abridgement of the original *Whispers* version.
- King wrote the following in an essay to accompany the *Whispers* publication:

I liked the prologue so well that I could feel it wanting to become a book itself; enough energy from the novel I had just written to make me feel as if I had just landed a powerful jet which still has enough fuel to take off again and do a few loops, power-turns, and barrel rolls. The feeling of my editor at Doubleday was that both the prologue and most of the epilogue could be cut, with the result that we could offer the book at a dollar less than if we included them (they would have brought the page total of *The Shining* to over five hundred). I agreed willingly enough, and although I don't regret the decision, I'm pleased that Stuart Schiff has elected to publish the prologue here (for the curious, the only part of the epilogue which remains in the book is the final chapter, set in Maine during the summer after the events at the Overlook).

- The *TV Guide* publication was to promote the upcoming miniseries *The Shining*, written by Stephen King and directed by Mick Garris.

- "After the Play" is the initially unpublished epilogue to *The Shining*. For years, it was believed to have been lost, but it was discovered and included in the special 2017 edition of *The Shining* published by Cemetery Dance.

Skybar

- "Skybar" includes the opening and concluding segments of a horror short story to which the reader contributes the middle section.

- King wrote "Skybar" for the book, *The Do-It-Yourself Bestseller*, which provided the reader/writer with the beginnings of a horror story and the final line—the first time he had ever contributed something so unusual to a book.

- King authority Dr. Michael Collings wrote that "Skybar" "suggests *IT*, as well as demonstrating traditional King stylistics and techniques: brand names and a painfully precise realism as a backdrop for fear."
- Several other well-known writers participated in *The Do-It-Yourself Bestseller*, including Isaac Asimov, Erskine Caldwell, Robin Cook, Irving Wallace, Ken Follett, William F. Buckley Jr., Barbara Taylor Bradford, Steve Allen, John Jakes, Alvin Toffler, and Colin Wilson. All contributed story fragments which the reader then had to complete.

For the Birds

- "For the Birds" is a comedic short-short King wrote for a pun-laden anthology.
- "For the Birds" is a very short (and very funny) piece which King describes as "a science fiction joke."
- He wrote it for a collection titled *Bred Any Good Rooks Lately?* in which well-known writers, including Annie Dillard, Roy Blount Jr., John D. MacDonald, Lawrence Block, Peter Straub, Robert Bloch, and others, all wrote short stories that ended with an absolutely horrendous pun. Editor James Charlton liked King's so much that he used it for the title of the book.
- Synopsis: By 1995, the air in London has gotten so bad that the rooks (an Old World bird related to the American crow and similar in size and color) are dying off and jeopardizing London's tourist trade. The London City Council hires a guy to breed rooks in Bangor, Maine, a city with a similar climate to London's, but without the pollution. The start-up materials for the Bangor-based North American Rook Farms were two cases of rook eggs. The rook-raiser was paid fifty thousand dollars a year by the London City Council to raise rooks so that London would not become "a rookless city." Since the Brits are especially eager to bring new life to their tourism business, they

send the Downeaster a telegram every day which reads, "Bred any good rooks lately?"

An Evening at God's

- *An Evening at God's* is a one-minute, one-act play King wrote in 1990 to benefit the American Repertory Theater's Institute for Advanced Theater Training. The entire play consists of two-and-a-half typescript pages and was auctioned off at the Hasty Pudding Theater on Monday, April 23, 1990.
- *An Evening at God's* takes place in God's living room.
- King was part of an elite contingent of fifteen writers tapped to contribute plays. Other literary luminaries participating included Art Buchwald, Don DeLillo, Christopher Durang, John Kenneth Galbraith, Larry Gelbart, David Mamet, David Rabe, John Updike, and Wendy Wasserstein.
- King did a lengthy interview with Gail Caldwell that ran in the *Boston Globe* on Sunday, April 15, 1990, a week before the auction. The two-page talk was titled "Stephen King: Bogeyman as Family Man," and in it, King discussed the benefit and his play.
- In King's *Boston Globe* interview he discussed a novel he wanted to write:
  - What I'd like to do at some point in the next year—this has never really let go of me—is to write a novel about Jonestown.
- In Guyana in 1978, the fanatical and messianic religious leader Jim Jones coerced 911 of his followers into drinking Flavor Aid laced with cyanide.
- In *An Evening at God's*, God mentions by name Alan Alda, Robin Williams, and Richard Pryor.
- The last line of the play is "My son got back, didn't he?"

Jhonathan and the Witches

- This is one of the first short stories Stephen King ever wrote. (Dr. Michael Collings, in his massive bibliography, *The Work of Stephen King*, describes this piece as "the *earliest* story King wrote." [emphasis added]) King wrote this tale when he was nine years old for his Aunt Gert, who would pay him a quarter for every story he wrote. "Naturally I inundated her!" he writes in the introduction to "Jhonathan and the Witches" in *First Words*.

- "Jhonathan and the Witches" is 545 words long and the first page of the manuscript is reproduced in *First Words*.

- "Jhonathan and the Witches" is a classic "Grimm's"-like fairy tale, and truly a significant work for someone so young, as well as being a sign of what was to come.

The Killer

- This short story was originally published in the spring 1994 issue of *Famous Monsters of Filmland*. It has not been reprinted.

- There are a couple of versions as to how this story ended up in print. King's version is that he submitted it to Forrest Ackerman, editor of *Spaceman* magazine, and that it might have been the first story he remembers ever submitting. Ackerman kept it and, according to King, showed up at a book-signing and asked King to sign the manuscript of the story, which King did. Ackerman's version is that he read part of the story to King during King's visit to his house and asked him to guess who wrote it. He then revealed to King it was his own story and King granted permission to Ackerman to publish it in Ackerman's magazine *Famous Monsters of Filmland*.

- In this story, a robot working on an assembly line suddenly becomes conscious and attacks one of his fellow robots. The PA blares the alarm, *"Killer! Killer! Killer!"* and the story ends with one of the guards at the factory saying, "One of them turns killer every now and then" as they take the killer away.

- "The Killer" is a re-imagined version of "I've Got to Get Away!" in *People, Places and Things*. (See the section on that story in this chapter.)

The Old Dude's Ticker

- This short story, which King calls a "crazed revisionist telling of Poe's 'The Tell-Tale Heart'," was published in the NECON XX Commemorative Volume in 2000. Only 333 copies of the booklet were printed.
- King writes that "The Old Dude's Ticker" was one of the stories that did not sell to the men's magazines in the two years after he was married (1971-1972). (The other was a modern-day revision of Nikolai Gogol's story "The Ring." King's version was called "The Spear" and it is lost.)
- "The Old Dude's Ticker" updates the Poe story to the Vietnam era.

Thin Scenery

- This short play's first appearance was in the summer 2017 issue of the literary journal *Ploughshares*.
- There's a lot to like in *Thin Scenery*, and it is likely we will be hearing about small theater group and school productions of this play. What is real and what is delusion? These are the questions Stephen King asks in the play and, as he's particularly good at it, he establishes a reality, and then makes us question it...*all* of it. Like, maybe that TV is something we can put our hand right through? Or maybe that wall is cardboard? Or not even there? Or maybe a child is not who her father believes she is? This is a chilling, multiple viewpoint story that literally makes you question: who's the audience? who are the actors? who are the characters? and is the play even really happening?

Early on, the psychiatrist says, "There's a difference between perception, which is subjective, and empiric reality, which is not." Yes. There certainly is.

Wimsey

- "Wimsey" comprises fifteen pages of manuscript in typescript consisting of the first chapter (fourteen pages) and the first page of the second chapter of a proposed "Lord Peter Wimsey" novel Stephen King was thinking of writing in 1977.
- In the summer of 1977, Stephen King and then-editor Bill Thompson (he acquired *Carrie*) discussed the possibility of King writing a novel using British novelist Dorothy Sayers's character of Detective Lord Peter Wimsey. This was at a time when King was preparing for a fall move to England for a year's stay that ended up lasting only three months.
- King and his family ended up renting a furnished house at Moorlands, 87 Aldershot Road, Fleet Hants in the county of Hampshire for fifty pounds a week. (This relocation— "abridged" as it ultimately was—would result in King's collaboration with Peter Straub on *The Talisman*.)

Aldershot Road, London, UK

- In the first chapter of King's novel, Lord Peter Wimsey and his faithful manservant, Bunter, are on their way in Lord Peter's Bentley to Sir Patrick Wayne's estate on the day before Halloween. Rain is coming down in torrents and the fog has begun to creep up, making driving even more difficult. Lord Wimsey is depressed: His beloved Harriet died during the German blitz of England; his friend Salcomb "Sally" Hardy had also recently died; Miss Climpson, a beloved member of his office staff, was suffering through her final days in a hospital; and, now, he was on his way to a dinner party he most definitely did not want to attend. As they drive through the English countryside on a pot-holed road also dotted with shell craters, the two men cross a terribly rickety bridge and Lord Wimsey asks Bunter to pull over so he can relieve himself. While waiting for his master, Bunter hears Lord Wimsey urgently call to him. Bunter ventures out into the rain, where he learns that Lord Wimsey has discovered that the supports on one side of the bridge they just crossed have been cut halfway through with a hatchet. Suspicious now, they get back in the car and continue on their way to Sir Patrick's estate. Suddenly, Bunter announces to Lord Wimsey that their vehicle no longer has any braking power. The two men end up crashing into a tree and the first chapter comes to a violent conclusion.

The Leprechaun

- "The Leprechaun" is a five-page short story in manuscript that King wrote for his son, Owen, and which he planned on someday expanding into a novel. It ends with no resolution, so these pages may actually be the first chapter of the planned novel.
- This story was written when Owen was five and tells the story of Owen's attempt to protect a real live leprechaun that was living in their front lawn from the family cat, Springsteen, a sly feline who liked to eat things (he had had his eye on Owen's

guinea pig, Butler, for quite some time) and who also liked to play with things before he ate them.

- King had written thirty pages of this story longhand in a notebook when he lost the precious pages off the back of his motorcycle somewhere in New Hampshire during a Harley-Davidson trip from Boston to Bangor.

Keyholes

- "Keyholes" is an unfinished short story (or possibly the opening scenes of a novel) consisting of two-and-one-half handwritten pages from a loose-leaf notebook. The text comprises twenty-six paragraphs and 768 words.
- "Keyholes" is one element of a collection of oddities found in a spiral-bound notebook that King initially donated to the May 1, 1988 American Repertory Theater Benefit Auction, and which has since traded hands several times on the secondary collector's market.
- *The Stephen King Notebook*, as the notebook has come to be known, contains the unfinished "Keyholes"; several notes from King to himself and his wife Tabitha; King's handwritten revision of the screenplay for his film *Silver Bullet* (based on his novel *Cycle of the Werewolf*); and page after page of King solving algebraic equations by hand.
- What there is of "Keyholes" is brief: The entire segment appearing in the *Notebook* takes place in the office of a psychiatrist named Doctor Conklin. Doctor Conklin is preparing for a session with a construction worker named Michael Briggs, a troubled man who wants to talk to the good doctor about his son Jeremy.
- The character of Michael Briggs is very reminiscent of another Stephen King troubled father character: Lester Billings from King's seminal *Night Shift* short story, "The Boogeyman."

Phil and Sundance

- *Phil and Sundance* is an unfinished eighty-page novella Stephen King wrote in 1987.
- One page of the manuscript is online and it begins Chapter 1, titled "Phil and the Thing on the Stairs," with "There were a lot of things the kid didn't like."
- There is a handwritten note on the first page of the manuscript:
    Jesse—This is what I wanted your opinion on. I dunno if grown-ups will let kids read it. But…is it any good? Drop me a line with your *honest* opinion. Steve King

Comb Dump

- This is a forty-one page incomplete manuscript for a mystery short story discovered by Rocky Wood during his research at the University of Maine's Stephen King Collection. This manuscript is set in a Maine psychiatric hospital and is undated.
- The story is about a young cocaine addict who checks into a rehab program with a comb that is missing teeth. The comb begins to "heal" itself, inexplicably replacing the missing teeth… and we're off to the races!
- Rocky Wood said it was highly unlikely King would ever return to the story and complete it.

George D X McArdle

- This is a 123-page partial novel stored in the Special Collection section of the Raymond H. Fogler Library at the University of Maine at Orono.
- George D X McArdle is a comic Western that King never finished. It is believed to have been written sometime in the 1980s.
- A multi-page, very detailed synopsis of the 123 pages of the manuscript is available in Rocky Wood's *Stephen King: Uncollected, Unpublished.*

But Only Darkness Loves Me

- This short story, of which only two pages exist, was written with King's eldest son, Joe Hill.
- The first part of the story (there's no way of knowing if there were more parts intended) is called "The Most Beautiful Girl in the World."
- The opening scene is of a boy talking to a girl in a bar in Ledge Cove, Maine whose beauty is so…something…she can only be looked at indirectly.

I Hate Mondays

- This story was written with King's son, Owen King.
- It is a completed story, five pages long and, along with "But Only Darkness Loves Me," is in the Special Collections section of the Raymond H. Fogler Library at the University of Maine in Orono.
- This story can only be accessed with Stephen King's written permission.

Squad D

- "Squad D" is an eleven-page, two-thousand-word unpublished Stephen King short story. It was written by King for Harlan Ellison's *The Last Dangerous Visions* anthology, a collection originally scheduled for publication in the late seventies.
- Harlan Ellison had this to say to George Beahm in the first edition of George's *The Stephen King Companion* about "Squad D":

    Stephen's sent me a story for *Last Dangerous Visions* that needs to be rewritten. The problem is, when you say, I'm going to talk to Stephen about rewriting, I'm going to make suggestions, it sounds as if you are trying to blow your own horn: Well, here I am, the smart, clever fellow who is going to teach Stephen King how to write. Well, I don't mean any such thing as that.

What I mean is that I was sent a short story, and I think there's a lot more in it than Stephen had time to develop. The story deserves better, the work deserves better, and Stephen's reputation deserves better.

- Dr. Michael Collings, writing in his *The Shorter Works of Stephen King*, has this to say about "Squad D":

  "Squad D" is a story of guilt and forgiveness, of peace growing out of turmoil. Josh Bortman finds the peace he has sought, among his only friends. Dale Clewson becomes reconciled to his son's death—and to the tragedy that took the lives of too many sons.

  While not a particularly "dangerous" vision, "Squad D" does deserve to be seen. With "The Reach," it is one of King's most penetrating statements on the relationship of life and death—and the tenuous border separating them.

- In December 2017, it was reported that "Squad D" would be officially published for the first time in Volume 8 of publisher Cemetery Dance's *Shivers* series, edited by Richard Chizmar, co-author with King of *Gwendy's Button Box*.

Remembering John

- "Remembering John" is Stephen King's moving eulogy for John Lennon, written shortly after Lennon's assassination on December 8, 1980 and published in the *Bangor Daily News* five days later.
- King begins this memorial with a slurry of no-nonsense facts about what John was not. He was not the first ex-Beatle to have a critical success. (George's *All Things Must Pass* album won that race.) He was also not the handsome former Beatle: We all know that award goes to Paul. And John wasn't a movie star, like Ringo was. "But somehow, for me," King writes, "he was the only ex-Beatle who really seemed to matter."

- From the essay:

  Lennon was a cynic, a poet, a sarcastic son of a bitch, a public figure, a private man. …And he had his fans like me, who looked at the paper on the morning of Tuesday the ninth of December and then sat down hard, unable to believe it at first…and then, horribly, all too able to believe it.

The Null Set and The Insanity Game

- These are the typed manuscripts of two Stephen King short stories: an unpublished science fiction short story ("The Null Set") and an unpublished short story ("The Insanity Game") that came into my possession through the generosity and good graces of a major Stephen King collector.

Laurie

- It isn't often that Stephen King gives stories away for free, yet on May 17, 2018, King released the new short story "Laurie" on his website as a PDF.
- King tweeted:

  "I'm posting a brand new short story, if you want to read it–think of it as an appetizer to the main course, THE OUTSIDER, coming next week. The story is free. Read, print, share, whatever. Enjoy!"
- Widower Lloyd Sunderland gets a puppy which he names Laurie. They go for a walk down Six Mile Path by the water one day and come upon a horrifying sight involving his neighbor and an alligator. Any more would be giving away the ending, but I will provide one small spoiler for animal lovers who have yet to read the tale: Laurie lives.

The Turbulence Expert

- Stephen King's most recent short story as of this writing (Summer 2018) is "The Turbulence Expert," which appeared in the 2018 Cemetery Dance anthology *Flight or Fright: 17 Turbulent Tales*, edited by Stephen King and Bev Vincent.

- The story is about people who have the capacity to literally believe they are going to die in a plane crash, a psychic power which allows the plane to survive in horrific turbulence. King refers to them as precognates, which harkens to the precognates Agatha, Dashiell, and Arthur in the 2002 film *Minority Report* and their ability to see "future crime." (The movie is based on the 1956 short story of the same name by Philip K. Dick.)

- These "turbulence experts" are paid incredibly well, and are given their assignments by someone they know only as the facilitator, a man with a slight lisp on the other end of the phone who none of them ever meet.

- The story recounts one particular flight on which Craig Dixon does his job, but also may have found a way to retire early.

- "The Turbulence Expert" could be categorized as science fiction, and I have always been a big fan of Stephen King's science fiction. He doesn't "let us down," (pun intended) with his latest effort.

ACKNOWLEDGMENTS

The most important things are the hardest things to say. They are the things you get ashamed of, because words diminish them—words shrink things that seemed limitless when they were in your head to no more than living size when they're brought out.
Gordie LaChance
The Body

Where do I begin? By thanking Stephen King, of course, without whom... And let me say that I think there is something quite wonderful about the fact that a community springs up, unbidden, around a writer. This has undeniably happened with Stephen King. (And many others, of course.)

I thank close to a hundred people in my *The Complete Stephen King Encyclopedia*, all of whom played a role in helping me complete that book and to whom I am eternally grateful. Without repeating that list, I re-thank them all now. And here are some *paesans* and *compadres* who I would like to single out for particular thanks for their help with this book, and for their love and support.

My Troika of the Essential...

- Valerie Barnes
- John White
- Mike Lewis

Cherished Family and Dearest Friends...

- George Beahm
- Helen Bennett and the *New Haven Register*
- Tyson Blue
- John Bogdal
- Justin Brooks
- Devon Brown
- Diana Carlyle
- Jennifer Spignesi Carreria
- Richard Chizmar
- James Cole
- Michael Collings
- Janet Spignesi Daniw
- Judi Dineen
- Jennine Dwyer
- Brian Freeman
- Robin Furth
- Mick Garris
- Cynthia Gwiazda
- Holly Newstein Hautala
- The late Rick Hautala
- Dave Hinchberger, LeeAnn Rhone Hinchberger, and the Overlook Connection
- Jay Holben
- Tonya Ivey
- Owen King
- Amy Lewis, Samantha Lewis, and Sydney Lewis
- Andrea Candela Lilburn
- Hans-Åke Lilja and Lilja's Library
- Tony Magistrale
- Lee Mandato
- The late Richard Matheson

- Richard Christian Matheson
- Mark McFadden and Katie McFadden
- Nancy McNicol
- Rachel Montgomery
- Anthony Northrup and Gena Northrup
- Yara Obeid
- Amber Pace
- Amanda Patterson
- Kevin Quigley
- Andrew Rausch
- Jenna Reilly
- Gayle Rienzo
- Amanda Spignesi
- Dave Spignesi
- Jennifer Spignesi Carreira
- Joe Spignesi and Caitlin Spignesi
- John Spignesi
- Paul Spignesi and Laura Spignesi
- Melanie Stengel
- Maddie Sturgeon
- Bev Vincent
- Hans Von Wirth
- Stanley Wiater and Iris Wiater
- Sabrina Williams
- The late Rocky Wood
- Anthony Ziccardi and my friends at Post Hill Press and Permuted Press

INDEX

U

ABOUT THE AUTHOR

Stephen Spignesi is a writer, retired university professor, and author of more than seventy books on popular culture, TV, film, American and world history, the paranormal, and the American Presidents and Founding Fathers. He is considered an authority on the work of Stephen King (five books), The Beatles (three books), and the *Titanic* (two books).

Spignesi was christened "the world's leading authority on Stephen King" by *Entertainment Weekly* magazine and has worked with Stephen

King, Turner Entertainment, the Margaret Mitchell Estate, Ron Howard, Andy Griffith, the Smithsonian Institution, George Washington's Mount Vernon, ITV, Viacom, and other personalities and entities on a wide range of projects.

Spignesi has also contributed short stories, essays, chapters, articles, and introductions to a wide range of books, his most recent being the short story "Lovely Rita" for the *Night of the Living Dead*-themed anthology *Rise of the Dead*, and a new foreword to the 2016 edition of the 1912 book, *The Sinking of the Titanic and Great Sea Disasters* by Logan Marshall.

He is the author of four of the acclaimed "For Dummies" nonfiction reference books. He is also a novelist whose thriller *Dialogues* was hailed upon release as "reinventing the psychological thriller," and which he has adapted into a screenplay.

Spignesi has appeared on CNN, MSNBC, the Fox News Channel, and many other TV and radio outlets. He also appeared in the 1998 E! documentary *The Kennedys: Power, Seduction, and Hollywood*, the A & E *Biography* of Stephen King that aired in January 2000, and the 2015 documentary *Autopsy: The Last Hours of Robin Williams*.

Spignesi's 1997 book *JFK Jr.* was a *New York Times* bestseller. Spignesi's *Complete Stephen King Encyclopedia* was a 1991 Bram Stoker Award nominee. Spignesi is a retired Practitioner in Residence from the University of New Haven in West Haven, Connecticut where he was nominated for an Excellence in Teaching Award and taught English Composition and Literature and other literature courses, several of which were based on his books.

He lives in New Haven, Connecticut. His website is www.stephen-spignesi.com.

STEPHEN SPIGNESI
BIBLIOGRAPHY

- *Mayberry, My Hometown* (1987)
- *The Complete Stephen King Encyclopedia* (1990)
- *The Stephen King Quiz Book* (1990)
- *The Second Stephen King Quiz Book* (1992)
- *The Woody Allen Companion* (1992)
- *The Official "Gone With the Wind" Companion* (1993)
- *The V. C. Andrews Trivia and Quiz Book* (1994)
- *The Odd Index: The Ultimate Compendium of Bizarre and Unusual Facts* (1994)
- *What's Your Mad About You IQ?* (1995)
- *The Gore Galore Video Quiz Book* (1995)
- *What's Your Friends IQ?* (1996)
- *The Celebrity Baby Name Book* (1996)
- *JFK Jr.* (1997)
- *The Robin Williams Scrapbook* (1997)
- *The Italian 100* (1997)
- *The Beatles Book of Lists* (1998)
- *Young Kennedys: The New Generation* (1998)
- *The Lost Work Of Stephen King: A Guide to Unpublished Manuscripts, Story Fragments, Alternative Versions, Oddities* (1998)
- *The Complete Titanic: From the Ship's Earliest Blueprints to the Epic Film* (1999)
- *How To Be An Instant Expert* (2000)
- *She Came In Through the Kitchen Window: Recipes Inspired by The Beatles & Their Music* (2000)

- *The USA Book of Lists* (2000)
- *The UFO Book of Lists* (2001)
- *The Essential Stephen King* (2001)
- *The Cat Book of Lists* (2001)
- *The Hollywood Book of Lists* (2001)
- *The Essential Stephen King: Complete & Uncut* (2001)
- *Gems, Jewels, & Treasures* (2002)
- *Catastrophe! The 100 Greatest Disasters of All Time* (2002)
- *The Evil 100* (2002)
- *Crop Circles: Signs of Contact* (with Colin Andrews, 2003)
- *The 100 Best Beatles Songs* (with Michael Lewis, 2004)
- *The Weird 100* (2004)
- *American Firsts* (2004)
- *What's Your Red, White & Blue IQ?* (2004)
- *Dialogues: A Novel of Suspense* (2005)
- *George Washington's Leadership Lessons* (with James Rees, 2007)
- *Second Homes for Dummies* (with Bridget McRae) (2007)
- *From Michelangelo to Mozzarella: The Complete Italian IQ Test* (2008)
- *Native American History for Dummies* (with Dorothy Lippert, 2008)
- *Lost Books of the Bible for Dummies* (with Daniel Smith-Christopher, 2008)
- *The Third Act of Life* (with Jerome Ellison, 2009)
- *The Titanic for Dummies* (2011)
- *Grover Cleveland's Rubber Jaw* (2012)
- *499 Facts About Hip-Hop Hamilton and the Rest of America's Founding Fathers* (2016)
- *In the Crosshairs: 75 Assassinations and Assassination Attempts* (2016)
- *635 Things I Learned from The Sopranos* (2016)
- *The ER Companion* (2017)
- *499 Words Every College Student Should Know* (2017)

- *Outdated Advertising: Sexist, Racist, Creepy & Just Plain Tasteless Ads from a Pre-PC Era* (with Michael Lewis, 2017)
- *Dr. Bizarro's Eclectic Collection of Strange & Obscure Facts* (2018)
- *The Big Book of UFO Facts, Figures & Truth* (2018)
- *Stephen King, American Master: A Creepy Corpus of Facts About Stephen King & His Work* (2018)

PERMUTED PRESS
needs **you** to help

SPREAD (THE) INFECTION

FOLLOW US!

Facebook.com/PermutedPress

Twitter.com/PermutedPress

REVIEW US!

Wherever you buy our book, they can be reviewed! We want to know what you like!

GET INFECTED!

Sign up for our mailing list at
PermutedPress.com

PERMUTED PRESS

KING ARTHUR AND THE KNIGHTS OF THE ROUND TABLE HAVE BEEN REBORN TO SAVE THE WORLD FROM THE CLUTCHES OF MORGANA WHILE SHE PROPELS OUR MODERN WORLD INTO THE MIDDLE AGES.

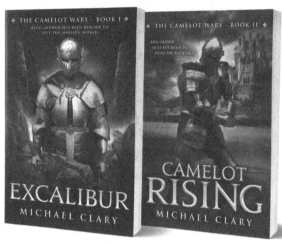

EAN 9781618685018 $15.99   **EAN** 9781682611562 $15.99

Morgana's first attack came in a red fog that wiped out all modern technology. The entire planet was pushed back into the middle ages. The world descended into chaos.

But hope is not yet lost— King Arthur, Merlin, and the Knights of the Round Table have been reborn.

PERMUTED
PRESS

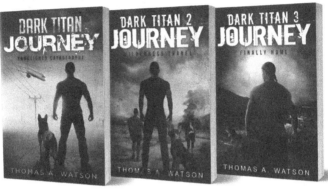

THE MORNINGSTAR STRAIN HAS BEEN LET LOOSE—IS THERE ANY WAY TO STOP IT?

An industrial accident unleashes some of the Morningstar Strain. The

EAN 9781618686497 $16.00

doctor who discovered the strain and her assistant will have to fight their way through Sprinters and Shamblers to save themselves, the vaccine, and the base. Then they discover that it wasn't an accident at all—somebody inside the facility did it on purpose. The war with the RSA and the infected is far from over.

This is the fourth book in Z.A. Recht's The Morningstar Strain series, written by Brad Munson.

PERMUTED
PRESS

GATHERED TOGETHER AT LAST, THREE TALES OF FANTASY CENTERING AROUND THE MYSTERIOUS CITY OF SHADOWS...ALSO KNOWN AS CHICAGO.

EAN 9781682612286 $9.99   EAN 9781618684639 $5.99   EAN 9781618684899 $5.99

From *The New York Times* and *USA Today* bestselling author Richard A. Knaak comes three tales from Chicago, the City of Shadows. Enter the world of the Grey–the creatures that live at the edge of our imagination and seek to be real. Follow the quest of a wizard seeking escape from the centuries-long haunting of a gargoyle. Behold the coming of the end of the world as the Dutchman arrives.

Enter the City of Shadows.

PERMUTED
PRESS

WE CAN'T GUARANTEE THIS GUIDE WILL SAVE YOUR LIFE. BUT WE CAN GUARANTEE IT WILL KEEP YOU SMILING WHILE THE LIVING DEAD ARE CHOWING DOWN ON YOU.

EAN 9781618686695 $9.99

This is the only tool you need to survive the zombie apocalypse.

OK, that's not really true. But when the SHTF, you're going to want a survival guide that's not just geared toward day-to-day survival. You'll need one that addresses the essential skills for true nourishment of the human spirit. Living through the end of the world isn't worth a damn unless you can enjoy yourself in any way you want. (Except, of course, for anything having to do with abuse. We could never condone such things. At least the publisher's lawyers say we can't.)

PERMUTED PRESS